Second Edition

Reading Strategies
for Elementary Students with
Learning Difficulties

Second Edition

Reading Strategies
for Elementary Students with
Learning Difficulties
Strategies for RTI

William N. Bender • Martha J. Larkin

CORWIN
A SAGE Company

For information:

Corwin
A SAGE Company
2455 Teller Road
Thousand Oaks, California 91320
(800) 233-9936
Fax: (800) 417-2466
www.corwinpress.com

SAGE Ltd.
1 Oliver's Yard
55 City Road
London EC1Y 1SP
United Kingdom

SAGE India Pvt. Ltd.
B 1/I 1 Mohan Cooperative
  Industrial Area
Mathura Road, New Delhi 110 044
India

SAGE Asia-Pacific Pte. Ltd.
33 Pekin Street #02-01
Far East Square
Singapore 048763

Printed in the United States of America.

Library of Congress Cataloging-in-Publication Data

Bender, William N.
Reading strategies for elementary students with learning difficulties : strategies for RTI / William N. Bender, Martha J. Larkin.—2nd ed.
        p. cm.
Includes bibliographical references and index.
ISBN 978-1-4129-6068-7 (cloth)
ISBN 978-1-4129-6069-4 (pbk.)

    1. Reading (Elementary)—United States. 2. Children with learning disabilities—Education—United States. 3. Reading—Remedial teaching—United States. I. Larkin, Martha J. II. Title.

LB1573.B424 2009
371.91′44—dc22   2008038186

This book is printed on acid-free paper.

        11   12   13   10   9   8   7   6   5   4   3   2

Acquisitions Editor:	David Chao
Associate Editor:	Cassandra Harris
Editorial Assistant:	Brynn Saito
Production Editor:	Eric Garner
Copy Editor:	Taryn Bigelow
Typesetter:	C&M Digitals (P) Ltd.
Proofreader:	Susan Schon
Indexer:	Sheila Bodell
Cover Designer:	Audrey Snodgrass
Graphic Designer:	Lisa Riley

Contents

Preface to the Second Edition

It is hard to imagine a field that has undergone more innovation and emphasis over the last two decades than the field of reading. Establishing that many reading problems result from phonemically based difficulties has allowed the field to identify benchmarks that can guide instruction throughout the early years, and the innovative instructional strategies presented here fit well within that instructional paradigm. The emphases that are stressed in the Report of the National Reading Panel (National Institute of Child Health and Development, 2000) likewise are presented here, with instructional strategies provided for each of the five major areas in reading.

More recently, the emphasis on how students respond to intensive interventions (RTI) has dominated the research on reading for students with reading difficulties, and in this new edition, the RTI emphasis is built into every chapter. Numerous case studies are presented to show how the reading instructional strategies presented here lend themselves to application in a multitier intervention plan. Data charts are presented with each case study so that the interventions are well integrated into the newly developed RTI procedures. We believe this approach will best prepare teachers for the exciting and dynamic world of RTI for reading, and we sincerely hope that educators nationwide will find this approach useful.

Acknowledgments

Corwin Press gratefully acknowledges the contributions of the following reviewers:

Kathryn Amacher
Special Education Teacher
Wheaton, Illinois

Mary Guerrette
Director of Special Education
M.S.A.D. #1
Presque Isle, Maine

Mary Reeve
Director, Services for Exceptional Students
Gallup McKinley County Schools
Gallup, New Mexico

Sandra Rief
Speaker, Author, Educational Consultant
Educational Resource Specialists
San Diego, CA

Sylvia Rockwell
Assistant Professor of Education
Saint Leo University, Madison Center
Madison, FL

About the Authors

 **William N. Bender,** PhD, taught special education in a junior high school for several years prior to receiving his PhD from the University of North Carolina. He has worked on the faculty at Rutgers University and at the University of Georgia, and has published more than 15 books, many of which have become best sellers. He has also written more than 60 research articles. Today he is writing several new books, and is traveling widely, conducting workshops for teachers and administrators on Response to Intervention, Differentiated Instruction, and Class Management and Discipline. His use of humor and emphasis on practical classroom strategies make him a favorite among workshop providers.

 **Martha J. Larkin** taught public school students in general education and special education at the elementary, middle, and secondary levels for several years. She then earned her PhD from the University of Alabama in 1999 and began a career in higher education. She has authored and coauthored 19 journal articles, 14 book and monograph chapters, and 6 research reports and commissioned papers in education and special education. She specializes in instructional strategies, particularly for students with learning disabilities. Her specific teaching and research interests include scaffolded instruction, content enhancement, learning strategies, graphic organizers, and grading rubrics. She especially enjoys pursuing these interests in the areas of reading, writing, and mathematics. She would like to receive your comments on this book and may be contacted at mlarkin@westga.edu.

Introduction

A New Age in Reading Instruction for Students With Learning Difficulties

Anew age in reading instruction has begun for students with learning disabilities and other reading disorders (Fuchs & Fuchs, 2007; Sousa, 2005). Although reading problems have been a concern for many years, increasing emphasis on effective reading instruction has been noted in several arenas—medical research, and political, to name only a few. In the 1990s, not only were new strategies being developed for reading instruction (e.g., phonemic-based instruction), but strategies developed in the 1980s were finding wide acceptance among teachers in elementary and middle school inclusive classes (e.g., metacognitive learning strategies). Further, several brain-scanning techniques were being developed and applied to the study of reading in students with learning disabilities (Sousa, 2005). Also, new research in genetics offered the promise of alleviating some reading problems in the future. On the political stage, several reports and legislative efforts created a major new emphasis on reading and early literacy instruction. Finally, with the new emphasis on documenting response to intervention in reading, teachers in every grade level across the nation are gearing up for increased responsibilities in reading instruction (Bender & Shores, 2007; Bradley, Danielson, & Doolittle, 2007; Fuchs & Fuchs, 2007). All these initiatives have created new demands on teachers and a new age in reading instructional techniques for today's classrooms.

NEW READING INSTRUCTIONAL STRATEGIES NEEDED NOW!

Reading and literacy skills are some of the most important skills a child with learning disabilities and other reading difficulties can master during the early years of schooling, because reading skills are the basis for subsequent mastery of almost every subject area (Kame'enui, Carnine, Dixon, Simmons, & Coyne, 2002; Sousa, 2005). For this reason, reading traditionally has received heavy emphasis in our nation's schools. However, research on the reading skills among children with learning disabilities and other reading difficulties has documented a higher rate of failure in reading instruction than any nation can

1

afford. For example, almost 20% of the nation's schoolchildren encounter some reading problems prior to Grade 3, and approximately 40% read below level for their grade (Kame'enui et al., 2002; National Institute of Child Health and Development [NICHD], 2000). From this group of students with reading difficulties come the students who eventually are placed in classes for students with learning disabilities.

THE GROWING NATIONAL EMPHASIS ON READING

Because of the reading problems noted above, a fundamental effort toward improving reading skills has been initiated at both the state and the national levels. The national emphasis on reading has resulted in two highly publicized efforts and one additional report that received somewhat less attention. First, in 1997, the federal government convened an expert panel—the National Reading Panel—to determine what instructional strategies work best in reading instruction (NICHD, 2000). The work of this group will be presented at numerous points throughout this book.

 ### REFLECTIVE EXERCISE
THE NATIONAL READING PANEL SYNOPSIS

At various points in the text, we will present a suggestion for an exercise or activity for you, which will enable you to reflect on the information and strategies provided. Of course, these exercises are optional, but taking a few minutes and exploring via these reflective exercises should assist you in developing a larger set of reading instructional ideas for students with learning difficulties.

As your first reflective exercise, visit the Web site (www.national readingpanel.org) of the National Reading Panel (NRP) and review the summary report of the NRP. You may wish to familiarize yourself with that Web site, since we will refer to these findings throughout this book.

Next, the federal initiative referred to as the "No Child Left Behind" legislation has added more emphasis to the incorporation of reading instruction into every elementary and middle school classroom (Bradley et al., 2007). Specifically, the No Child Left Behind legislation mandated that each state receiving federal funding in education submit a plan for reading instruction to the federal government. These state reading plans were required to stipulate the specific research-based reading instructional curricula that the state planned to use to assess and address early literacy deficits among students with learning disabilities as well as other students at risk for reading failure. After a review at the federal level of 40 such state plans, only 11 plans were approved, and of those plans that were not approved, the Department of Education, which conducted the review, indicated that most did not show how the funds would be spent on research-based reading programs (Manzo, 2002). Clearly, this represents a new emphasis on research-driven best practices in reading for each and every classroom, to which all educators must attend.

Based on this legislation, teachers are now expected to use only research-proven reading instructional strategies and to intervene for every child (hence the "no child left behind" language) as soon as a reading problem is noted. Across the nation, schools are providing professional development opportunities to prepare teachers for this emphasis on research-proven strategies, and this emphasis will increase during the next few years.

Finally, because of the increasing numbers of students who are identified with learning disabilities based on reading problems, President Bush appointed a presidential commission to review special education practices. In 2001, that Commission on Excellence in Special Education produced its report, titled *Revitalizing Special Education for Children and Their Families*. That report highlighted the fact that the vast majority of students identified as learning disabled are identified based on a reading deficit. One recommendation of this group involved the implementation of response to intervention (RTI) procedures for documenting the eligibility of students for services for learning disabilities (Bradley et al., 2007; Division of Learning Disabilities, 2007). That recommendation became law in December of 2004, when President Bush signed the reauthorization of the federal special education legislation, Individuals With Disabilities Education Act (IDEA). Thus, RTI is now allowed as an eligibility procedure for students suspected of having a learning disability. Further, RTI procedures are typically implemented by general education teachers, so in virtually every state in the nation, general education teachers are undergoing additional inservice on implementing RTI for reading disabilities (Bender & Shores, 2007; Fuchs & Fuchs, 2007). One purpose of this book is to provide teachers with concise, up-to-date information on how to do an RTI procedure in various areas of reading.

With these three national initiatives noted, the nation has experienced a new, critically important emphasis on reading instruction. All elementary and middle school educators will be expected to provide research-proven reading instruction for students with learning disabilities and other reading problems in general education classes and special education classes. Teachers will be expected to provide a range of instructional options, including whole class, small group, and individual instructional strategies within the context of the inclusive general education class. Further, teachers will need to emphasize reading skills much more, across all subject areas in the elementary and middle grades. This book is intended to facilitate research-based reading instruction implemented in an RTI model, from the early grades through middle school.

LEARNING DISABILITIES AND EARLY READING PROBLEMS

Learning Disabilities or Learning Difficulties?

It is no secret that students with learning disabilities present an array of reading problems from the earliest years of their schooling. However, because the term *learning disabilities* traditionally has been defined as a discrepancy between reading achievement and intelligence, students who have this disability often are not identified until their second or perhaps even their third year in school (Bender, 2008). In fact, in most cases a reading problem must develop prior to specifically identifying a particular child as demonstrating a learning disability. This presents a problem for many children since children must fail in reading— or in some other subject area—prior to identification and subsequent assistance with their reading problems. The Commission on Excellence in Special Education (2001) noted that this "wait-to-fail" basis of services for students with learning disabilities was unfair and inadequate, and that was the major reason for the recommendation of the RTI procedures as an eligibility tool.

This wait-to-fail arrangement is even less satisfactory when one considers the fact that so much critical and essential reading instruction takes place during the first several years of schooling, beginning in early kindergarten and continuing throughout the early grades. Clearly, teachers have a moral obligation to provide effective, enhanced reading instruction from the first signs of difficulty on the part of the child, and the RTI procedure is intended to facilitate that from the earliest days of kindergarten through the early school years (Fuchs & Fuchs, 2007).

To address reading problems among students with learning disabilities, who may not have been identified in kindergarten, we have chosen in this book to discuss students with learning difficulties or reading difficulties rather than exclusively use the term *learning disabilities*. Clearly, it would be incorrect to use the term for students who have not been so identified, and for our purposes here we view many students with early reading problems as students who eventually may be identified and placed in classes for students with learning disabilities. The broader terms *learning difficulties* and *reading difficulties* should be taken to mean all students who have reading problems, many of which may date from their earliest schooling. Further, this group of students with learning difficulties also would include students who may later be identified as students with Attention Deficit Hyperactivity Disorder (ADHD) or other reading problems. We hope the use of terms other than learning disabilities will ease communication throughout this text. Also, note that all the reading tactics, strategies, and assessments presented in this text are equally useful for all those students with reading problems that manifest in the elementary or middle grades.

Cognitive Deficits and Learning Difficulties

With that qualification of terms in mind, there are several learning characteristics of students with learning difficulties that negatively impact reading success. First, students with learning difficulties often demonstrate problems in attention skills; this particularly is true for students who eventually are identified as ADHD or learning disabled. Further, the attention deficits demonstrated by these students will negatively impact reading achievement over time (Sousa, 2001, 2005). Clearly, if a child with learning difficulties does not—or cannot— pay attention during instruction on letter recognition or other early reading skills, that child will have reading difficulties later on. Many such attention problems lead eventually to significant reading problems.

Next, the memory skills of many children who manifest reading problems in the elementary and middle grades are quite weak (Bender, 2008; Sousa, 2005). Of course, every teacher in the elementary grades has experienced at least one child who seemed to grasp the meaning of new vocabulary terms on one day, only to seem clueless the very next day when the same terms are presented again. Also, students with memory problems often manifest the ability to decode a word (i.e., sound out a word using letter sounds), but seem to forget the new term within a period of days. These memory problems can be identified as the root of many subsequent reading problems. Thus, many students with learning difficulties will need to receive much more applied practice to memorize new terms in reading.

Finally, many students with learning disabilities demonstrate cognitive deficits in visual or auditory processing skills. Students with visual processing problems often have trouble copying information from the dry-erase board or from their text. For some students, the letters in words seem to move across the page as students read. Obviously, these deficits will have a negative impact on reading (Sousa, 2005).

For example, one subgroup of students with learning disabilities manifests a reading disorder referred to as dyslexia (Bender, 2008). Historically, dyslexia has been associated with visual processing problems that interfere with letter and word identification in reading. Clearly, if a student perceives letters to be swimming across the page or if recognition of one letter interferes with recognition of subsequent letters in the word, that student will have problems in reading. This brief discussion highlights only a few of the cognitive processing problems that may negatively impact reading, and other brain-based cognitive processing problems are presented in more detail.

THE PURPOSE OF THIS BOOK

Our purpose in writing this book is to provide for elementary and middle grade teachers a practical set of research-based instructional strategies for use in the newly mandated RTI procedures in the general education class for students suspected of having learning disabilities and other reading difficulties. Teachers need practical strategies that will help document how a child is responding to instruction, and these strategies must be grounded in effective research and work in the real context of today's classrooms. The strategies and tactics presented herein are proven in elementary and middle school classes across the nation. Within the book, teachers will find strategies and instructional examples for use in inclusive classrooms, as well as in RTI procedures.

We should note that throughout this book we use the term *strategy* for an involved instructional idea or concept that takes some degree of teacher time to develop for use in the classroom. In contrast, we use the term *tactic* to represent a series of toss-out ideas that can be easily and immediately implemented with little or no preparation. Often tactics are presented in lists or teaching tips throughout the text, while more involved strategies are described in more detail within the text.

While research-proven reading strategies are now mandated nationally, our intention is not to provide extensive research reviews of these strategies, nor do we review all the available curricula on the commercial market. Rather, this book presents a one-stop source for reading instructional ideas for use in RTI procedures throughout the elementary and middle grades (approximately Grades K–7), with the research reviewed only sparingly. We hope this will provide teachers with a ready reference for their increasingly important role in reading instruction for students with learning difficulties.

REFERENCES

Bender, W. N. (2008). *Learning disabilities: Characteristics, identification and teaching strategies* (6th ed.). Boston: Allyn & Bacon.

Bender, W. N., & Shores, C. (2007). *Response to intervention: A practical guide for every teacher.* Thousand Oaks, CA: Corwin Press.

Bradley, R., Danielson, L., & Doolittle, J. (2007). Responsiveness to intervention: 1997 to 2007. *Teaching Exceptional Children, 39*(5), 8–13.

Commission on Excellence in Special Education. (2001). *A new era: Revitalizing special education for children and their families.* Washington, DC: U.S. Department of Education. Viewable online at http://www.ed.gov/inits/commissionsboards/whspecialeducation.

Division of Learning Disabilities. (2007). *Thinking about response to intervention and learning disabilities: A teacher's guide.* Arlington, VA: Author.

Fuchs, L. S., & Fuchs, D. (2007). A model for implementing responsiveness to intervention. *Teaching Exceptional Children, 39*(5), 14–23.

Kame'enui, E. J., Carnine, D. W., Dixon, R. C., Simmons, D. C., & Coyne, M. D. (2002). *Effective teaching strategies that accommodate diverse learners* (2nd ed.). Upper Saddle River, NJ: Merrill-Prentice Hall.

Manzo, K. K. (2002, October 2). Majority of states told to revise reading plans. *Education Week,* p. 10.

National Institute of Child Health and Development. (2000). *Teaching children to read: An evidence-based assessment of the scientific research literature on reading and its implications for reading instruction* (Report of the National Reading Panel). Retrieved May 23, 2002, from http://www.nichd.nih.gov/publications/nrp/findings.cfm.

Sousa, D. A. (2001). *How the special needs brain learns.* Thousand Oaks, CA: Corwin Press.

Sousa, D. A. (2005). *How the brain learns to read.* Thousand Oaks, CA: Corwin Press.

The Reading Brain, Literacy Instruction, and RTI 1

Strategies Presented in This Chapter Include

✓ Big Ideas From Reading Research

✓ Several Informal Early Literacy Assessments

✓ A Phonics Literacy Checklist

✓ DIBELS

✓ Ten Tactics for the Brain Compatible Classroom

✓ Brain Compatible Research Results for the Classroom Teacher

✓ The Basics of RTI in Reading

THE GOOD NEWS IN READING RESEARCH!

Although the initial picture of reading success among students with learning disabilities and other reading difficulties, as presented by the National Reading Panel (NRP), was not overly positive, there is much good news to report (King & Gurian, 2006; National Institute of Child Health and Development [NICHD], 2000; Sousa, 2005). Research on reading instruction has exploded in the past two decades, resulting in major advances in several related areas including the brain and central nervous systems bases for reading, literacy instruction, phonological awareness research, and reading comprehension instructional tactics for students with reading difficulties (Bender, 2008; Bhat, Griffin, & Sindelar, 2003; Chard & Dickson, 1999; Joseph, Noble, & Eden, 2001; Kemp & Eaton, 2007; Rourke, 2005; Sousa, 2005; Sylwester, 2001; Wood & Grigorenko, 2001). Much of this research (e.g., brain functioning during reading) is rather esoteric in nature and generally not readily accessible for the practicing teacher. In fact, a major emphasis of this book is to make this research—and the instructional ideas that are based on it—readily available to every elementary teacher in the classroom.

There is more good news. Because of the passage of the Individuals With Disabilities Education Act (IDEA) of 2004, teachers across the nation now are beginning to implement response to intervention (RTI) procedures that more closely track how struggling students are doing in their reading and early literacy (Bender & Shores, 2007; Bradley, Danielson, & Doolittle, 2007; Fuchs & Fuchs, 2007; Kemp & Eaton, 2007). As teachers "ramp up" their efforts in this regard, reading instruction will improve for many struggling readers as earlier interventions are provided that are specifically targeted to address their reading problems.

Within this growing body of research, three emerging emphases will provide the basis for this text—the emphasis on a holistic view of early literacy instruction (Haager, 2002; McCutchen et al., 2002; Shaker, 2001), the growing literature on brain compatible reading instruction in the classroom (King & Gurian, 2006; Prigge, 2002; Rourke, 2005; Sousa, 2001, 2005; Sylwester, 2001), and the recent RTI mandate (Bradley, Danielson, & Doolittle, 2007; Fuchs & Fuchs, 2007). Each of these emphases is presented below to provide a backdrop for the strategies discussed in this and each subsequent chapter.

BIG IDEAS FROM EARLY LITERACY RESEARCH

As mentioned previously, there has been an explosion of research in the area of reading within the past decade (Bender, 2008; King & Gurian, 2006; Rourke, 2005; Sousa, 2005). As a result, a number of recent research-based conclusions have been developed concerning how reading skills progress among learners without reading difficulties. A number of points about reading instruction from a variety of sources are presented to provide a basis for discussion of the reading strategies and tactics for students with reading problems (Fuchs & Fuchs, 2007; Kame'enui, Carnine, Dixon, Simmons, & Coyne, 2002; NICHD, 2000; Sousa, 2005). These big ideas represent our best understandings of reading difficulties, as well as the best practices in reading instruction for all students today. These seven ideas are

- Reading is not natural.
- There is no "reading" area in the brain.
- Reading disabilities result from both genetic and environmental influences.
- Development of reading skill is complex and long term.
- Students must learn the alphabetic principle and the alphabetic code.
- Phoneme manipulation and phonics are the most effective ways to teach reading.
- Students must develop automaticity with the code.

Reading Is Not Natural

Unlike sight, hearing, cognition, or the development of language, reading is not a natural process. For example, an infant isolated on an island will develop sight, hearing, attention skills, rudimentary numeration and counting skills, and language of some sort, but reading will not develop naturally (Sousa, 2001, 2005). Of course, a human infant isolated on an island probably would not survive, but give us some literary flexibility here! In short, reading skills will not develop unless these skills are specifically taught, so teachers should emphasize them in every aspect of the school curriculum throughout the earliest instruction in kindergarten, as well as the early and middle school years.

There Is No "Reading" Area in the Brain

Although regions of the brain can be associated with sight, hearing, physical movement, or language, there is no single reading area within the brain. Rather, reading involves many more areas of the brain than does language development but must be understood as a function of linguistic capability (Armstrong, 2007). While speech and language seem to be "hardwired in the brain," with specific areas related to these skills, reading is not hardwired in only one or two brain areas (Sousa, 2001). This is one reason that reading skill does not develop naturally.

Reading Disabilities Result From Both Genetic and Environmental Influences

The evidence for a genetic abnormality that may lead to a reading disability has grown stronger over the years (Wood & Grigorenko, 2001), and various research studies have implicated a variety of specific regions within specific chromosomes—particularly chromosomes 1, 2, 6, 13, 14, and 15—as possible genetic problem areas for students with learning disabilities (Raskind, 2001). However, much more research is needed prior to isolating a specific genetic basis for either learning disabilities or reading disabilities. Further, although teachers cannot control genetic influences in a child's life, they can control the environment in which reading instruction occurs, and manipulating that reading environment offers teachers the best option to assist students in developing reading skills. For our purposes, we will concentrate on environmental strategies such as RTI, phonemic instruction, and tactics for enhancing reading comprehension, rather than the growing literature on genetic causes of reading problems for students with learning disabilities. Teachers also would be well-advised to adopt such an emphasis on environmental-instructional bases of reading development.

Development of Reading Skill Is Complex and Long Term

All children speak (or communicate in some fashion) before they read, and speech sounds serve as the basis for reading (Sousa, 2005). A *phoneme* is the briefest discrete sound that can communicate meaning. In total, all the languages in the world include only about 150 phonemes (Sousa, 2005). For the

English language, some researchers report 41 phonemes (NICHD, 2000), whereas others suggest there are 44 discrete phonemes (Sousa, 2001). Reading involves making brain connections between phonemes and *graphemes*, or the squiggly lines on a page that represent printed letters. This transition is very difficult for some 30% of children, and these children develop reading problems to some degree; this group also includes children who are later identified as students with learning disabilities.

Just to confuse matters further, there is no one-to-one relationship between the phonemes and the specific letters in our alphabet. Thus, learning to read is both a complex and a long-term endeavor for all students, and students with learning disabilities in particular (Kame'enui et al., 2002). Teachers in kindergarten through middle school should build reading instruction into every instructional period as a primary and major emphasis, and recent federal and state initiatives are emphasizing that instructional need.

We now know that reading is based on the brain's ability to detect and manipulate phonemes, and that students who have not mastered these prereading skills will have great difficulty in reading (Sousa, 2005). Further, phonemic-based skill is a prerequisite for teaching phonics (which is the pairing phonemic skill and letter recognition), and even as late as middle school, phonemic instruction can be an effective component of reading instruction (Bhat, Griffin, & Sindelar, 2003).

Students Must Learn the Alphabetic Principle and the Alphabetic Code

The *alphabetic principle* involves the fact that most phonemes, and all speech sounds in English, can be represented by letters, and the pairing of speech sounds to printed letters is referred to as phonics instruction. Further, a child's ability to decode unknown words is based on those letter-sound relationships. The *alphabetic code* thus represents the relationships between letters and the sounds they represent. Research has documented that students with learning disabilities must learn the alphabetic principle to read effectively across the grade levels; merely memorizing words and word meanings is not enough for successful reading long term (Kame'enui et al., 2002; Sousa, 2005). Further, the alphabetic principle is not learned merely from exposure to print, but must be specifically taught (Sousa, 2005).

Phoneme Manipulation and Phonics Are the Most Effective Ways to Teach Reading

Although debate has raged for decades over phonics versus sight word instructional techniques, the evidence has clearly shown that an emphasis on phonemic instruction, and phonics (as represented by the alphabetic principle involving discrete sound manipulations and sound-letter relationships), is the most effective instructional method for reading for almost all children with and without reading problems (NICHD, 2000). Elementary and middle school teachers should emphasize the relationships between sounds and letters in every subject area whenever possible.

Students Must Develop Automaticity With the Code

While phoneme manipulation, phonetic decoding, word segmentation, and use of context clues to determine word meaning are all essential skills in early reading, rigorous application of these skills for every letter or word on the page would result in a highly cumbersome reading process. Rather, to develop effective reading skills, students must learn the alphabetic principle and the alphabetic code extremely well, so that the brain processing involved in decoding these letter sounds is "automatic" (Kame'enui et al., 2002)—this is referred to as *automaticity*. In that fashion, the student's brain may process many letters, sounds, or words at one time, and fluent reading is possible. Teachers should build their instruction such that every child with reading problems can attain automaticity in reading. Various reading programs described in subsequent chapters (e.g., Academy of Reading by AutoSkill, or Fast ForWord) focus directly on developing automaticity and fluency in all aspects of reading skill, from phonemic awareness and manipulation up through reading comprehension.

 REFLECTIVE EXERCISE 1.1
USING THE BIG IDEAS FROM READING RESEARCH

Pause for a moment and consider the big ideas presented above. Almost all these ideas can suggest instructional activities within the classroom for students with learning disabilities and other reading difficulties, and we encourage you to reflect on how many of these ideas are currently implemented in your class. Remember that, with the growing national emphasis on reading, all teachers in elementary and middle grades should be teaching reading skills and should be building an emphasis on these skills into every lesson plan.

THE EMERGING EMPHASIS ON LITERACY

Within the last decade, an emphasis on early literacy instruction—versus merely an emphasis on reading—has emerged (Armstrong, 2007; McCutchen et al., 2002; Shaker, 2001). Literacy approaches focus not only on the discrete skills in reading such as phonics and reading comprehension (Bos, Mather, Silver-Pacuilla, & Narr, 2000; Patzer & Pettegrew, 1996; Smith, Baker, & Oudeans, 2001), but also on the more holistic set of skills that enhances and supports a student's skill in reading, such as the student's ability to speak, write, and listen effectively, as well as to use these literacy skills in reading and communicating (Winn & Otis-Wilborn, 1999). The emphasis in a literacy approach is on the interrelationship between reading, writing, and language and the interdependence of these systems within the human brain. However, this certainly does not mean that the particulars of phoneme manipulation, phonics, word attack, or comprehension are not taught—they are. Rather, the emphasis is on the end goal of reading—the ability to derive meaning from the written word and to use that skill as a communication tool.

Further, within the literacy emphasis, there is a growing emphasis on assisting struggling readers to improve their literacy skills, rather than merely a focus on remediation of specific and discrete reading deficits (Dayton-Sakari, 1997). In most cases, this results in an emphasis on the phoneme manipulation skills that have not been mastered previously or on instruction on the alphabetic principle. Smith et al. (2001) delineated several components of early literacy instruction that constitute an effective literacy program. Notice the emphasis on discrete skill instruction on letter names and sounds in the following skills.

1. Allocation of time for daily, highly focused literacy instruction

2. Consistent routines for teaching the big ideas of literacy

3. Explicit instruction for new letter names and sounds

4. Daily scaffolded or assisted practice with auditory phoneme detection, segmenting, and blending

5. Immediate corrective feedback

6. Daily application of new knowledge at the phoneme and lettersound levels across multiple and varied literacy contexts

7. Daily reviews

A word of explanation may be in order for several of these skills. First, examples of big ideas in literacy instruction may include things such as teaching the alphabet as code or teaching students that all stories have structure (e.g., character, story problem, climax) and using story structure as a basis for instruction. Next, the term *scaffolded* in Point 4 refers to the supports that a teacher provides to an individual child in assisting that child to improve his or her current reading skill. Typically, scaffolded instruction involves an in-depth, individualized examination of the reading skills, instructional support from the teacher to the child for the next skill to be mastered, and a planned withdrawal of support from the student to ensure that the student masters each successive skill independently (Larkin, 2001).

Research on Literacy Instruction

Consistent with the broader research results reported earlier, research on early literacy instruction has supported a strong phoneme-based instructional approach for students with reading problems (Bender, 2008; Bos et al., 2000; NICHD, 2000; Patzer & Pettegrew, 1996; Smith et al., 2001). The research supports the use of group-based oral reading, or choral reading, as an instructional technique to enhance reading fluency, because reading is dependent upon a student's language ability. Also, choral reading practice is recommended because students often are called upon to read orally in class across the grade levels (NICHD, 2000). This emphasis will be discussed in more detail later in the book.

Next, early instruction in reading should be quite robust; that is, instruction in each area of reading skill should be undertaken with sufficient intensity to assist students in reaching their early reading goals. Research has also shown that, for young readers who lag behind others in kindergarten and first grade, phonological instruction is even more important in their early literacy instruction (AutoSkill, 2004; Kame'enui et al., 2002). In fact, students who miss early phonological instruction always will lag behind in reading, and phonological instruction may be necessary in the late elementary or middle school grades for those students with reading problems.

McCutchen et al. (2002) used an experimental design and studied teachers' awareness of these newly emerging literacy emphases by investigating teachers' instruction and student outcomes in 44 classrooms scattered throughout the western states. These researchers not only assessed teacher knowledge of these literacy skills, but also observed how teachers instructed their students and noted the students' outcomes in phonological awareness, listening comprehension, and word reading. The results indicated that teachers were, in many cases, unaware of this emerging emphasis on phonemic instruction. However, based on a two-week instructional workshop, the teachers in the experimental group quickly grasped the importance of this emphasis, as well as the instructional techniques involved. Those teachers then implemented these practices, and students' reading skills improved rather dramatically in each area.

The good news from this study, as well as other research, is that phonological awareness is a teachable skill—teachers can learn these instructional techniques and students can learn the phonological manipulation skills that will improve their overall reading skill. Many of these instructional techniques are presented in Chapter 2, which concentrates on phonemic instruction, as well as subsequent chapters. Further, these results document that adequate instruction in that area will enhance the reading of students who display subsequent reading disabilities (Kame'enui et al., 2002; Smith et al., 2001). Thus, as teachers become aware of this broader emphasis on early literacy instruction, as well as the need to emphasize the alphabetic principle and phonemic instruction, the prognosis for remediation improves considerably across the grade levels (Bhat, Griffin, & Sindelar, 2003).

Further, phonemic instruction can be managed very effectively in a technology format (AutoSkill, 2004). Various computer-based reading programs have been developed that emphasize a student's ability to detect, compare, and manipulate phonemes, and this will save teachers considerable instructional time.

 ### REFLECTIVE EXERCISE 1.2
DEVELOPING LITERACY INSTRUCTIONAL SYSTEMS

With the emerging emphasis on literacy in recent years, coupled with the No Child Left Behind legislation from the federal government in 2001, a number of comprehensive literacy programs have been developed. These new literacy programs involve a wide array of skills ranging from early phoneme instruction to reading and writing skills. As one example, you may wish to review the Four Blocks program by Patricia M. Cunningham and Dorothy P. Hall (www.four-blocks.com). The four blocks involve (1) guided reading, (2) self-selected reading,

(3) writing, and (4) working with words. The early research on this project indicated strong initial results in one school in North Carolina. The Four Blocks program is a comprehensive program that involves the entire range of literacy skills.

Word Play and the Development of Early Literacy Skills

With the continuing research efforts in reading, as well as the advent of several newly developed research technologies (described below), we have gained a more complete picture not only of how reading skills develop, but of the dependent relationship between reading and the development of language. A representation of the development of these interrelated skills is presented below.

A List of Early Literacy Skills	
Development of oral language	Birth to 24 months
Phoneme discrimination	Birth to 11 months
Says first words	6 months to 11 months
Follows simple verbal directions	12 months to 17 months
Pronounces first vowels and most consonants	18 months to 24 months
Enjoys having a story read	18 months to 24 months
Awareness of certain letters (such as letters presented in advertising; i.e., *M* stands for McDonald's and *K* for Kellogg's)	24 months to 36 months
Complex phoneme manipulation	48 months to 8 years
Can tell a story	36 to 48 months
Becomes aware of the alphabetic code (i.e., letters stand for specific sounds)	48 months to Grade 1
Begins to read first words	48 months to Grade 1
Can grasp meaning from reading short paragraphs	Grade 1 to Grade 3
Begins to comprehend longer texts	Grade 1 to Grade 3

As you can see, reading is dependent upon the development of language in most children, and children with learning difficulties are no different in terms of these general milestones. However, children at risk for reading failure do progress through these milestones somewhat later than other children. Likewise, children who are hearing impaired do not follow this sequence, but the placement of oral language at the top of this list of skills correctly presents language as a fundamental basis for reading for almost every child.

Also, note that informal reading instruction begins prior to school. In our society, children—including children with learning difficulties in reading—learn that a *K* means breakfast cereal (can't every three-year old grab the cereal from the cabinet under the sink?) and an *M* means McDonald's. Children are surrounded by letters and many pick up the correct meaning of those letters at an early age. Of course, parents are well-advised to engage in word play or letter play whenever young children show an interest in these letters. This can prepare a child for later work in reading. Finally, teachers should make letter play and word play a fun aspect of the classroom from the prekindergarten programs through the elementary grades. This will greatly enhance the reading skills of the students with learning disabilities in the class and will develop reading skills that will stay with those children throughout life.

ASSESSMENTS OF EARLY LITERACY

Using Informal Literacy Checklists

As an example of a comprehensive literacy strategy, teachers may wish to consider using a literacy checklist. Literacy checklists are available from many sources and have been offered by a number of authors in the literature. The skills on the checklists may reflect the entire array of reading skills ranging from early phonemic awareness to higher-order reading comprehension. However, rather than depend on checklists devised by a reading scholar, Winn and Otis-Wilborn (1999) suggest the use of individually developed checklists for monitoring the literacy of individual students. An individually developed checklist allows the teacher to develop individually the items on the checklist and thus to specifically tailor the checklist to the needs and strengths of the student. A sample of such a literacy checklist is presented in Teaching Tip 1.1.

As you can see, this informal literacy checklist encompasses a wider variety of literacy skills, in this case phonemic and phonics skills, than would a traditional reading instructional lesson, and this broader view is the perspective supported by proponents of literacy instruction. Of course, teachers should vary the reading skills on the checklist for each student to reflect specifically those literacy skills that are relevant for that particular student. For some students, the indicators on the checklist would be exclusively comprehension, and for other students a mix of decoding or word attack skills and comprehension skills may be noted. A checklist for comprehension skills that would be useful for elementary and middle school students is presented in Teaching Tip 1.2. Teachers should feel free to alter or adapt these checklists to exclude or include any skills relevant for a particular student.

DIBELS: An Informal Assessment of Basic Literacy

The *Dynamic Indicators of Basic Early Literacy Skills* (DIBELS; Good & Kaminski, 2002) is an informal assessment of early literacy skills that can be obtained from Sopris West (in Longmont, CO). Although we do not intend to discuss large numbers of curricula or assessments in this book, we will present commercial materials that are research based and can enhance reading assessment and instruction for students with learning difficulties. On that basis, we recommend that every teacher of kindergarten through Grade 3 take the time to investigate this informal assessment of early literacy skills.

☞ **TEACHING TIP 1.1**

A Sample Literacy Checklist

Name _____ Date _____ Reading Material _____

   While listening to a child read, the teacher should note below specific examples of the successes and difficulties experienced. Completing this checklist during several reading activities will present a more complete picture of the child's reading skills. The teacher may also complete this checklist at the end of the grading period, as a postinstructional assessment.

1. Attempts to decode unknown words _____
   _____
   _____
   _____

2. Difficulty with initial consonant sounds _____
   _____
   _____
   _____

3. Difficulty with vowels _____
   _____
   _____
   _____

4. Difficulty with consonant blends _____
   _____
   _____
   _____

5. Difficulty with multisyllabic words _____
   _____
   _____
   _____

6. Demonstrates self-correcting _____
   _____
   _____
   _____

7. Demonstrates understanding _____
   _____
   _____
   _____

☞ TEACHING TIP 1.2

A Comprehension Checklist for Elementary Textbook Reading

Name _____ Date _____ Reading Material _____

   While listening to a child read from a subject area textbook, the teacher should note below specific examples of the successes and difficulties experienced. Completing this checklist during several reading activities will present a more complete picture of the child's reading skills. The teacher also may complete this checklist at the end of the grading period, as a postinstructional assessment.

1. Reflects on the relationship between the current chapter and previous or subsequent chapters _____
_____
_____

2. Reviews chapter headings and subheadings prior to reading _____
_____
_____
_____

3. Reviews vocabulary lists or review questions prior to reading _____
_____
_____
_____

4. Reflects on pictures and picture captions presented in text _____
_____
_____
_____

5. Makes predictions about information which may be found in various sections of the chapter text _____
_____
_____

6. Reads the chapter reflectively _____
_____
_____
_____

7. Answers comprehension or review questions after reading with 85% accuracy
_____
_____
_____

DIBELS is a research-based assessment that teachers love because it is quite easy to administer. Individual sections of this assessment take approximately two to three minutes to complete, which makes this assessment a user-friendly approach to early literacy instruction (Langdon, 2004).

DIBELS is based on a number of early indicators of literacy success (Haager, 2002). Its four stepping-stones indicate with a high degree of accuracy which students will display learning difficulties and eventual learning disabilities in reading. For example, by two months into kindergarten, students should master onset recognition—referred to as initial sounds fluency—and that measure becomes a benchmark. Students who do not master initial sounds fluency by several months into kindergarten are quite likely to develop later reading difficulties (Langdon, 2004). Other stepping-stones through the first several years of school, such as those presented below, represent similar benchmarks.

Onset fluency (initial sounds)	Two months into kindergarten
Phoneme segmentation fluency	End of kindergarten
Nonsense words fluency	Middle of Grade 1
Oral reading fluency	End of Grade 1

The DIBELS assess students' performance on these benchmarks and can predict, with a high degree of accuracy, which students will develop subsequent reading problems. This assessment also includes some higher-level reading skills such as oral reading fluency through Grade 3. Other DIBELS measures include word-use fluency and retelling fluency (story retelling frequently is used as an indicator of early reading comprehension). Again, for students who meet these benchmarks on time, reading difficulties are not likely to develop. However, for students who do not master these skills by the times mentioned above, reading problems are quite likely to develop. Thus, for teachers to determine which students are having difficulty or may be likely to have difficulty, DIBELS is quite useful as an information measure of early literacy skill. Further, with the emerging emphasis on RTI across the nation, many states (e.g., Ohio and West Virginia) have chosen to use this instrument as the early screening instrument for all students in kindergarten through Grade 3.

BRAIN COMPATIBLE READING INSTRUCTION

With the growing national emphasis on early literacy in mind, we can turn to the emerging information on how the human brain learns to process information during the reading process. This area of research—commonly known as brain compatible instruction—has emerged only within the past 15 years and is based primarily on improvements in the medical sciences (Bhat, Griffin, & Sindelar, 2003; King & Gurian, 2006; Leonard, 2001; Prigge, 2002; Sousa, 2001, 2005; Sylwester, 2001).

Specifically, several brain measurement techniques have emerged that have added to our understanding of brain functioning. First, much of our increasing understanding of the human brain has come from the development of functional magnetic resonance imaging (fMRI). This is a nonradiological technique—and thus a relatively safe brain-scanning technique—that has allowed scientists to study the performance of human brains while the subject concentrates on different types of learning tasks (Richards, 2001; Sousa, 2005).

The fMRI measures the brain's use of oxygen and glucose during the thinking process, and from that information, physicians can determine which brain areas are most active during various types of educational tasks (Richards, 2001; Sousa, 2005). For example, specialists have now identified brain regions that are specifically associated with various learning activities such as language, math, auditory processing, motor learning, listening to music, or verbally responding to questions in a classroom discussion (Leonard, 2001). Further, a body of research on students with learning disabilities or other reading disorders also has emerged (Sousa, 2001).

As one example of this research, researchers working with Shaywitz at Yale University compared brain functioning of 29 dyslexic readers and 32 nondisabled readers (Shaywitz et al., 1996). Dyslexia readers had great difficulty in reading nonsense rhyming words (e.g., "lete" and "jeat"), whereas normal readers had no such difficulty. Further, using fMRI scans while readers were performing these tasks, these researchers showed that brains of the dyslexic readers were underactivated in the brain region that links print to the brain's language areas, compared to normal readers. However, the brains of the dyslexic readers were overactivated in Broca's area—a brain region associated with spoken language. These researchers suggested that readers with dyslexia were "overcompensating" in Broca's areas for the lack of activation in other areas. Thus, a clear functional difference has been shown between normally reading brains and brains that are challenged by reading.

Another recently developed technique for studying the brain is referred to as PEPSI, which stands for proton echo-planar spectroscopic imaging (Posse, Dager, & Richards, 1997). This technique measures activity in various brain regions by assessing lactate changes in various brain regions, related to a mismatch of the delivery of oxygen to those regions. Richards et al. (1999) compared six dyslexic and seven nondyslexic readers and demonstrated not only differences in brain functioning, but also the brain's ability to modify brain functioning as a result of intensive phonemically based reading instruction.

Many researchers have suggested that the research has developed to a point where specific teaching suggestions may be made (Richards et al., 2000; Shaywitz et al., 1996; Sousa, 2005). Based on this growing understanding of how students with learning difficulties learn, teachers across the nation have begun to restructure their classroom practices based on these brain compatible instruction guidelines (Goldstein & Obrzut, 2001; Leonard, 2001; Sousa, 2005). Although various authors make different recommendations, the ten tactics for a brain compatible instruction classroom, presented in Teaching Tip 1.3, represent some of the accumulated thought in this area; these tactics can enhance your reading instructional practices for all students, in particular students with reading difficulties (Gregory & Chapman, 2002; Prigge, 2002; Richards, 2001; Sousa, 2005).

TEACHING TIP 1.3

Ten Tactics for the Brain Compatible Classroom

1. Provide a safe, comfortable environment. Research on learning has demonstrated that the brain serves as a filter on several levels. The brain selectively focuses on sounds, sights, and other stimuli that threaten our safety, often to the exclusion of other stimuli. A second priority is information resulting in emotional responses, and only as a last priority does the brain process information for new, nonthreatening learning tasks (Sousa, 2001). Thus, students with reading problems must not be distracted by either a sense of danger in their learning environment or emotional threats in the classroom. Unsafe classes and emotional threats or challenges can prevent learning.

2. Provide comfortable furniture. As a part of structuring a comfortable learning environment, many teachers bring house furniture into the classroom and set up reading areas with a sofa and perhaps several comfortable chairs for students with learning difficulties. Lamps also are used in brain compatible classrooms for more home-like lighting, and some research has suggested that lighting closer to the red end of the light spectrum functions like a wake-up call for the brain (Sousa, 2001).

3. Provide water and fruits. Research has shown that the brain requires certain fuels—oxygen, glucose, and water—in order to perform at peak efficiency (Sousa, 2001). Water is essential for the movement of neuron signals through the brain. Research has shown that eating a moderate amount of fruit can boost performance and accuracy of word memory (Sousa, 2001). Thus, in brain compatible classrooms teachers offer students water and dried fruits quite frequently.

4. Require frequent student responses. Students with learning difficulties will learn much more when work output is regularly expected from them, because students generally are much more engaged in the process of learning when they must produce a product of some type (Bender, 2001). Products may include a range of activities such as pictures to demonstrate comprehension of an 1860s Midwestern farm or development of a one-act play to show Washington crossing the Delaware River in the battle of Trenton, New Jersey, during the Revolutionary War.

5. Base instruction on bodily movements when possible. Motor learning takes place in a different area than do higher order thought processes within the brain. Motor learning is based in the cerebellum and motor cortex whereas higher order learning and planning takes place in the frontal lobes of the cerebrum. Thus, motor learning takes place in a more fundamental or *lower* brain area than does learning languages and other *higher* brain functions. Also, the brain considers motor skills more essential to survival, because our evolutionary ancestors often had to run from predators or to hunt for prey. Consequently, motor skills (e.g., swimming, riding a bike), once learned, are remembered much longer than cognitive skills (e.g., foreign language) without a motor basis. This suggests that whenever possible teachers should pair factual memory tasks of higher order with physical movements to assist in memory for students with learning difficulties.

As an example of movement-based learning in an elementary class, the first author developed the following movement-based teaching idea. Students had read a text selection on the functions of a cell wall in protecting the cell. The lesson required an instructional demonstration that represented a cell wall in the processes of protecting the cell from bacteria while letting in various food enzymes. Initially three students stood together facing inward and locked their elbows tightly to represent the cell wall. The teacher then pointed out, "The cell wall is very strong to protect the cell." Next, the teacher selected a bacteria (i.e., another student) to try to break into the cell, with the cell wall holding that bacteria out. The teacher stated, "Cell walls protect the cell from bacteria." Finally, the teacher had a student representing the friendly enzyme move toward the cell wall to gain entrance. The cell wall let her in without delay! The teacher concluded, "Cell walls let in food and friendly enzymes." Elementary students who participate in this motor learning example will never forget this simple demonstration, because movement was used as the basis for comprehending this reading selection on the functions of a cell wall.

6. *Emphasize visual novelty.* The human brain is specifically attuned to seek out novelty and differences in stimuli (Sousa, 2001). In elementary grade reading instruction teachers should use color enhancements, size, and shape enhancements in developing worksheets or material posted in the classroom. However, in order to make this an effective learning tool, teachers should specifically discuss with the students why certain aspects of the material are colored differently and the importance of those colored items. Students with reading disabilities will benefit greatly from color and other novelties in the reading passages. Teachers should consider coloring every topic sentence in paragraphs for students with reading disabilities.

7. *Use chanting, rhymes, and music to increase novelty in learning.* Because music and rhythms are processed in a different area of the brain from language, pairing facts to be learned to a musical melody or a rhythmic chant can enhance memory for reading comprehension. Most adults, upon reflection, can remember the song that was frequently used to memorize the ABCs—the tune to *Twinkle, Twinkle, Little Star*—and many students used that same song for other memory tasks in the higher grades (e.g., multiplication or division math facts).

8. *Increase your wait time.* Different brains process information at different rates, independent of intelligence. Of course, elementary students have learned that teachers often will call on the first one or two students who raise their hand after the teacher has asked a question in class. On average, teachers will wait only two or three seconds before calling on someone for an answer, and this period of time between the question and when an answer is called for is defined as "wait time" (Sousa, 2001). However, the brain research has demonstrated the importance of waiting for a few seconds (perhaps seven to ten seconds) after asking a question, prior to calling on someone for the answer. This increased wait time gives students with reading disabilities, many of whom process information more slowly and deliberately, a longer period of time to consider their answer and hopefully raise their hand to volunteer a response to the teacher's question.

9. *Increase students' choices.* Sylwester (2001) emphasized the use of choices for students. In short, if teachers want their students to make reasonable and informed choices when they are not in the context of the school, teachers must offer choices and coach students in making informed choices within the context of the classroom. Such choices may involve options for demonstrating competence or understanding of a set of facts or other choices among assignments on a particular topic.

(Continued)

TEACHING TIP 1.3 (Continued)

10. Use students to teach other students. Teachers should present some information and then pause and let students discuss it and synthesize it (Sousa, 2001). Alternatively, teachers may wish to have students read a short text selection and then discuss it with a peer buddy. One good idea is to have students discuss the information after every five minutes of reading or discussion.

Teachers may say something like the following:

Turn to your learning buddy beside you and take turns explaining the four points I just made and that we just read about. Let me know if you uncover any disagreements in what each of you heard.

The teacher should then move around the room for one to two minutes, listening to the discussions between the students and checking that the students have a correct understanding of the information just presented.

 REFLECTIVE EXERCISE 1.3
MY BRAIN COMPATIBLE TEACHING

Consider the ten tactics for brain compatible instruction described in Teaching Tip 1.3 in terms of your current teaching. The research on brain compatible instruction, while emphasizing many of these tactics, was not the origin for many of these ideas, and you may be currently using many of these tactics in either small group instruction or whole class instruction for students with learning difficulties. Which tactics can you identify as representative of your methods this year? Which would you like to use more often? The emerging research does suggest that the more we use these ideas, the stronger our instruction in reading will be. Which new ideas would you like to try?

A BRAIN-BASED MODEL OF READING

Although no one argues that teachers should become "brain experts," a general insight into the basic brain processes involved in reading does help to understand many types of reading difficulties for students with learning difficulties. As noted previously, reading is a very complex process. We believe that reading instructional strategies for students with learning difficulties should be presented within the context of this broader emphasis on brain compatible instruction. Further, Sousa's model of the reading brain can provide teachers with numerous insights for instruction, as well as a guide for selection of strategies and tactics for students with reading problems who may demonstrate different instructional needs within the class. Sousa (2001) presented this model in his work, *How the Special Needs Brain Learns.* Within Sousa's model of the reading brain, four areas of the brain, working simultaneously, seem to be most heavily involved in reading: the visual cortex, Wernicke's area, the angular gyrus, and Broca's area (Sousa, 2001).

Beginning on the left of the top section of the model of the reading brain in Figure 1.1, the brain perceived the word *dog* via the visual cortex, which is located at the rear of the brain. The actual brain areas are shown on the sketch of the brain in the figure, which presents both the left and right hemisphere of the brain. The visual stimulus *dog* is immediately transferred to several parts of the brain. These include the angular gyrus, which is involved in this process of phoneme interpretation (Joseph et al., 2001). Next both Broca's area and Wernicke's area become involved in interpretation of those phonemic sounds into meaningful sounds, combinations of sounds, and word. Wernicke's area has traditionally been associated with various types of language function, including auditory processing, comprehension of words, and deriving meaning from words (see Joseph et al., 2001; Sousa, 2001).

Next, Broca's area becomes involved in the translation of the sounds into meaningful language. Broca's area has been associated with not only language, but also grammar and syntax, so while Broca's area is involved in the linguistic aspects of reading a one-word stimulus such as *dog*, it is also searching for and identifying meanings for this word, as well as relationships and meanings that relate this word to other previously read words. Thus, Broca's area is believed to be the language area in which meaning is attached to the stimulus word, *dog*.

Notice that, from the outset, several areas of the brain are heavily involved in the process of reading, that is, the process of translating graphemes (letters on the page) into phonemes (sounds). Even when a student is reading silently, this translation into letter sounds takes place in the brain during the initial stages of reading, and mistranslation can take place throughout this system, leading to reading errors. Of course, one must realize that while these four major areas of the brain are involved in noting the word, decoding the word by

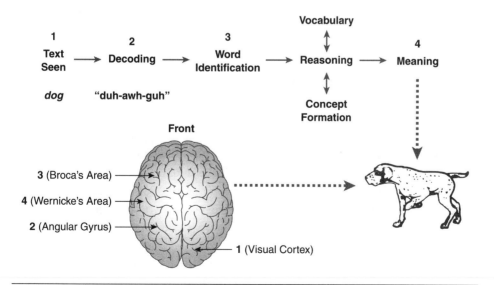

Figure 1.1   Sousa's Model of Reading

SOURCE: Sousa (2001).

sounding it out, and attaching meaning to the word, the eyes and brain continue to scan the page for other words to begin the process all over again. Thus, this word reading process is repeated many times each minute when a student reads, and often the eyes and visual cortex are scanning a word prior to the association of meaning with words read previously. Therefore, the timing of these mental processes becomes involved in reading, and the process becomes even more complex. In fact, with only one or two misread letters or words, the reading process can become very confusing.

REFLECTIVE EXERCISE 1.4
TEACHING STUDENTS ABOUT THEIR BRAINS

Prigge (2002) suggested that teachers should teach students with learning difficulties about their brains. For example, even young children can be taught the importance of water, appropriate sleep, appropriate diet, and so on, whereas older children can be taught to informally assess their own learning styles and preferences. Knowledge of one's learning styles and preferences can assist students with learning difficulties in understanding how they should study textual material or prepare for exams.

As a guide for instruction about the brain, the ten tactics for brain compatible classrooms could be used initially. Also, many interesting Internet research possibilities could be explored. The Web site at www.brainconnection.com, for example, provides a series of brain diagrams that can be used as worksheets for identifying various parts of the brain. As an interesting activity, you may wish to develop several lesson plans for instruction on how the brain thinks (or reads) based on this information, Sousa's (2001) model of the reading brain, and the sample worksheets at the Web site mentioned above.

For students who manifest reading difficulties, reading problems can occur at any point in this highly interactive reading process (Sousa, 2001, 2005). Perhaps because of quick scanning, a child thinks he or she sees the word *bale* instead of the word *tale* in a sentence—the visual cortex has thus introduced an error into this complex process that will, in all probability, lead to a lack of comprehension on the other end. Alternatively, either Wernicke's area or Broca's area could introduce an error with any word read, which will also lead to comprehension problems in the final reading of the text.

With this level of reading complexity in mind, this book will follow the basic processes of the brain noted above, emphasizing specific instructional tactics that may be associated with each major area. First, reading strategies will be presented that assist students in mastering the decoding auditory processing skills that emerge somewhat early in this reading sequence. Specifically, Chapters 2 and 3 present information on phoneme-based instruction and phonics, respectively, two sets of skills that are heavily involved in auditory processing, which takes place in Wernicke's area and the angular gyrus, as noted above. Chapters 4, 5, and 6 present information on vocabulary development, reading fluency, and reading comprehension during reading instruction in the lower grades, and reading comprehension in elementary and middle grades. This comprehension emphasis corresponds to the later involvement of Broca's area in the reading process. Thus, this overall model of the reading brain will serve as an organizer for the remainder of this book of reading strategies in various reading areas.

WHAT THE BRAIN RESEARCH ON READING HAS FOUND

With this model of the reading brain as a basis, several specific results from the emerging brain research on reading can assist teachers in understanding the reading performance of students with reading problems in the lower and middle grades. Also, this brief list of research results emphasizes the contributions of the brain research to reading instruction. These research conclusions by no means represent the extent of understanding from research on the reading brain, but these results are interesting and some may surprise you. Further, these research findings can inform teachers on how we should manage students with reading problems in our classes.

Reading Problems May Be Speech-Timing Problems

Brain research on students with reading problems and learning disabilities has shown that a dysfunction in how the brain processes information concerning letter sounds or speech sounds may lead to reading problems. In fact, when one group of researchers used a computer program to pronounce words more slowly than normal, some children with reading problems were able to advance their reading levels by two years in only four weeks of training (Tallal et al., 1996). Thus, their reading problem was a brain-based, language-timing problem—they needed to hear the words more slowly than usual to process the information, even when they themselves were doing the reading. This would seem to implicate Wernicke's area—the auditory processing area—in the reading problems of some students with reading difficulties. Recently, a number of phonemically based, computer-delivered reading programs have incorporated these findings into a practical reading curriculum by allowing teachers to vary the timing on pronunciation of phonemes and/or syllables while students learn to read. These include programs such as Fast ForWord and Academy of Reading by AutoSkill.

Poor Readers Often *Are* Trying Harder

Have we, as teachers, ever told a student to "try harder" in reading? While encouraging students in their reading efforts is essential, recent brain research suggests that teachers of students with learning difficulties may wish to find another phrase to use. Brain scans have shown more frontal lobe activity in the brains of poor readers than in the brains of good readers. In fact, these data show that poor readers are putting forth additional effort—indeed more effort than good readers—in decoding. For example, many students with reading problems subvocalize (e.g., softly pronounce) what they read to interpret words correctly (Sousa, 2001; Tallal et al., 1996). This work requires extra brain processing and can be shown using fMRI technology among many students with reading difficulties.

This sheds new light on the admonishment from teachers or parents for students with reading problems to "try harder." For poor readers, the automaticity with the alphabetic code that good readers have developed is not yet present; consequently, these poor readers are, in many cases, already trying harder.

A further note is required on this research result. Because of a lack of automaticity with the alphabetic code, the reading problems of many poor readers tend to grow and compound. Thus, students who have not developed automaticity with phonemes, letters, or letter sounds will experience increasing problems in reading throughout the elementary and middle school years.

Letters Can Be Confused Because They Sound Alike

The brain essentially pronounces phonemes associated with specific letters during the early decoding process—transferring phonemes into graphemes—and this process, if not successful, can result in reading problems. While early research in dyslexia concentrated on letter confusion as a visual processing problem (e.g., confusing *b* and *d* because these letters look similar), recent research in dyslexia has implicated the angular gyrus, the location for interpreting letters that sound alike, as the basis for some letter confusion problems. In addition to looking alike, the letters *b* and *d* also sound alike, and if the angular gyrus mistranslates one of these letters in a particular word or text, a reading error will occur. Thus, a problem of the dyslexic reader, which previously was viewed as a visual discrimination problem involving these two mirror image letters, may in fact be an auditory discrimination problem based on the similar sounds they represent. In that context, the term *dyslexia* takes on an entirely new meaning—a language-based reading problem!

Nonlinguistic Deficits May Cause Some Reading Problems

We like to think that most reading problems are caused by language deficits, and language problems do result in reading problems. However, we now know that nonlanguage problems (i.e., nonlinguistic deficits) can also cause reading problems. Wright, Bowen, and Zecker (2000) suggest that auditory problems in the perception of sequential sounds can lead to reading problems. In effect, while reading a passage, the child may be subvocalizing and if certain sounds are held in auditory memory too long, the letters those sounds bring to mind may actually be superimposed over other letters, resulting in considerable reading confusion. This would represent a problem in Wernicke's area involving auditory processing. Further, this type of reading problem will create numerous errors in reading.

Some Reading Interventions Result in Measurable Changes in the Brain

Research has shown that reading begins at the phonemic level (Sousa, 2005), because brains detect and interpret phonemes, independent of viewing letters. Brains detect phonemes all the time when listening to others speaking, and consequently, reading begins, in some fundamental sense, with listening to the language of others, and generating language oneself. Consequently, it should come as no surprise that effective reading interventions impact a brain's actual processing, but only recently have we had various technologies that would allow neuroscientists to measure those changes in brain function (UniSci, 2000). As one example, research has shown only recently actual changes in brain functioning resulting from as few as 15 two-hour reading instruction sessions in a phonologically driven instructional treatment involving systematic instruction in analysis of the structure of spoken and written words (Richards et al., 2000). We are at a point today when measures of actual brain functioning can tell us which reading intervention programs work best, and what this research has shown is that reading programs should be phonemically based. More on these exciting discoveries is presented below in this chapter.

These findings represent only a few of the notable research results from the brain research on reading and are presented only to show the types of insight that can be derived from powerful new research technology. In fact, various authors have identified other reading problems that have been identified using the newly developed fMR1 technologies (Joseph et al., 2001; King & Gurian, 2006; Leonard, 2001; Richards et al., 1999, 2000; Shaywitz et al., 1996; Sousa, 2005; Tallal et al., 1996), and this area of research will continue to lend insight into the reading problems noted among students with reading difficulty.

RESPONSE TO INTERVENTION: THE NATIONAL MODEL

What Is RTI?

Given recent research on the reading brain, coupled with the increasing national emphasis on reading instruction, teachers today must understand the newly emerging response to intervention instructional model. This has become the model for reading interventions across the nation in programs such as Reading First, and RTI is now allowed by the federal government as one option for identification of students with learning disabilities (Bender & Shores, 2007). Although RTI can be used to document a student's learning disability, as described below, the basic emphasis of RTI is remediation of reading problems prior to diagnosis of a disability.

Traditionally, learning disabilities were identified by noting a difference between an IQ score and a reading achievement score for a particular child. Whereas other academic scores were sometimes used, in well over 90% of the cases, learning disabilities were diagnosed on the basis of reading deficits (Bender, 2008). In short, if a child had an IQ score that was considerably higher than his or her reading score, coupled with some indication among the IQ subtest scores of various auditory or visual processing problems, a learning disability was believed to exist. Over the years, many researchers expressed dissatisfaction with this diagnostic procedure, and in 2004, the federal government passed legislation that allowed the use of another procedure, commonly referred to as response to intervention, or RTI. Note that the federal legislation does not mandate RTI, but rather, allows RTI as an indication of a learning disability. Subsequent research (Barkeley, Bender, Peaster & Saunders, in press) has indicated that most states are implementing RTI statewide, or pilot testing RTI as an eligibility tool for documenting a learning disability.

Using an RTI process, schools will be required to document how a child responds to several scientifically based educational interventions. It is hoped that more intensive educational interventions will meet the needs of most children, who will not then be documented as learning disabled. However, should a child not respond to two or more scientifically based reading interventions, that child may be suspected of having a learning disability.

What Does RTI Look Like?

The RTI process is typically described in terms of a pyramid that includes multiple tiers of instructional interventions (Barkeley et al., in press; Bender & Shores, 2007; Fuchs & Fuchs, 2007; Kemp & Eaton, 2007), and most models involve three such intervention tiers, as presented in Figure 1.2. The purpose of the multiple tiers is to document that the child had more than one opportunity to respond to a scientifically based reading curriculum, when instruction was presented in an appropriate fashion, consistent with the instructions in the teacher's manual. To protect the interests of the child, and prevent a diagnosis of learning disability based on only one supplementary instructional intervention, every model used in the various states and described in the instructional literature mandates a minimum of two supplemental instructional interventions prior to a diagnosis of learning disability (Barkeley et al., in press). These multiple intervention tiers are required to ensure that the child had several adequate opportunities to respond to instruction.

In the RTI procedure, a student who is struggling in reading is identified by the general education teacher, who then provides supplementary, more intensive instruction as the tier one intervention. Note that this intervention must be offered as a supplementary intervention in reading—not a replacement for the reading class, and it must be more intensive than the intervention provided for all students in the general education class. As indicated in Figure 1.2, the instruction provided for all students in the general education class is believed to meet the instructional needs of approximately 80% of all students.

Whereas most learning needs for most struggling students can be addressed at the first intervention tier, some students will not progress adequately, even

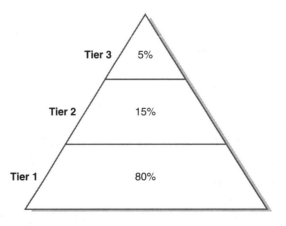

Figure 1.2 RTI Pyramid of Interventions

with the supplemental intervention. These students will require a second, more intensive tier of intervention, which may involve small group instruction for an additional period each day. This tier two intervention, in some school districts, will be a function of the student support team, and while it will be managed by the general education teacher, most districts are providing considerable support for teachers to meet this need for more intensive interventions for a limited number of students in the classroom. While one may expect 20% of students to be exposed to tier two, the tier two intervention adequately will meet the needs of some 15% of the school population (Bender & Shores, 2007).

Finally, for students who do not progress in the first two intervention tiers, another more intensive intervention will be required. In some cases, school districts are viewing this third tier of intervention as an intervention that is provided in the context of special education, and is thus offered only after a child has been identified as learning disabled. Other districts, however, are presenting this third intervention tier as a general education intervention tier that is more intensive than the first two interventions, but still managed by general education teachers, with the support of perhaps a reading specialist or an inclusion teacher who is co-teaching in the same classroom. Approximately 5% of students are expected to need a third intervention tier.

Issues to Consider in RTI

Teachers should be aware of a number of issues when they plan for implementing RTI interventions. First, this is the first time in history in which the interventions managed by the general education teacher will play such a significant role in determining the eligibility of students for learning disability status. Although general education teachers have been sitting on child eligibility teams for decades, only under RTI do general education teachers provide one of the two most critical pieces of data documenting the eligibility—a chart of the child's daily or weekly performance in response to the first targeted intervention.

Next, many different models of RTI currently are being implemented. For example, the three-tier model described above is being used in Texas, whereas both Georgia and North Carolina are implementing a four-tier model. Teachers should check with their own state department of education and school district to obtain a description of the RTI model used in their district.

One issue will be how general education teachers can make the time to undertake these additional interventions. In a typical third grade class, with 24 students, there may be five to six students who are struggling in reading, and those students will need a tier one intervention, which is provided above and beyond their typical reading instruction. Moreover, the general education teacher in that class is expected to provide that intervention, monitor the weekly or daily performance of those students, and be prepared to present those data (which are typically presented in the form of an x-y axis chart with days or weeks at the bottom and achievement on the side) to the student support team in a matter of weeks. Finding or making the time to do that is a critical concern, and fortunately technology can assist. Once teachers identify students who need the tier one or tier two intervention, teachers may be able to find and implement a computer-based reading program, such that the teacher can continue teaching the class, while those five or six students work on computer-assisted instruction on their targeted reading skills.

A final issue to consider involves treatment fidelity, which may also be referred to as treatment validity. This addresses the question, "Did this child receive instruction that was presented as it should have been presented, or in accordance with the instructor's manual for the curriculum used?" Clearly, even the best scientifically validated curriculum is not effective unless it is taught appropriately, and if it is not implemented appropriately, the child will not have an appropriate opportunity to respond to instruction. Thus, educators will have to address the issue of treatment fidelity in the RTI process (Bender & Shores, 2007).

As can be seen from the discussion above, solutions for a number of issues on implementation of RTI have not been determined as yet, and in all likelihood, various districts will develop different approaches to RTI. What is certain is that general education teachers will be playing an increasing role in documentation of the effectiveness of reading instruction for students suspected of having a learning disability, and we must all prepare for that.

One major purpose of this text will be to describe various RTI procedures in reading and relate these to various reading strategies. These case studies will vary according to the content of the chapter. For example, a phonemically based tier of interventions will be presented in the next chapter, while subsequent chapters will present RTI procedures dealing with phonics, reading fluency, or reading comprehension. Also, this text will present a number of instructional procedures that can be the basis for interventions in the RTI process. This should help all general education teachers prepare for the full and complete implementation of RTI.

CONCLUSION

This chapter has presented a series of research-based conclusions on the development of reading skill, as well as several areas within which reading instructional strategies may be discussed: early literacy instruction, brain compatible instruction, and RTI. A series of general research results has been presented in each of those areas, as those results provide a further framework for the strategies discussed throughout this book. Finally, the RTI model presented here will serve as our organizer for the remainder of the book, as we present research-based reading strategies and suggest how those might fit into an RTI procedure. Each subsequent chapter will include at least one RTI case study, and these may be used as models for educators struggling to implement RTI.

WHAT'S NEXT?

In the next chapter, you will find a series of instructional strategies to enhance phoneme awareness and phoneme manipulation skills among students with reading difficulties. These skills are essential for the effective auditory processing of letter sounds, which takes place in the angular gyrus and Wernicke's area of the brain. Further, these skills also serve as a basis for all subsequent reading. The RTI example in that chapter will focus on early literacy skills for kindergarten teachers, involving phonemic recognition activities.

REFERENCES

Armstrong, T. (2007). *The multiple intelligences of reading and writing: Making words come alive.* Alexandria, VA: Association for Supervision and Curriculum Development.

AutoSkill. (2004). *Focus on research: A paper on the scientific validation of effective reading programs and the development of the AutoSkill Academy of Reading.* Ottawa, Canada: Author.

Barkeley, S., Bender, W. N., Peaster, L., & Saunders, L. (in press). Implementation of responsiveness to intervention: A snapshot of progress. *Journal of Learning Disabilities.*

Bender, W. N. (2001). *Learning disabilities: Characteristics, identification and teaching strategies* (4th ed.). Boston: Allyn & Bacon.

Bender, W. N. (2008). *Differentiating instruction for students with learning disabilities* (2nd ed.). Thousand Oaks, CA: Corwin Press.

Bender, W. N., & Shores, C. (2007). *Response to intervention: A practical guide for every teacher.* Thousand Oaks, CA: Corwin Press.

Bhat, P., Griffin, C. C., & Sindelar, P. T. (2003). Phonological awareness instruction for middle school students with learning disabilities. *Learning Disability Quarterly, 26*(2), 73–88.

Bos, C. S., Mather, N., Silver-Pacuilla, H., & Narr, R. F. (2000). Learning to teach early literacy skills collaboratively. *Teaching Exceptional Children, 32*(5), 38–45.

Bradley, R., Danielson, L., & Doolittle, J. (2007). Responsiveness to intervention: 1997 to 2007. *Teaching Exceptional Children, 39*(5), 8–13.

Chard, D. J., & Dickson, S. V. (1999). Phonological awareness: Instructional and assessment guidelines. *Intervention in School and Clinic, 34*(5), 261–270.

Dayton-Sakari, M. (1997). Struggling readers don't work at reading: They just get their teachers to! *Intervention in School and Clinic, 32*(5), 295–301.

Fuchs, L. S., & Fuchs, D. (2007). A model for implementing responsiveness to intervention. *Teaching Exceptional Children, 39*(5), 14–23.

Goldstein, B. H., & Obrzut, J. E. (2001). Neuropsychological treatment of dyslexia in the classroom setting. *Journal of Learning Disabilities, 34,* 276–285.

Good, R. H., & Kaminski, R. (2002). *DIBELS: Dynamic Indicators of Basic Early Literacy Skills* (6th ed.). Longmont, CO: Sopris West.

Gregory, G. H., & Chapman, C. (2002). *Differentiated instructional strategies: One size doesn't fit all.* Thousand Oaks, CA: Corwin Press.

Haager, D. (2002, October 11). *The road to successful reading outcomes for English language learners in urban schools.* A paper presented at the annual meeting of the Council for Exceptional Children, Denver, CO.

Joseph, J., Noble, K., & Eden, G. (2001). The neurobiological basis of reading. *Journal of Learning Disabilities, 34*(6), 566–579.

Kame'enui, E. J., Carnine, D. W., Dixon, R. C., Simmons, D. C., & Coyne, M. D. (2002). *Effective teaching strategies that accommodate diverse learners* (2nd ed.). Upper Saddle River, NJ: Merrill-Prentice Hall.

Kemp, K. A., & Eaton, M. A. (2007). *RTI: The classroom connection for literacy: Reading intervention and measurement.* Port Chester, NY: Dude Publishing.

King, K., & Gurian, M. (2006). Teaching to the minds of boys. *Educational Leadership, 64*(1), 56–61.

Langdon, T. (2004). DIBELS: A teacher friendly basic literacy accountability tool for the primary classroom. *Teaching Exceptional Children, 37*(2), 54–58.

Larkin, M. J. (2001). Providing support for student independence through scaffolded instruction. *Teaching Exceptional Children, 31*(1), 30–35.

Leonard, C. M. (2001). Imaging brain structure in children: Differentiating language disability and reading disability. *Learning Disability Quarterly, 24,* 158–176.

McCutchen, D., Abbott, R. D., Green, L. B., Beretvas, N., Cox, S., Potter, N. S., et al. (2002). Beginning literacy: Links among teacher knowledge, teacher practice, and student learning. *Journal of Learning Disabilities, 35*(1), 69–86.

National Institute of Child Health and Development. (2000). *Teaching children to read: An evidence-based assessment of the scientific research literature on reading and its implications for reading instruction* (Report of the National Reading Panel). Retrieved May 23, 2002, from http://www.nichd.nih.gov/publications/nrp/findings.cfm

Patzer, C. E., & Pettegrew, B. S. (1996). Finding a "voice": Primary students with developmental disabilities express personal meanings through writing. *Teaching Exceptional Children, 29*(2), 22–27.

Posse, S., Dager, S. R., & Richards, T. L. (1997). In vivo measurement of regional brain metabolic response to hyperventilation using magnetic resonance proton echo planar spectroscopic imaging (PEPSI). *Research in Medicine, 37,* 858–865.

Prigge, D. J. (2002). Promote brain-based teaching and learning. *Intervention in School and Clinic, 37,* 237–241.

Raskind, W. H. (2001). Current understanding of the genetic basis of reading and spelling disability. *Learning Disability Quarterly, 24,* 141–157.

Richards, T. L. (2001). Functional magnetic resonance imaging and spectroscopic imaging of the brain: Application of the fMRI and fMRS to reading disabilities and education. *Learning Disability Quarterly, 24*(3), 189–204.

Richards, T. L., Corina, D., Serafini, S., Steury, K., Echeland, D. R., Dager, S. R., et al. (2000). The effects of a phonological-driven treatment for dyslexia on lactate levels as measured by proton MRSI. *American Journal of Neuroradiology, 21,* 916–922.

Richards, T. L., Dager, S. R., Corina, D., Serafini, S., Heide, A. C., Steury, K., et al. (1999). Dyslexic children have abnormal brain lactate response to reading-related language tasks. *American Journal of Neuroradiology, 20,* 1393–1398.

Rourke, B. P. (2005). Neuropsychology of learning disabilities: Past and future. *Learning Disability Quarterly, 28*(2), 111–114.

Shaker, P. (2001). Literacies for life. *Educational Leadership, 59*(2), 26–31.

Shaywitz, B. A., Shaywitz, S. E., Pugh, K. R., Sukdlarski, P., Fulbright, R. K., Constable, R. T., et al. (1996). The functional organization of brain for reading and reading disability (dyslexia). *The Neuroscientist, 2,* 245–255.

Smith, S. B., Baker, S., & Oudeans, M. K. (2001). Making a difference in the classroom with early literacy instruction. *Teaching Exceptional Children, 33*(6), 8–14.

Sousa, D. A. (2001). *How the special needs brain learns.* Thousand Oaks, CA: Corwin Press.

Sousa, D. A. (2005). *How the brain learns to read.* Thousand Oaks, CA: Corwin Press.

Sylwester, R. (2001). *A biological brain in a cultural classroom: Applying biological research to classroom management.* Thousand Oaks, CA: Corwin Press.

Tallal, P., Miller, S. L., Bedi, G., Bvma, G., Want, X., Nagarajan, S., et al. (1996). Fast-element enhanced speech improves language comprehension in language-learning impaired children. *Science, 271,* 81–84.

UniSci. (2000, May). Brain shown to change as dyslexics learn. *Daily University Science News,* p. 26.

Winn, J. A., & Otis-Wilborn, A. (1999). Monitoring literacy learning. *Teaching Exceptional Children, 32*(1), 40–45.

Wood, F. B., & Grigorenko, E. L. (2001). Emerging issues in the genetics of dyslexia: A methodological review. *Journal of Learning Disabilities, 34,* 503–511.

Wright, B. A., Bowen, R. W., & Zecker, S. G. (2000). Nonlinguistic perceptual deficits associated with reading and language disorders. *Current Opinion in Neurobiology, 10,* 482–486.

Phonological and Phonemic Instruction 2

The Key to Early Reading and Literacy

Strategies Presented in This Chapter Include

- ✓ Ten Tactics for Teaching Basic Phonemic Instruction
- ✓ Lindamood-Bell Phonemic Programs
- ✓ Fast ForWord
- ✓ The Academy of Reading
- ✓ The Wilson Reading System
- ✓ A Phonemic Segmentation Activity
- ✓ A Syllable-Blending Game
- ✓ Phonemic Substitution Strategy
- ✓ The Guess-the-Word Blending Game
- ✓ A Change-the-Letter Game
- ✓ RTI Case Study in Phonemic Instruction

PHONOLOGICAL INSTRUCTION AND PHONEMIC INSTRUCTION

Phonological instruction involves manipulation of the sounds in language and manipulation of the letters that represent the sounds in language. As discussed in Chapter 1, the emerging emphasis on early literacy for students with learning difficulties has been tied heavily to phonological instruction. This level of reading instruction addresses several of the initial brain processes in reading—the discrimination of speech sounds, the association of phonemes and graphemes involving both visual- and language-processing areas of the brain, and the manipulation of the sounds that form the basis of language (Abbott, Walton, & Greenwood, 2002; Sousa, 2005). Thus, the visual cortex (which visually interprets the letters on the page), together with Wernicke's area (the brain area that is responsible for auditory discrimination), are both involved in—and activated by—effective phonological instruction (Sousa, 2005). First, some general definitions and concepts are presented below. Next, a variety of instructional strategies and tactics for phonological instruction are described.

Misunderstandings About Phonological Instruction

There are three terms that are often confused—indeed some teachers mistakenly use these terms interchangeably. The terms are *phonics*, *phonemic* instruction, and *phonological instruction* (National Institute of Child Health and Development [NICHD], 2000). To truly understand the process of learning to read, we need to refine our understanding of the relationship between these three discrete emphases in early literacy instruction.

Phonics is the mapping of letters to speech sounds or phonemes. Until very recently, perhaps five or ten years ago, teachers were trained to begin reading instruction with instruction in phonics—that is, instruction in reading began with instruction in letters and letter sounds and thus involved the mapping of individual sounds to specific letters in our alphabet. However, this instructional emphasis presented some degree of difficulty for many children with learning difficulties, because some students did not have the sound discrimination skills that would allow them to detect differences in speech sounds. For example, distinguishing the differences in the initial sounds between the following paired words, when spoken, would represent a problem in the auditory discrimination of students with reading problems and thus may not involve letter recognition at all. Needless to say, this situation could be quite problematic in early reading instruction for a child with reading problems. Note that only the initial phoneme in the following words changes in each pair.

B/i/g	H/a/t	S/u/n
W/i/g	B/a/t	F/u/n

If students with early reading problems cannot detect such initial sound differences, it is extremely difficult to teach them to read these words. In other words, it is quite difficult to teach which sounds are represented by particular letters until and unless some prerequisite phoneme discrimination skills are present. Further, for many young students with reading problems and/or learning disabilities this deficit in phoneme detection is quite pronounced. These deficits result in a need to specifically teach sound differences, and this emphasis on detection and manipulation of discrete speech sounds is referred to as *phonemic instruction.* As you will recall from Chapter 1, phonemes are the smallest, most discrete sounds in our language that can change the meaning of a word. Thus, phonemic instruction involves detecting and manipulating the smallest sounds in our language that can change meaning, independent of instruction on letters and letter shapes.

Only a few years ago, teachers began to understand that phonemic instruction had to precede phonics instruction for many children with learning difficulties in order for phonics instruction to proceed at a reasonable pace (Abbott et al., 2002; Sousa, 2005). In fact, teachers often find that students who succeed in phonics-based reading programs during the early grades without specific instruction in phonemes come from language-rich home environments in which phonemic instruction has already taken place informally. However, for children with reading problems, many researchers suggest that some 20% to 30% of all children need specific instruction in phonemes, either prior to or coupled with instruction in phonics (Abbott et al., 2002; Sousa, 2001, 2005).

From the perspective of brain research, this sound discrimination weakness would seem to represent a weakness in Wernicke's area of the brain—the area that is responsible for auditory discrimination (Sousa, 2005). For example, while there are 41 (or 44) phonemes in our language, there are only 26 graphemes (letters) that must be used in combination to represent these phonemes. Again, there is no one-to-one correspondence between phonemes and graphemes, and students cannot proceed successfully with phonics instruction unless and until they can detect differences in speech sounds or phonemes (Abbott et al., 2002; NICHD, 2000). Resulting from this research, the emerging emphasis on early literacy involves an extensive emphasis on phonemic instruction, because a strong basis here facilitates reading instruction throughout the school years.

In addition to the distinction between phonemic instruction and phonics, teachers need to understand that phonemic instruction and phonological instruction are two different things (NICHD, 2000). Whereas phonemic instruction involves instruction in awareness and manipulation of discrete speech sounds, *phonological instruction* is a much broader concept that involves not only speech sounds, but also the identification and manipulation of other sounds such as syllables or other parts of words (e.g., prefixes or suffixes) in spoken form. Thus, much work in early reading may be considered phonological instruction, whereas phonemic instruction is limited to manipulation of discrete phonemes.

Within the past several years, research has documented that skills in phonemic manipulation are critical components of early reading and language arts skills (Bos, Mather, Silver-Pacuilla, & Narr, 2000; Chard & Dickson, 1999; Davis, Lindo, & Compton, 2007; Kame'enui, Carnine, Dixon, Simmons, & Coyne, 2002; Langdon, 2004; Sousa, 2005). Further, a deficit in phonemic manipulation skill has been identified as a primary causal factor for learning disabilities among many students experiencing reading problems (Kame'enui et al., 2002; Moats & Lyon, 1993). Recently, a general consensus emerged in which students with learning disabilities demonstrate an early inability to manipulate phonemes and this language-based inability seems to be the primary cause of subsequent learning disabilities in a wide variety of areas. From this perspective, one easily can see the critical need for instruction in phonemes for many students with reading problems.

There are a number of other terms that cause some confusion in this general area of early literacy. Initially, some theorists used the term *phonemic awareness* to represent a child's ability to detect different phonemes, but it quickly became apparent that children needed to do more than merely become aware of the different sounds that make up our language. Rather, skills in phonemic detection, phonemic blending, or phonemic segmentation (i.e., in taking apart words to isolate specific phonemes) are all a part of phonemic instruction. The term *phonemic manipulation* recently has been used to represent this array of skills.

Additional new terminology now is used for phonological instruction for young children. Onsets and rimes are parts of spoken language that are smaller than syllables but larger than phonemes (NICHD, 2000). An *onset* is the initial consonant sound of a syllable (e.g., the /p/ sound in the word *pan*). A *rime* is the part of a syllable that includes the vowel and everything that follows (e.g., the /a/i/n/ sounds in the word *pain*). These terms are used quite extensively in phonological instruction and subsequent phonics instruction, and teachers may need to become familiar with this emerging terminology.

The Importance of Phonological Skill in Early Literacy

Research over the last decade has documented the importance of phonological skills in early literacy. Among young children, phonological awareness and emergent print knowledge are the strongest early predictors of reading (Davis et al., 2007; Langdon, 2004). To develop reading skill, students must be sensitive to speech sounds and sound segments. Further, once sounds can be recognized and identified, students must partner those understandings with letters and words on the printed page. Also, phonological awareness includes many skills that reach beyond sound/letter pairings, including rhyming sounds, alliteration, blending of syllables, blending of other speech sounds, and manipulation of speech sounds such as adding "endings" of words (e.g., an "s" makes most nouns plural, and thus changes their meaning).

Over the last few years, research has focused on these phonological skills, and documented the complex interrelationships between these skills, and early literacy success. For example research has suggested that the blending tasks noted above are more accurate determinants of phonological skill in younger children, whereas deletion/substitution tasks (e.g., eliminating the final consonant sound from a word, and substituting another) are better predictors in older children (Schatschneider, Francis, Foorman, Fletcher, & Mehta, 1999). Also, recent work has shown that a child's ability to recognize and name letters, that is "rapid letter naming," is a critical reading skill that is highly correlated with reading fluency in later years. As this research continues, we will develop better understandings of early literacy skill.

As children grow in their reading ability, additional skills become involved in their overall reading success. For example, the amount of time a child is exposed to printed material is critically important in developing reading skill.

Also, emergent print knowledge seems to be one of the best predictors of early reading ability (Davis et al., 2007), and this is one reason that adults (parents, preschool and kindergarten teachers) are strongly encouraged to read to children, and emphasize that printed matter is important. As children grow, their own exposure to printed material takes on increasing importance. As children interact with written material, they are exposed to various spelling relationships and begin to understand those relationships. As early as Grade 1, students become sensitive to spelling sequences and constraints in our language system. For example, when first grade children are presented with two letter groups (e.g., ffeb and beff) and asked which looks more like a word, emergent readers can correctly identify the latter (Davis et al., 2007), indicating they are sensitive to various rules in our written language system. This mental collection of spelling patterns—referred to as orthographic knowledge—is critical for early reading skill, and continues to grow over time.

A Hierarchy of Phonological Skills

Instruction on phonological manipulation skills typically proceeds in a predictable, hierarchical fashion (Edelen-Smith, 1997; Kame'enui et al., 2002; Langdon, 2004; NICHD, 2000). For example, theorists suggest that detecting similar sounds in the middle and at the end of words (i.e., rhyming) is a phonological skill that precedes detecting different initial sounds (i.e., the difference between the first sound and the rhyme sound in /c/a/t/ versus /h/a/t/). Each of these skills precedes the child's ability to break up a word into component sounds (typically referred to as segmentation) or to substitute one phoneme for another. This continuum of skills varies somewhat from one researcher to another, but the ten phonological manipulation skills presented in Teaching Tip 2.1 represent this general hierarchical concept.

 TEACHING TIP 2.1

A Hierarchy of 10 Phonemic Manipulation Skills

1. Detecting rhyming sounds

2. Recognizing the same initial sound in words

3. Isolating initial sounds

4. Categorizing onsets and rimes

5. Isolating middle and ending sounds

6. Blending sounds into words

7. Segmenting or dividing sounds within words

8. Phoneme addition

9. Phoneme deletion

10. Phoneme substitution

Of course, a variety of instructional activities may be used to teach these skills, and most teachers seem to prefer some type of gaming or fun, classwide instructional exercises (Abbott et al., 2002; Chard & Dickson, 1999; Edelen-Smith, 1997). Teaching Tip 2.2 presents a variety of ideas from a number of sources (Bender, 2008; Chard & Dickson, 1999; Edelen-Smith, 1997) that teachers may find useful in teaching some of the early phonemic awareness and manipulation skills to young readers.

 TEACHING TIP 2.2

Ten Tactics for Basic Phonological and Phonemic Instruction

Tactics for Detecting Rhyming Sounds

1. Ask students to raise their hand when they hear a pair of rhyming words as the teacher says various word pairs together.

2. Pair students up, and when one student says a word, his or her partner is required to say a rhyming word. Then the second student picks a word and the first partner must say a rhyming word.

3. Ask students to identify rhyming words they hear in a song or a poem in class.

Tactics for Recognizing the Same Initial Sound in Words

1. Ask students to raise their hand (or stand up—some visible class signal) when they hear two words that begin with the same sound in a one-sentence passage. The teacher should read a story passage and pause briefly at the end of each sentence to allow children the time to consider each word in the sentence.

2. Students may be requested to provide another word that has the same initial sound as the word spoken by the teacher or a partner.

3. Divide the class into teams, with each team including the children that sit in one row of desks. After the teacher reads a sentence, call on students in one team to give the initial sound in each word sequentially. For example, after reading the sentence, "The ball rolled under the large truck on the highway," the first student would be expected to give the initial sound in the word *the:* the /t/h/ consonant blend. The child in the second seat would need to give the initial sound in the word *ball,* and so on. For each initial sound given correctly, the team earns one point. After completing a sentence with students in one row, Team 2 (or the students in the next row) is given another sentence. Depending on the grade level, teachers may wish to write the sentence on the dry-erase board to help students with poor memory skills.

A Tactic for Isolating Initial Sounds

Students should be required to isolate phonemic sounds, particularly at the beginning of syllables and words. For example, teachers should stress letter sounds in simple reading passages by asking questions about phoneme sounds:

"What is the first sound in /b/a/l/l/?"

"Can someone give me another word with the same first sound?"

A Tactic for Categorizing Onsets and Rimes

The teacher should verbally present sets of three or four words in which one or more of the words do not fit or sound different. Word sets such as the following would be a good choice.

bat	bill
hat	pan
ham	still
cat	pill

In the first set of words, the word *ham* sounds different, whereas in the second set the word *pan* is different.

Tactics for Isolating Middle and Ending Sounds

1. Students should be required to identify middle and ending sounds in words. Most of the activities that were used above in recognizing the same initial sound may be used as instructional tasks for middle and ending sounds in words. Asking questions about middle and ending sounds in any reading passage is also a good teaching technique (e.g., "What is the last sound in *house*?").

2. When the teacher comes to a new vocabulary word in the reading, he or she should pause a moment and discuss the sounds in the word.

SOURCE: These ideas and activities came from "Phonological awareness: Instructional and assessment guidelines" by D. J. Chard and S. V. Dickson (1999), in *Intervention in School and Clinic, 34,* pp. 261–270, and from "How now brown cow: Phoneme awareness activities for collaborative classrooms" by P. J. Edelen-Smith (1997) in *Intervention in School and Clinic, 33,* pp. 102–111, by ProEd, Inc. Reprinted with permission.

Advanced Phonological Manipulation Skills

The more complex phonological manipulation skills would include many of the skills listed in the ten phonemic manipulation skills above. These are blending sounds into words, segmenting or dividing sounds within words, phoneme addition, phoneme deletion, and phoneme substitution. In general, these skills are founded on the prerequisite skills—the first five skills of the hierarchy. Further, for students who have not mastered phonemic awareness and manipulation skills, even as late as elementary grades and middle school, this instruction must precede higher-level instruction in reading (Kame'enui et al., 2002).

Many students master phonological and phonemic manipulation skills prior to beginning school and may not need specific instruction in phonemic manipulation. Rather, those students should move directly into phonics. Estimates of the number of children who have problems manipulating phonemes range from 10% to 20% of the kindergarten and first grade population. However, even for the students who need specific instruction in phonemes, not all of the skills in the hierarchy above should be offered. The Report of the National Reading Panel (NICHD, 2000) cautioned teachers against attempting to offer specific instruction in all ten skills in the hierarchy. Rather, the research has shown that offering instruction for children on only one or two of the several skills in the hierarchy is more effective than attempting to teach all these skills. When instruction is offered to students with early reading problems, teachers generally should provide instruction at the higher end of the skill hierarchy, unless the child is functioning at a very low reading level. If the child is functioning at a low level, instruction should be provided on the first five skills in the hierarchy, and for those students with reading problems the tactics described in Teaching Tip 2.2 may be used.

With these concerns noted, a number of advanced instructional strategies for teaching phonological and phonemic manipulation are presented in Teaching Tip 2.3. Several of these ideas were adapted from Chard and Dickson (1999), whereas others are presented for the first time. Each of these ideas is presented in a lesson plan format (i.e., an objective is listed, as are the necessary materials and a description of the activity) that may be implemented easily in most elementary classes.

 TEACHING TIP 2.3

Advanced Phonological Instructional Lesson Plans

A Syllable Blending Game

Type of Activity

This is a good activity for either the entire class or for smaller instructional groups.

Objective

Students will blend and identify a word that is stretched into component sounds.

Materials Needed

List of 20 to 30 multisyllable words.

Activity

The teacher should identify two teams in the class and have each team number its members. Next, the teacher will call out words one syllable at a time for the first student in Team 1 and have that student "put the word together and say the whole word." The team gets two points if that student can put the word together correctly and then pronounce the word. If the student cannot, or tries and fails in the correct pronunciation, the other team members can help, and if the team subsequently gets the word correct, the team is awarded one point. Call out the syllables in the next word for the first student in Team 2 and then return to Team 1 for the next word.

To initiate this exercise the teacher may say something like, "What word do you have if you put the following sounds together?"

HO – may – ker	Homemaker
AN – ten – a	Antenna
LET – er	Letter
BOT – le	Bottle

The Guess-the-Word Blending Game

Type of Activity

This works best as a small group activity in either the inclusive class or a special education class.

Objective

Students will blend and identify a word that is stretched out into component sounds. This game was developed by Chard and Dickson (1999).

Materials Needed

Picture cards of objects that students are likely to recognize such as sun, bell, fan, flag, snake, tree, book, cup, clock, plane.

Activity

Place a small number of picture cards before the children. Tell them you are going to say a word using "snail talk"—a slow way of saying words (e.g., fffff lllll aaaaa ggggg). They have to look at the pictures and guess what the snail is saying. It is important to have the children guess the answer in their head so that everyone gets an opportunity to try it before hearing other answers. Alternate between having one child identify the word and having all children say the word aloud in chorus in order to keep the children engaged.

A Phonemic Segmentation Instructional Strategy

Type of Activity

This works best as a small group activity since certain aspects of this activity (e.g., hand clapping) can get quite loud in a whole class setting. This may be used in either the inclusive class or a special education setting.

Objective

Students will be able to segment various parts of oral language. This game was developed by Chard and Dickson (1999).

Materials Needed

List of brief phrases or poems children would know (e.g., "I scream. You scream. We all scream for ice cream" or "Ring around the rosy").

Activities

(a) Early instruction involves teaching the children to segment sentences into individual words. Have the children clap hands with each individual word.

(b) As children advance, teach them to segment words into syllables. You may wish to start with children's names (Al-ex-an-der, Ra-chel). Have the groups state the syllables together while clapping hands in rhythm—the rhythmic aspect of this work keeps the children pronouncing the syllables together.

(c) When children have learned to remove the first phoneme from a word, teach them to segment short words into individual phonemes (s-u-n, s-t-o-p).

The Change-the-Letter Game

Type of Activity

This activity works best in a group but can also be used when a teacher and student are working one-on-one or in a peer buddy or pair learning situation. This can be a loud activity, so using it in an inclusive class may present problems if other students are doing other activities.

(Continued)

TEACHING TIP 2.3 (Continued)

Objective

Students will segment various parts of oral language. This game was developed by Chard and Dickson (1999).

Materials Needed

List of word cards, each of which presents a simple noun with three letters and a picture of that object (consonant–vowel–consonant words; e.g., bat, cup, hat, ham).

Activities

"Students, Mr. Sound will show you a word and then change the first letter of the word." Show a picture of a bat. Say this word together. (Students say *bat*.) "Mr. Sound wants to change the first sound to an /h/" (teacher says the letter sound for *h* and not the letter name). "If Mr. Sound changes that sound, what would be the matching picture?" Encourage each student to decide on the answer prior to calling on a student for the answer.

A Phoneme Substitution Activity

Type of Activity

This is appropriate for whole class or small group instruction.

Objective

Students will correctly say a word after substituting one phoneme for another.

Materials Needed

List of multisyllable words and a list of letters to use as initial consonants.

Activity

The teacher should identify two teams in the class and have each team number its members. Call out a word and suggest a substitute for the initial consonant sound, and then have the first child in Team 1 "put the word together and say the whole word." The team gets two points if that student can put the word together correctly. If he or she cannot, the other team members can help. If the team gets the word correct, the team is awarded one point. Call out the next word and substitute the consonant sound for the first student in Team 2. Return to Team 1 for the next word.

A Phonological Rhyme Game

Type of Activity

Small group or whole class instruction.

Objective

Students will identify why words rhyme, based on either a syllable rhyming or on only a few letters at the end of a syllable rhyming.

Materials Needed

Several sets of single and multisyllable rhyming words.

Activity

Explain to your students that rhymes may or may not involve a set of letters that constitute an entire syllable. Whereas some words rhyme because of only a vowel and ending consonant, other words rhyme because the entire last syllable is the same. When presenting words verbally to your students, request that they tell you the difference; i.e., is the entire last syllable the same or merely the last few sounds in the word? Here are some words you may use to get started; in each column below, the words rhyme—see if your students can tell you why.

rocket	pan	bat	bottle
pocket	can	hat	myrtle
locket	tan	cat	humble

SOURCE: These ideas and activities came from "Phonological awareness: Instructional and assessment guidelines" by D. J. Chard and S. V. Dickson (1999), in *Intervention in School and Clinic, 34*, pp. 261–270, and from "How now brown cow: Phoneme awareness activities for collaborative classrooms" by P. J. Edelen-Smith (1997) in *Intervention in School and Clinic, 33*, pp. 102–111, by ProEd, Inc. Reprinted with permission.

REFLECTIVE EXERCISE 2.1
ADAPTATION OF THESE ACTIVITIES

While the activities in Teaching Tip 2.3 range across the early grade levels, teachers often can adapt various instructional ideas for different grades. Select two of the activities above and consider how you would adapt these for the students with reading difficulties in your classroom. For teachers in Grades 4 through 7, perhaps more complex word lists would be one adaptation that could make the Phonological Rhyme Game more appropriate for your grade level. Make some notes on these lesson plans and consider using one or more of these activities in your reading program this year.

Instructional Planning for Phonological and Phonemic Instruction

Kame'enui et al. (2002) combined the idea of the hierarchy of phonological skills with the instructional concept of scaffolding. As described previously, scaffolding involves providing differential support to students, based on their individual needs (Larkin, 2001), and sequentially withdrawing the support as appropriate until the students can complete the task unassisted. Kame'enui and his coworkers recommended a series of instructional scaffolds designed to support students in learning various complex phonemic skills for the latter portion of the hierarchy. Since these activities involve presenting actual letters to students, as well as the sounds of the letters, these activities may be considered a bridge between phonological instruction and subsequent instruction in phonics.

Scaffold 1—Model	The teacher says the sounds in a word while touching each letter: "My turn to sound out this word. When I touch a letter, I'll say its sound. I'll keep saying the sound until I touch the next letter."
Scaffold 2—Over Sound Out	The teacher touches under each letter while students say each sound: "Your turn to sound out this word. When I touch a letter, you say its sound. Keep saying the sound until I touch the next letter."
Scaffold 3—Internal Sound Out	The teacher touches under each letter while students say each sound in their head: "You are going to read this word without saying the sounds out loud. As I point to the letters, sound out this word to yourself."
Scaffold 4—Whole Word Reading	The teacher points to the word and students sound it out independently: "You are going to read this word the fast way. When I point to a word, sound it out to yourself. When I signal, say the word the fast way."

Note that both the sounds and the letters are emphasized. Also, the scaffolded concept here incorporates a shift in emphasis from teacher modeling to student completion of the behavior, in four steps.

1. *Modeling:* The teacher models the sounds of the word.

2. *Repetition:* The teacher says the individual sounds of the word as the student repeats these discrete sounds.

3. *Segmenting the word:* The student says the discrete sounds of the word in a segmented fashion.

4. *Blending the word:* The student says the entire word as a whole.

Should you wish to use this type of scaffold without emphasizing letters, perhaps for lower-functioning students with learning difficulties in kindergarten or first grade, you could complete this entire activity using pictures of common items rather than letters. Thus, this activity would emphasize exclusively the phonemes involved and not phonics.

 REFLECTIVE EXERCISE 2.2
A PHONEMIC GAME ACTIVITY

How much "reading" instruction should kindergarten teachers do? While kindergarten curricula generally emphasize some work in letter recognition, many kids do recognize many letters early in the kindergarten year. Teachers in kindergarten should foster a sense of fun in learning to use letters in various games. For example, teachers may pick a classroom object (e.g., desk), and tell the class to identify as many things as they can that begin with the same sound.

This can be changed to emphasize sound endings, rimes, and so on. Teachers may emphasize the importance of these games by writing answers on the board and then having the class say the letters of that answer in unison. While not explicitly teaching letters and sounds, teachers can still emphasize the importance of them in a fun and exciting format.

GUIDELINES FOR PHONEMIC INSTRUCTION

Based on the hierarchy of phonemic skills, and on the accumulated research on phoneme instruction for students with learning difficulties, teachers need to remember several points or guidelines when considering a phonemically based instructional program (Abbott et al., 2002; Edelen-Smith, 1997; NICHD, 2000; Sousa, 2005). These are presented below.

1. *Cover the bases!* In phonemic instruction, leaving out one simple skill can result in gaps in a student's ability to manipulate phonemes effectively, and it is critical for students who require such instruction to provide comprehensive instruction that covers all of the necessary skills. Teachers must consider the child's reading problem and the various skills within the hierarchy. Some children with reading problems can detect different phonemes but cannot blend sounds together, whereas others can blend sounds but need assistance in word segmentation. All of these skills are important for subsequent reading success. The teacher should understand which specific skills present problems for the child. Of course, one oft-repeated truth about students with learning disabilities is that no two students demonstrate the same types of reading problems! Teachers will need to search for the specific phonemic problems shown by the individual students and tailor the instruction to those specific problems, while offering instruction in one or two such skills at a time.

   Abbott et al. (2002) recommend an "instructional fidelity" checklist that teachers can use to ensure that all of the appropriate skills are covered. Instructional fidelity addresses the question, was the content taught in a way that allowed the student an appropriate opportunity to learn? Thus, all teachers should be concerned with instructional fidelity, and using checklists can benefit teachers to ensure that they have covered the material completely. Another alternative is for teachers to use the prescribed lesson plans in phonemically based reading or language curriculum materials, while, of course, using a scientifically validated instructional curricula. Teaching Tip 2.4 presents an instructional fidelity checklist for instruction in early phonemic skills; teachers may use this checklist as is, or adapt it in any fashion that proves useful.

☞ **TEACHING TIP 2.4**

An Instructional Fidelity Checklist for Early Phonemic Skills

_____1. Teacher ensures that the student is oriented to the teacher and paying attention.

_____2. Teacher reviews prior work and makes connections with today's work.

_____3. Teacher identifies which individual or group of phonemic skills (listed below) will be practiced, given the development and prerequisite skills of the child.
   a. Picture/sound matching activities on onsets
   b. Picture/sound matching activities on rimes
   c. Matching of onset of two words (_bake_ and _bear_ or _bake_ and _house_)
   d. Segmentation: Isolating onset
   e. Segmentation: Isolating rime
   f. Segmentation: Identifying all phonemes in a word and counting them
   g. Blending: Combining onset and rime
   h. Substitution: Changing onset of words to make new words with same onset as picture
   i. Substitution: Changing rimes of words to match sample word

   Note that this list of skills could be lengthened to include more skills at various levels or more complex skills in the phonological area such as syllabication, suffixes, prefixes, and so on.

_____4. Teacher models selected activity, while discussing answer selections out loud.

_____5. Teacher guides student through first activity, coaching student to "think aloud" while making answer selections.

_____6. Teacher presents multiple examples for student to complete.

_____7. Teacher keeps a written record of student performance on each example, carefully monitoring performance, and inquiring about student's errors. Consider charting performance over time.

_____8. Teacher reviews all examples with the student, offering feedback on errors, and then complimenting the student on a good job!

2. _Select only one or a few skills to teach at a time._ Teachers should select only one, two, or three skills from the hierarchy for the child with reading difficulties to work on, bearing in mind that mastery of those skills probably will improve the child's work on the other skills as well. Activities should be fun and should seem like play rather than drill (Edelen-Smith, 1997). In fact, the classrooms of effective teachers are often word-rich environments in which wordplay (e.g., creation of puns, questions about multiple meanings) is encouraged. Once the initial skills are mastered, instruction may proceed on to more complex skills.

3. _Consider working on phonemic skills in isolation._ Whereas some students with reading problems need specific work on phoneme detection (e.g., identification of initial onset sounds), others may need to work on

phonemes in combination with phonics. The teacher must determine the appropriate level to emphasize for each student, but teachers must recognize that many students have failed in reading because we educators have moved directly into phonics without adequate preparation on phonemic manipulation as a prerequisite. Most of the games and activities described in this chapter emphasize exclusively work on phonemes and can provide a good set of strategies for students who need to work only on phonemes.

4. *Use phoneme sounds.* When doing phoneme instruction, it is easy for teachers to slip into using letter names rather than sounds for the instruction, and this should be avoided (Edelen-Smith, 1997). Rather, the teacher should use the sounds of the letters for the instruction, and it may help to represent those sounds by putting the letters between slash lines or brackets in the teacher's lesson plan (e.g., the teacher should say /h/a/t/ rather than "Say hat").

5. *Consider the age of the child.* Many teachers in the elementary grades have asked, "What is the age at which teachers should stop using phonemic instruction with a particular child who has reading problems?" This question has not been adequately answered by the research to date (NICHD, 2000). Because most of the extant research on phonological and phonemic instruction described tactics for young children, generally prekindergarten up through about Grade 2 (Bos et al., 2000; Chard & Dickson, 1999; Fuchs et al., 2001; Kame'enui et al., 2002; NICHD, 2000), there is some question as to when such instruction might be appropriate for older students. However, at least some research suggests that phonemic manipulation instruction will enhance reading for struggling readers even as high as the middle school grades. In particular, Bhat, Griffin, and Sindelar (2003) provided phonological instruction for middle school students with learning disabilities in reading, and demonstrated that such instruction would enhance the students' ability to understand and manipulate phonemes. Based on this work, teachers who work with struggling readers, even during the late elementary or middle school grades, should consider some phonemic or phonological instruction, coupled with more traditional phonics, fluency, or comprehension instruction for older, less successful readers.

PHONEMIC-BASED READING PROGRAMS

Although the Resources section in this book presents information on several reading programs for students with learning difficulties, we wanted to highlight several reading programs here that are based primarily on phonemic instruction. Several programs that have received wide attention are presented below: the Lindamood-Bell Learning Processes, Academy of Reading, Fast ForWord, and the Wilson Reading System. These are some of the most widely used phonemically based supplemental reading programs.

The Lindamood-Bell Reading Programs

Nanci Bell, Pat Lindamood, and Phyllis Lindamood have authored a series of Lindamood-Bell programs designed to help students develop the sensory-cognitive processes for language and literacy skills (see www. LindamoodBell.com for products and information). These phonemic-based reading programs are well researched and quite comprehensive. The goal of the programs is to develop the processes that underlie reading, spelling, and language comprehension. The various programs have been designed for use with all students, from those with severe learning disabilities to those who are academically gifted. The Lindamood-Bell programs can be used with individuals ages five through adult. One strength of the Lindamood-Bell programs is that they provide ways to assess specific reading and phonemic-based difficulties and then provide solutions tailored toward the needs of the specific student in the specific deficit area. There are several reading programs in a variety of areas and each involves phonemic-based instruction.

The Lindamood Phoneme Sequencing (LiPS) program is designed for students having difficulty with decoding, spelling, and speech or who lack phonemic awareness or the ability to judge sounds within words. This program presents various instructional procedures to develop the ability to identify and sequence individual sounds and the order of those sounds within words. Letters are categorized into groups with kid-friendly names for each group (e.g., some are identified as lip poppers, such as the /p/ sound). The instructional activities focus on the use of the lips, tongue, and mouth in pronouncing the various sounds, and this results in phonemic awareness and correct production of these sounds, as students become conscious of how to produce these sounds. Self-correction of speech sounds also is emphasized. Components of the program include the following:

- A teacher's manual
- A classroom kit (all materials needed to implement the program)
- A clinical kit (smaller version of classroom kit)
- A practice CD-ROM

The Lindamood Auditory Comprehension Test

The second program, Seeing Stars: Symbol Imagery, is designed to improve the skills of students who lack phonemic awareness and have poor sight-word vocabulary, difficulty with spelling, and poor reading fluency. This is a program that addresses the needs of students with learning difficulties at a slightly higher level than the LiPS program described earlier. Using this program will help students to establish phonological awareness and contextual fluency. Materials are designed to teach students to self-correct reading errors and improve reading fluency. Components of this program include the following:

- Seeing Stars teacher's manual
- My Stars words boxes
- Seeing Stars kit (all materials needed to implement the program)
- Seeing Stars decoding workbooks

In addition to the products available, extensive workshops also are offered to assist teachers in making the most of the programs. Workshops may be taken at selected locations or onsite at individual schools.

The Academy of Reading

- The Academy of Reading (AutoSkill, 2004) is a comprehensive, computer-based reading and literacy program that is founded on extensive research from the neurosciences (www.autoskill.com). It is intended as a supplementary program, and the curriculum is structured to be consistent with the five basic areas of reading identified by the National Reading Panel report (NICHD, 2000). The program recommends a commitment of 20 to 30 minutes per session, with three to five sessions per week. Within the program, specific sections address
  - o The Phonemic Awareness Training
  - o The Reading Subskills Section
  - o The Reading Comprehension Section

- Initially, a screening assessment within the program may be utilized to place a student at an appropriate level within the Phonemic Awareness Training section of the curriculum. Once the appropriate level or placement is determined, the student begins a series of instructional activities tailored to his or her specific needs.

- The phonemic awareness portion of the program consists of word matching, sound matching, and blending/segmenting phonemes. Activities in the program begin with initial phoneme recognition, and progress through fluency and reading comprehension. This curriculum builds skills as students progress through the computerized activities. For example, the curriculum begins with phoneme recognition on initial sounds by presenting match-to-sample activities in a computerized format. A cartoon character initially is presented and says the name of the target item. The character then asks the student to "touch" another item on the computer screen that begins with the same sound. This activity is repeated a number of times, and over time the research has shown that students build automaticity in initial sound recognition.

- While more research on this program is needed, the initial research has supported this reading intervention system. In fact, several studies have shown impressive gains in early literacy and/or reading in relatively brief periods of time (AutoSkill, 2004; Fiedorowicz, 1986; Fiedorowicz & Trites, 1987; Loh, 2005). Although the research is still preliminary, it is scientifically valid (see synopsis at the Florida Center for Reading Research at www.fcrr.org). Further, because many elementary general education teachers are concerned about finding the time to undertake a tier one supplementary literacy intervention for struggling students, this curriculum is worthy of consideration, since it is, in large measure, computer based.

- In consideration of RTI implementation, teachers often lament, "What will the other students do when I'm working with that struggling group of readers?" A computer-based curriculum that focuses on phonemic activities and mastery of the alphabetic code to a high level of automaticity may be one answer to that concern. For that reason alone, educators should consider this supplementary curriculum as an affordable option in their school's general education program.

- Finally, this curriculum is somewhat less expensive than other similar curricula. In most cases, this program is sold in terms of a schoolwide license, but educators can purchase this program for as few as ten students, making this computer-based intervention fairly affordable.

Fast ForWord: A Brain Compatible Phonemic Instruction Program in Reading

The Fast ForWord reading program is a computer-based curriculum that was developed by Scientific Learning Corporation (see the Web site at www.scilearn.com). It is likewise built upon the latest research on how the human brain learns, and it focuses on phonemic-based instruction for students with reading difficulties, over several levels of reading.

The Fast ForWord program involves a series of comprehensive computer-driven programs that cover reading skills from preschool through the elementary grades (aspects of this program are appropriate for students with reading problems even in high school). The program must be purchased at the school level and has been criticized by some as being somewhat expensive.

In the early phoneme instructional programs for early grade students with reading difficulties, a stimuli picture is presented on the screen, and the student hears a series of phoneme sounds that represent the picture. One task involves the blending of these sounds to recognize the correct pronunciation of an entire word. Other tasks involve word segmentation and oral reading fluency. The computer program tracks the progress of the students with reading difficulties individually and generates progress reports for the teacher. Subsequent programs present different skills in a variety of ways, most of which involve game-like formats. The Fast ForWord program also includes a series of reading instructional packages.

Basics	Intended for four- to seven-year-olds with reading problems who need to develop early reading skills such as phonemic awareness, letter naming, and letter-sound skills.
Language	Used for students with learning difficulties to develop the basic language skills that are the basis of reading, including working memory, reasoning, phoneme discrimination, and sound processing. These are weakness areas for many students with learning disabilities.
Language to Reading	Used for students to make the connection between oral and written language, including decoding, vocabulary, grammar, and beginning word recognition.
Reading	Concentrates on word recognition and fluency, advanced decoding, spelling, vocabulary, and passage comprehension.
Middle and High School	Emphasizes sustained focus and attention, listening comprehension, sequencing, and organization.

These programs have been piloted by Scientific Learning Corporation in a number of school districts, and the early research results on applications of these programs among students with learning difficulties are quite impressive. A bibliography of journal articles from this research is available at the company Web site. Many students with learning difficulties in early literacy skills have demonstrated one- to three-year gains in reading and language in just two months, and such improvement in reading warrants considerable discussion of this innovative program. According to the literature on the Web site, the following results were obtained.

- In New York City, New York (Public School 87), students gained two to four years in reading skills in just eight weeks.
- In Tiffin, Ohio, 77% of the students in the program passed the Ohio Proficiency Test.
- In Houston Public Schools, Texas, 92% of students at-risk for reading failure at Cornelius Elementary passed the Texas statewide assessment.
- In Fort Lupton, Colorado, public schools, 50 students gained between two and two-and-a-half years in reading skills in just six weeks using Fast ForWord.

The Fast ForWord reading program is solidly based in highly effective software and is of further interest in this context because it does represent the merger of brain compatible instructional research, reading research, and literacy and language development research. Further, with reading gains among students with learning difficulties such as those reported above, one may well expect to hear much more about this program. Finally, because many educators anticipate that effective instruction increasingly will be based to some degree on effective software, reading programs such as this example may well represent this century's approach to reading instruction. This would mean that the current generation of educators may well see schools retire the long-practiced and venerated basal reading instructional approach.

The Wilson Reading Program

The Wilson Reading System, written by Barbara Wilson (www.wilsonlanguage.com) has received fairly extensive research support and been widely hailed as one of the most effective supplementary reading programs for struggling readers available (Banks, Guyer, & Guyer, 1993; Bursuck & Dickson, 1999; Moats, 1998). The Wilson Reading System is both a reading and writing system, that begins with phonemic instruction, but is quite comprehensive in that it includes skills up to and including comprehension and written expression. Initially, instruction in phonemic skills and the alphabetic code is emphasized, beginning with phoneme segmentation and other phonemic skills. The structure of the English language system is taught in a systematic fashion, using a multisensory structured language program. Each lesson is structured similarly, in a ten-part lesson plan, designed to be highly interactive between the student and the teacher.

Twelve steps are used to teach the structure of words. Steps 1 and 2 emphasize phonemic segmentation and blending skills, and are thus directly relevant to phonemic instruction. Using monosyllabic words initially, a student learns to segment sounds within words. In addition to using sound cards, this program uses a "sound tapping" system that students seem to enjoy. For example, in teaching the word "cap" three lettered cards are put on the table to represent the three sounds in the word. The student is taught to say each sound while tapping a different finger to his or her thumb, as follows:

- As he says the /c/ sound, he taps his index finger to his thumb.
- As he says the /a/ sound, he taps his middle finger to his thumb.
- As he says the /p/ sound, he taps his ring finger to his thumb.
- He then says the sounds as he drags his thumb across the three fingers starting with his index finger and ending with his ring finger.

Thus, the sensory stimulation associated with touching fingertips in an order that represents the phonemes in a particular word, tends to emphasize the blending together of the phonemes in the word. Both real words and nonsense words are used in this fashion, to instruct the child in such blending skills. The student would then move on to words with four sounds, then five sounds. At the end of Step 2, the student is able to fluently blend and segment up to six sounds in a syllable.

Step 3 moves beyond phonemic instruction to phonological instruction, while focusing on multisyllable words. Here students are taught to segment words into syllables. Steps 4–6 emphasize phonics instruction involving vowel-consonant-*e* syllables, open syllables, suffix endings, and consonant-*le* syllables. Later skills address vocabulary, fluency, and comprehension. In steps 7–12, complex word structure is taught.

Research has supported this curriculum for a wide variety of areas in reading and literacy ranging from early reading skill to higher-order skills such as fluency and reading comprehension (Banks et al., 1993; Bursuck & Dickson, 1999; Moats, 1998; O'Connor & Wilson, 1995). Some of the research demonstrates reading gains of over four years in word attack, and more than one year in overall reading after the implementation of approximately 60 lessons from the Wilson Reading System (O'Connor & Wilson, 1995). Needless to say, these results are quite impressive, and similar results have made this program one of the more popular among teachers. Further, given the highly structured nature of this program, teachers find this relatively easy to implement, and extensive professional development is available for this program at the company Web site (www.wilsonlanguage.com).

RTI CASE STUDY IN PHONEMIC SKILLS

Because of the increased emphasis on early phonemic and phonological reading skills, every general education teacher today must be prepared to implement response to intervention procedures in early literacy at any point beginning in the early months of kindergarten (Abbott et al., 2002; Bender & Shores, 2007; Etscheidt, 2006). In most cases, such a procedure will not ultimately result in a diagnosis of a learning disability, since many early literacy and early reading problems can be alleviated by systematic supplemental instruction targeted specifically at the skill deficit. Also, a wide variety of instructional assessments and curricula lend themselves to just this type of intervention beginning with early literacy skills in kindergarten, including several of the curricula described above. Here is an example of an RTI procedure for a student struggling in early literacy.

Noting and Documenting an Early Reading Problem

For this example, let's imagine a young boy in kindergarten, Juan, who is having some difficulty with early literacy skills. His parents are Hispanic, but Juan was born in the United States. A mix of English and Spanish is spoken at home, and Juan is showing some difficulty in his literacy skills during the first two months of kindergarten. Ms. Snipes, the kindergarten teacher, regularly screens all of her students using the DIBELS assessment that was described in Chapter 1 (Langdon, 2004). For early kindergarten, DIBELS involves two quickly administered assessments, initial sound fluency (a phonemic assessment) and letter naming fluency (a letter recognition or phonics assessment). When Ms. Snipes screened Juan on October 10, she noted that Juan was at risk in both areas, and that an "intensive" need was indicated by the DIBELS assessment.

To be more specific, when Juan was shown a picture of a common item, and told the word for that item (e.g., tree), he could not identify, from among four possible answers, another picture that began with that same phoneme (a "t" sound). Note that this exercise was not dependent upon his recognition of letters, but rather was a "pure" measure of his phonemic ability—the ability to recognize and match the same initial phoneme or initial sound in a word. Likewise, whereas most kindergarten students could name at least three or four letters, Juan named only two letters. According to the benchmark early literacy goals for kindergarten students, Juan was below level on both of these skills (see Langdon, 2004, for discussion of these benchmarks).

The Tier One Intervention

Ms. Snipes was aware of the research that shows quite convincingly that students who do not meet the early literacy benchmarks, even as early as beginning kindergarten, would be at risk for later reading problems, and she did not wish to wait to see such failure prior to assisting Juan. Therefore, she was determined to begin a structured intervention on these benchmark skills and also to monitor his performance more closely. Moreover, she had several other students who likewise were at risk, so she decided she would begin a set of supplemental literacy activities with a group of four students who needed the extra help. She wrote a description of what she intended to do and solicited the parents' permissions for that supplemental work. The portion of that parent permission letter describing the instruction is presented next.

A Portion of Ms. Snipes's Letter to Parents

Working with your child and three other students, I will provide them with sup-plemental practice in recognition of initial sounds in words. I plan on pulling this group together three times each week for approximately 20 minutes each session, and I'll continue to work with them for approximately six weeks. There, the students will be presented with a target picture of a common household item, such as a bed, and told the name of that item. They then will have to select another item from four pictures of other household items that begins with the same sound. Among those four pictures, only one item will start with the "b" sound. In each case, the student will be expected to correctly point to the item that begins with the same sound as "bed." I will give every student many opportunities to practice that skill each time we meet, along with practice in naming letters in the alphabet. Finally, I'll use ten such items at the end of each week as a performance monitoring check on how well your child is doing, and I'll share those data with you when we meet again.

Intensity of the Tier One Intervention

We should note several things about Ms. Snipes's intervention plan, and the first is the issue of the intensity of the intervention (Bender & Shores, 2007). When a child is having difficulty in literacy, merely working with that child for 10 to 15 minutes each week is much less likely to alleviate the problem than working with that child for 20 minutes three times per week, because the latter intervention plan is more intensive. In the description in the letter above, a variety of indicators on intensity are addressed by Ms. Snipes.

First of all, teachers initiating a tier one intervention in a general education class should describe and document exactly what they intend to do as the intervention exercises for the student or students. Also, since this intervention should be "more intensive" than merely the general instruction offered for the whole class, teachers should state explicitly that this is supplemental instruction and that participating students will not be removed from their other literacy instruction—rather, tier one interventions should be a supplement to the traditional class instruction. Teachers should note explicitly the "intensity" of the instruction by indicating exactly how many minutes per day, how many days per week, and how many weeks will be used for the intervention. Each of these factors was addressed in the note above.

Should a student progress all the way through the intervention tiers without success in developing literacy skills, it is possible that this initial intervention may become a significant piece of information on which a later eligibility determination may be made. Thus, documenting the intensity of the intervention is critical.

Next, the level of performance monitoring should be noted (Etscheidt, 2006), and again, it should reflect a more intensive performance monitoring than is received by other members of the class. In this case, Ms. Snipes uses DIBELS with all class members to screen for literacy skills three times each year, as recommended by the manufacturer. However, the students receiving this tier one intervention will be assessed additionally each week as described above, resulting in more intensive performance monitoring. Finally, note that Ms. Snipes stated specifically the student-teacher ratio for this group—four students and one teacher. Again this indicates that Juan and the other students will receive very intensive supplemental instruction. Again, to document an intensive tier one or tier two intervention, these indicators of intensity must be described:

Supplemental instruction

Specific time commitment to the supplemental instruction

Increased performance monitoring

Student-teacher ratio

Implementing a Scientifically Validated Curriculum

The next overriding issue in planning an RTI procedure is the issue of implementing scientifically validated curricula (Fuchs & Deshler, 2007). Teachers today realize that interventions should be based on scientifically proven instructional tactics, and in most cases, teachers probably will use a commercially available curricula that has received scientific support. However, in this instance, Ms. Snipes chose to develop her own set of instructional activities for this tier one intervention. She was aware of the instructional recommendations for activities that improve phonemic matching skill, and the fact that various assessments use such activities as benchmark indicators. Based on her expertise and those model exercises, she was confident she could develop similar exercises. Further, Juan was still participating in the general education literacy curriculum used by the entire class, so clearly Juan was exposed to scientifically validated curricula, as were all class members.

Instructional Fidelity

A third issue to consider in implementing tiered instruction in an RTI procedure is the issue of instructional fidelity (Bender & Shores, 2007; Fuchs & Deshler, 2007). This issue addresses the question, "Was the instruction offered appropriate for a student and of sufficiently high quality to provide a student with an appropriate opportunity to learn?" In the case above, Ms. Snipes chose to develop some curricula activities similar to those that were used as benchmarks for kindergarten literacy, so clearly the instructional fidelity question would be paramount; would Juan receive high-quality instruction tied directly to his learning needs?

To address that question, Ms. Snipes did several things. First, she was highly fluent with instructional procedures from the professional literature on which types of instructional activities had been scientifically validated for enhancing phonemic skills. Thus, based on that knowledge, she developed a series of picture-based activities to measure the student's ability to recognize initial letter sounds on ten trials each day (see her description above in the letter to the parents). She also showed her learning practice activities to the reading lab coach in her school—Ms. Askew. Ms. Askew provided her input on those activities, as they were developed. Ms. Snipes also invited Ms. Askew to come and observe her as she instructed the small group during those activities. Thus, another knowledgeable reading specialist in the school could attest that the curricula activities used represented scientifically valid practice, and that they were taught in an appropriate fashion. In this way, instructional fidelity was ensured.

As Ms. Snipes progressed through this intervention, she noted that three students were moving toward increased success with this supplemental assistance in literacy skills. However, Juan was not progressing as quickly as she would like, and Ms. Snipes believed that Juan would need more assistance. At this point, Ms. Snipes summarized her intervention with Juan by writing a brief intervention report, and creating a data chart to summarize his progress (see Figure 2.1). She then took that summary report and the data chart to the student support team in her school and she used those data to recommend a tier two intervention for Juan.

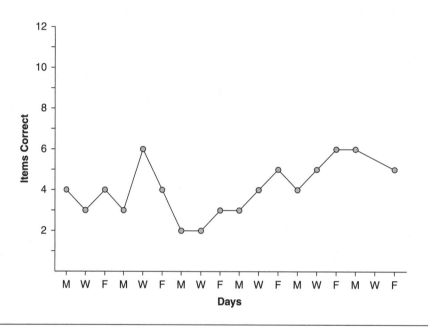

Figure 2.1   Juan's Initial Phoneme Recognition

Data Review and Tier Two Intervention Planning

Ms. Snipes met with members of the student support team for her school, including Ms. Askew, the Reading Lab Coach, Ms. Bullock, the school principal, and Ms. Jones, the Team Captain for Kindergarten Classes. Ms. Snipes presented the data summarized in Figure 2.1 and discussed her intensive instruction with the team. She noted that while Juan seemed to be progressing somewhat, he was not moving forward quickly enough to have a realistic opportunity to "catch up" with the other kindergarten students by the end of the year, since most of her other students had totally mastered initial phoneme sounds, whereas Juan had never scored higher than 60%. Therefore, other class members moved on to final phoneme sounds or phoneme substitution exercises.

Next, Ms. Askew told the team that she'd participated in development of the instructional activities Ms. Snipes had used. She then stated that she had observed one class period when Juan received the supplemental instruction. She indicated that the instructional activities were the correct type of activities for Juan, but that he'd need more time on those types of initial phonemic recognition activities, as well as considerable time on other phonemic work. Therefore, she and Ms. Snipes recommended that the team consider a tier two intervention that would address the same two benchmark early literacy skills, but would offer a more intensive supplemental intervention program for Juan. After all team members concluded that such a tier two intervention seemed reasonable, Ms. Askew suggested one possibility for such a program.

In the reading lab, Ms. Askew was using the Academy of Reading program described previously in this chapter. In particular, that program presented phonemic awareness matching activities that were very similar to the activities developed by Ms. Snipes and Ms. Askew. Ms. Askew suggested that Juan should be included in that program, noting that it was a computer-based, highly interactive individual phonemic matching and phonemic manipulation program. To make certain that Juan received intensive instruction, Ms. Askew recommended that Juan participate in the Academy of Reading for at least 30 minutes each day in the reading lab for the next four weeks, without removing him from the literacy instructional program in kindergarten. She also pointed out that the Academy of Reading assessed the child continually, and thus she could print out data either every week, or even every day to monitor Juan's performance in the program.

The team decided to go with that recommendation and meet at the end of the next grading period in four weeks to consider Juan's progress. Ms. Snipes and Ms. Askew then worked out the time that Juan would come into the reading lab for 35 minutes each day.

Note that, in describing the tier two intervention above, the team attended to the RTI expectation that higher number tiers provide more intensive instruction. The chart below compares the tier one intervention and the tier two intervention on several measures of intensity of instruction.

Indicator of Intensity	Tier One	Tier Two
Supplemental program	Teacher made	Computer based
Time commitment	20 minutes 3 times per week for 6 weeks	35 minutes daily for 4 weeks
Performance monitored	3 days per week	Daily
Student-teacher ratio	4 to 1	Individual

As this comparison indicates, the tier two intervention is more intensive than the tier one intervention in every respect. Thus, it was reasonable to believe that Juan's literacy problems could realistically be addressed by providing this supplemental phonemic literacy program for Juan. Also, in addition to addressing the intensity of intervention issue, the issues of a scientifically validated curriculum and instructional fidelity were both addressed. As noted previously, the Academy of Reading has been supported by scientific research. Also, with implementation of a computer-based curriculum of this nature, one can be relatively comfortable that the curriculum will be taught in an appropriate fashion, consistent with the instructions of the curriculum developers, because most of the actual teaching will be delivered in an electronic environment.

In the case of Juan, implementation of the Academy of Reading was exactly what he needed. As the data in Figure 2.2 indicate, the weekly performance of Juan showed impressive progress on phonemic matching for initial sounds, and he progressed to detection of final phonemes before the grading period was over. Thus, Juan was receiving instruction at the intensity level he needed to make progress and catch up with his classmates by the end of the year. When the team reviewed the data in Figure 2.2, they determined to keep Juan in the reading lab, and working on the same curriculum while Ms. Snipes would continue to work with him on literacy, and monitor his progress using DIBELS every two weeks.

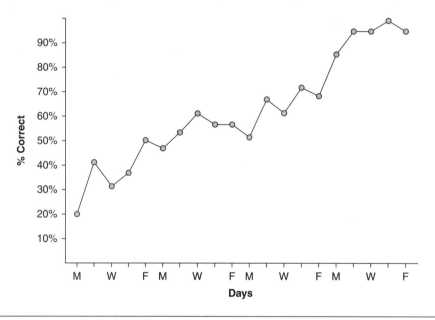

Figure 2.2   Juan's Initial Phoneme Recognition Percentage in a Computerized Reading Program

Important Points From This RTI Case Study

In the RTI procedure above, we should note several things. First, a general education teacher typically will initiate the tier one supplemental intervention, and for most students that typically will be an intervention in early literacy or reading skills. In this case, the intervention that Ms. Snipes could offer, while seemingly the appropriate type of intervention, could not be provided to Juan as intensively as he needed, as the progress monitoring data demonstrated. Thus, a tier two intervention was necessary. In most states, general education teachers will be responsible for both the tier one and tier two interventions for students struggling with reading (Bender & Shores, 2007; Fuchs & Deshler, 2007), but that does not necessarily mean that those general education teachers must implement those interventions alone. In fact, the time pressures in the typical general education classroom would become unbearable in most cases, and it is unrealistic to expect general education teachers to teach reading/literacy for an entire class, implement a tier one intervention for a small subgroup of struggling readers within the class, and also implement a more intensive tier two intervention for other class members.

As the example above indicates, while general education teachers probably will implement the first supplemental intervention for struggling students, they should request and receive some type of support to implement the second tier intervention. Here, Ms. Askew actually implemented the second tier intervention, and not Ms. Snipes.

Of course that brings up another question: Should a student participate in more than one supplementary reading/literacy intervention at any one time? Our recommendation is that they should not. In the example above, Juan was participating in traditional class instruction with Ms. Snipes, and for one grading period was also receiving a tier one intervention from Ms. Snipes. Once the data demonstrated that this intervention was not working, the tier one intervention ceased, and Juan moved to a tier two intervention in the reading lab. Given that the tier two intervention succeeded, it would be advisable for that intervention to continue for the remainder of the year, or until Juan catches up with his classmates. Thus, struggling students may be participating in the general education curriculum and a supplemental tier one intervention at one point, and at a later point participating in the general education curriculum and a supplemental tier two intervention. However, the student should not be participating in more than one "tier" or more than one supplemental intervention at any one time.

Next, we should consider this procedure and how it might fit within a diagnosis of learning disability, and for that we'll need to "modify" the results discussed above for Juan. Specifically, let's imagine that the data in Figure 2.2 indicated a lack of progress for Juan. Had that been the case, the student support team would review the tier one and tier two intervention data, and would then conclude that Juan's early literacy problems had not been adequately remediated—that is, he had failed to respond to two separate tiered interventions. Based on those data, the student support team should consider recommending that the eligibility team in the school convene and consider the possibility that Juan might have a learning disability.

Note that the student support team in this example has not stated that Juan definitively has a learning disability, just that they suspect he might have based on his failure to respond to two separate interventions. At that point, a psychological assessment to examine Juan's auditory and visual processing skills, his memory skills, and other psychological processes that may underlie a learning disability would be necessary. Also, the teacher would wish to consider various medical or home factors that might have impacted Juan's performance. To be specific, after a student has not succeeded in two interventions (i.e., tier one and tier two), a learning disability may be suspected, but at that point the learning disability has not been demonstrated. The determination of the existence of a learning disability is the responsibility of the eligibility team, based on the evaluation of the data from tier one and tier two interventions, coupled with their interpretation of the psychological processes (as demonstrated in a psychological report) that may underlie a learning disability, along with other relevant data.

Next, note that this example was a kindergarten example. Whereas traditionally, most students with learning disabilities were diagnosed in Grades 3 or 4, the proponents of RTI expect that that "age of onset" for learning disability diagnosis will go much lower. In fact, given the RTI procedure, it is quite possible to diagnose a learning disability in the first one-half of the kindergarten year. In that fashion, students with learning disabilities probably will receive more intensive instruction much sooner than in the past.

Finally, we should point out the serious responsibility that general education teachers now have in the eligibility process when documenting a learning disability. Of course, general education teachers have always participated in determining the eligibility of students for such services; they have historically participated in meetings, brought in work samples, and done error analysis and/or task analysis of student learning skills. Still, those general education teachers, under RTI, will have an increasingly serious responsibility. They will now be responsible for providing one of the two most critical pieces of data in that learning disability determination—the performance monitoring assessment data chart for the tier one intervention. General education teachers should be made aware of that increased responsibility, and the need to understand the intricacies of RTI, and in particular monitoring a child's performance repeatedly in tier one interventions.

CONCLUSION

This chapter has presented a series of instructional strategies to assist teachers in implementing phonemic instruction in the classroom, in addition to demonstrating how a response to intervention procedure might look for a student who is struggling with early literacy phonemic manipulation skills. A consensus has emerged over the past decade that phonemic instruction must serve as the basis for effective reading and literacy skills for students with reading problems. With this in mind, every teacher should have a series of instructional activities and tactics that can assist students in developing this important set of skills. Further, the recent implementation of RTI procedures for students in kindergarten suggests that almost every general education teacher—kindergarten throughout the lower elementary grades—will be expected to initiate an RTI procedure for students in his or her class. Therefore, mastery of RTI implementation is critical for every teacher in the classroom today.

WHAT'S NEXT?

While this chapter has concentrated on phonemic manipulation instructional activities, the next step involves phonics instruction based on matching phonemes with letters and letter combinations. These phonics and word attack skills represent the next step in reading mastery, and formulation of RTI procedures in those areas likewise is critical for general education teachers.

REFERENCES

Abbott, M., Walton, C., & Greenwood, C. R. (2002). Phonemic awareness in kindergarten and first grade. *Teaching Exceptional Children, 34*(4), 20–27.

AutoSkill. (2004). *Focus on research: A paper on the scientific validation of effective reading programs and the development of the AutoSkill Academy of Reading.* Ottawa, Canada: Author.

Banks, S. R., Guyer, B. P., & Guyer, K. E. (1993). Spelling improvement by college students who are dyslexic. *Annals of Dyslexia, 43*, 186–193.

Bhat, P., Griffin, C. C., & Sindelar, P. T. (2003). Phonological awareness instruction for middle school students with learning disabilities. *Learning Disability Quarterly, 26*(2), 73–88.

Bender, W. N. (2008). *Differentiating instruction for students with learning disabilities* (2nd ed.). Thousand Oaks, CA: Corwin Press.

Bender, W. N., & Shores, C. (2007). *Response to intervention: A practical guide for every teacher.* Thousand Oaks, CA: Corwin Press.

Bos, C. S., Mather, N., Silver-Pacuilla, H., & Narr, R. F. (2000). Learning to teach early literacy skills collaboratively. *Teaching Exceptional Children, 32*(5), 38–45.

Bursuck, W., & Dickson, S. (1999). Implementing a model for preventing reading failure: A report from the field. *Learning Disabilities Research and Practice, 14*(4), 191–202.

Chard, D. J., & Dickson, S. V. (1999). Phonological awareness: Instructional and assessment guidelines. *Intervention in School and Clinic, 34*(5), 261–270.

Davis, G. N., Lindo, E. J., & Compton, D. L. (2007). Children at risk for reading failure: Constructing an early screening measure. *Teaching Exceptional Children, 39*(5), 32–39.

Edelen-Smith, P. J. (1997). How now brown cow: Phoneme awareness activities for collaborative classrooms. *Intervention in School and Clinic, 33*, 103–111.

Etscheidt, S. K. (2006). Progress monitoring: Legal issues and recommendations for IEP teams. *Teaching Exceptional Children, 38*(3), 56–60.

Fiedorowicz, C. (1986). Training of component reading skills. *Annals of Dyslexia, 36*, 318–334.

Fiedorowicz, C., & Trites, R. (1987). An evaluation of the effectiveness of the computer-assisted component reading subskills training. Toronto, Canada: Queens' Printer for Ontario.

Fuchs, D., & Deshler, D. D. (2007). What we need to know about responsiveness to intervention (and shouldn't be afraid to ask). *Learning Disabilities Research and Practice, 22*(2), 129–136.

Fuchs, D., Fuchs, L., Al Otaiba, S., Thompson, A., Yen, L., McMaster, K., et al. (2001). K-Pals: Helping kindergartners with reading readiness: Teachers and researchers in partnerships. *Teaching Exceptional Children, 33*(4), 76–80.

Kame'enui, E. J., Carnine, D. W., Dixon, R. C., Simmons, D. C., & Coyne, M. D. (2002). *Effective teaching strategies that accommodate diverse learners* (2nd ed.). Upper Saddle River, NJ: Merrill-Prentice Hall.

Langdon, T. (2004). DIBELS: A teacher friendly basic literacy accountability tool for the primary classroom. *Teaching Exceptional Children, 37*(2), 54–61.

Larkin, M. J. (2001). Providing support for student independence through scaffolded instruction. *Teaching Exceptional Children, 34*(1), 30–35.

Loh, E. (2005). *Building readers proficiency in high school students: Examining the effectiveness of the Academy of Reading for striving readers.* Retrieved December 7, 2007, from http://www.autoskill.com.

Moats, L. C. (1998). Reading, spelling, and writing disabilities in the middle grades. In B. Wong (Ed.), *Learning about learning disabilities.* Orlando, FL; Academic Press.

Moats, L. C., & Lyon, C. R. (1993). Learning disabilities in the United States: Advocacy, science, and the future of the field. *Journal of Learning Disabilities, 26,* 282–294.

National Institute of Child Health and Development. (2000). *Teaching children to read: An evidence-based assessment of the scientific research literature on reading and its implications for reading instruction* (Report of the National Reading Panel). Retrieved May 23, 2002, from http://www.nichd.nih.gov/publications/nrp/findings.cfm.

O'Connor, J., & Wilson, B. (1995). Effectiveness of the Wilson Reading System used in public school training. In C. McIntyre & J. Pickering (Eds.), *Clinical studies of multisensory structured language education.* Salem, OR: International Multisensory Structured Language Education Council.

Schatschneider, C., Francis, D. J., Foorman, B. R., Fletcher, J. M., & Mehta, P. (1999). The dimensionality of phonological awareness: An application of item response theory. *Journal of Educational Psychology, 91,* 439–449.

Sousa, D. A. (2001). *How the special needs brain learns.* Thousand Oaks, CA: Corwin Press.

Sousa, D. A. (2005). *How the brain learns to read.* Thousand Oaks, CA: Corwin Press.

Phonics and Word Attack Strategies 3

> ## Strategies Presented in This Chapter Include
>
> ✓ Word Boxes
>
> ✓ Analyzing Words
>
> ✓ Picture Sorts
>
> ✓ Word Sorts
>
> ✓ Making Words
>
> ✓ Word Banks
>
> ✓ Word Study Notebooks
>
> ✓ RTI Case Study for Word Attack Strategies

PHONICS AND THE BRAIN

Once students have mastered the phonemic awareness skills used to detect and discriminate between phonemes, they must learn the letters that are associated with those phonemes. Phonics instruction helps "beginning readers understand how letters are linked to sounds (phonemes) to form letter-sound correspondences" that are used in reading and spelling (National Institute of Child Health and Development [NICHD], 2000, p. 8). Mapping letters to phonemes involves the activation of several brain areas in the reading process including the visual cortex (to see and interpret the printed form of the letter, to "image" the shape of the letter for other brain areas, and to interact with other brain areas), Wernicke's area (to interpret the phoneme associated with the letter), and Broca's area (to seek meaning for the letter-sound set; Sousa, 2005).

Students with learning difficulties in reading may have deficits in phonemic awareness and the alphabetic principle (Sousa, 2001, 2005). In other words, their brains may not understand that words consist of segmented sounds that can be connected to letters (i.e., the alphabetic principle). These students have difficulty pronouncing words, read with frequent starts and stops, and have low comprehension. Such deficits may be due to genetic and neurobiological problems in the angular gyrus or to lack of exposure to spoken language patterns and usage in preschool. Some children have dysfunction in the timing of speech sounds that makes processing those sounds difficult. Brain scans have shown that poor readers' brains exhibit more activity during reading than the brains of good readers; thus, poor readers put forth more effort to pronounce and interpret words correctly (Merzenich et al., 1996; Tallal et al., 1996).

Sousa (2001) noted that approximately 2% to 5% of elementary-age students have dyslexia, a developmental reading disorder in which they cannot process graphic symbols. Dyslexia is not attributed to eye problems or low intelligence. Some students with dyslexia may confuse letters because they sound alike; in other words, their brains may process what is heard rather than what is seen. Brain imaging studies have shown that this decoding problem occurs in the angular gyrus, which has a significantly reduced blood flow in persons with dyslexia. Students who have difficulty decoding print to sound and sound back to print need intensive practice to establish correct phonemic connections. Other individuals with dyslexia may have a visual magnocellular deficit that may cause the visual images of letters to be held longer than usual and thus other images may be superimposed (Stein, Talcott, & Walsh, 2000). Such blurry letters make reading difficult for these individuals. Wright, Bowen, and Zecker (2000) stated that, to individuals with dyslexia, the letters on a page might overlap or appear to move.

Wright et al. (2000) reviewed research on nonlinguistic perceptual deficits that impact one's ability to be a good reader. For example, problems in the detection and discrimination of sounds presented in rapid succession are common in persons with reading and language disorders. Some persons with reading disorders may be unable to hear differences in sound frequency or to detect tones within noise. These findings indicate that auditory functions play a substantial role in reading disorders.

PHONICS INSTRUCTIONAL OPTIONS

We have learned that students with learning difficulties in reading put a great deal of effort into making the connections of spoken language with the alphabet and with word recognition (Sousa, 2001, 2005). In addition, these learning difficulties may be manifested in different ways or attributed to various genetic, neurobiological, or environmental factors. Although brain research has provided some interesting and meaningful findings, we still have much to learn about how the brain functions in reading and why persons with dyslexia have such reading difficulties. In the meantime, research has shown some promising practices that can help many struggling readers, including those with learning difficulties. While some debate occurred in the 1970s about the effectiveness of phonics instruction, research has answered the age-old question on the relative efficacy of whole-language versus phonics instruction in favor of phonics for almost all students. Some of the principles of whole-language instruction may be incorporated for readers at later developmental stages (Moats, 2000), but beginning readers and students with learning difficulties in reading need explicit phonemic awareness and phonics instruction.

Imaginative teachers may provide a systematic phonics approach in which phonics elements are taught explicitly in a sequential manner or they may select incidental phonics instruction in which they highlight particular phonics elements as needed. Several phonics instructional approaches include the following (NICHD, 2000):

- *Analogy phonics:* Students are taught unfamiliar words by using analogies to familiar words. For example, if students are familiar with the word *cat* and know the sound that the rime portion (*at*) of that word makes, then they should be able to read unfamiliar words from the *at* family. This is done by sounding out the onset portion of the word and blending it with the rime. Thus, the onset *b* blended with *at* becomes *bat*.
- *Analytic phonics:* Students are taught to "analyze letter-sound relations from previously learned words to avoid pronouncing sounds in isolation" (NICHD, 2000, p. 8). Thus, students learn whole-word units first and then learn how to link word letters with their respective sounds.
- *Embedded phonics:* Students learn phonics when it is embedded in text reading. This approach is implicit and may rely on incidental learning.
- *Phonics through spelling:* Students are taught to spell words phonemically (i.e., dividing words into phonemes and selecting the appropriate letters for those phonemes).
- *Synthetic phonics:* Through explicit instruction, students are taught to convert letters into sounds or phonemes and blend them to form words. Thus, students first learn the sounds and then use them to create words.

A meta-analysis of research literature conducted by the National Reading Panel (NRP) found that systematic phonics instruction helped children learn to read and provided benefits for students in Grades K–6 (NICHD, 2000). Systematic synthetic phonics particularly was helpful for students with learning disabilities, low-achieving students, and students with low socioeconomic status. The NRP concluded that explicit, systematic phonics instruction is an essential component of a successful reading program, but educators should not interpret this finding as a blanket endorsement of all phonics instruction. For example, phonics programs that are too focused on the letter-sound relations without applying them to real reading situations are likely to be ineffective. Although we often hear the need for "intensive, systematic" phonics instruction, the NRP indicated that future research is needed to define this term (NICHD, p. 10). In other words, we do not have a magic formula that indicates how long single phonics sessions should last, how many letter-sound relations should be taught, and at what grade level phonics instruction should no longer be emphasized. Teachers must assess individual student needs and tailor phonics instruction to meet these needs. In addition, teachers should make sure that phonics instruction is integrated with other reading components such as phonemic awareness, fluency, and comprehension to create a complete reading program (NICHD).

As mentioned in Chapter 1, Cunningham and Hall developed a framework for beginning reading instruction called the Four Blocks approach, whose purpose was to meet the needs of students who had a wide range of literacy levels and to combine major approaches to reading (Cunningham, Hall, & Defee, 1998). In the Four Blocks approach, the language arts segment (typically 2 1/4 to 2 1/2 hours daily) is divided into four 30- to 40-minute blocks: (1) Working With Words, (2) Guided Reading, (3) Self-Selected Reading, and (4) Writing. The purpose of the Working With Words block is to help students review high-frequency words, participate in phonics-based activities, and learn strategies for decoding words and spelling. If you use a Four Blocks balanced approach to reading in your classroom, many of the activities discussed in this chapter would fit nicely into the Working With Words block. Even if you are not using the Four Blocks approach, we believe you will find the activities in this chapter of value in helping students with learning difficulties practice their decoding skills and learn appropriate strategies for decoding.

This chapter will address specific strategies tailoring developmentally appropriate instruction to increase students' word attack skills. Be sure to read or skim through all sections of this chapter because some of the strategies such as word boxes, picture sorts, word sorts, and making words activities that are introduced early on can enhance phonics and word study instruction for students at a variety of developmental stages. Examine these strategies, because they are some that we are beginning to see used more often for students with learning difficulties. (These strategies are good for all students, too!) You will find this chapter full of a number of individual student and class ready-to-use activities and games that require little preparation, so select those that best fit your students' learning needs. Finally, be sure to read Teaching Tip 3.10 at the end of the chapter about assessing the decodability of text materials.

STRATEGIES FOR DEVELOPMENTAL READING AND SPELLING STAGES

Word study must be related to students' developmental needs to be appropriate (Vacca et al., 2003). To determine appropriate word study activities, you will need to be familiar with your students' reading and spelling levels. Bear, Invernizzi, Templeton, and Johnston (2000, 2008) noted that individuals move along a continuum from the alphabet to pattern to meaning as they become more proficient readers and spellers.

Alphabet ⟶		*Pattern* ⟶		*Meaning* ⟶	
Grade level	PreK–mid 1	K–mid 2	1–mid 4	3–8	5–12
Reading stage	Emergent	Beginning	Transitional	Intermediate	Advanced
Spelling stage	Emergent	Letter-name alphabetic	Within word pattern	Syllables and affixes	Derivational relations

SOURCE: Adapted from Bear et al. (2000).

Although this continuum represents the typical progression and grade levels for reading and spelling development, students with learning difficulties may progress along the continuum at a slower pace and encounter many difficulties along the way. Some of these struggling readers may appear to be stuck in one of the stages. Therefore, when planning word study instruction, teachers need to select activities that are appropriate for students' particular stages of reading and spelling development. Bear et al. (2000, 2008) noted characteristics for each of the reading and spelling stages and the corresponding reading and writing activities, as well as ideas for word study focus. This framework will provide the structure for the strategies and tactics discussed in this chapter. The first or emergent stage is mentioned here to illustrate the progression from one stage to the next. Please refer back to Chapter 2 for more information regarding emergent literacy strategies on phonemic instruction.

1. Emergent Stage

Characteristics	Reading and writing activities	Word study focus
• Scribbles letters and numbers • Lacks word concepts • Lacks letter-sound correspondence • Pretends to read and write	• Read to students • Model writing • Encourage pretend reading and writing	• Play with speech sounds • Participate in alphabet activities • Sort pictures by beginning sound • Encourage invented spelling

SOURCE: Adapted from Bear et al. (2000).

Once children begin leaving the emergent reading and spelling stage at approximately kindergarten to mid–first grade, they move toward the beginning reading, letter-name alphabetic spelling stage. Note that students with learning difficulties who have not had intensive phonemic instruction still may have difficulty with some of the emergent reading and spelling tasks.

2. Letter-Name Alphabetic Stage

Characteristics (early)	Reading and writing activities	Word study focus
• Identifies beginning and ending sounds • Has basic concept of word • Reads word by word	• Read to students • Provide practice with patterned trade books, rhymes, and dictations • Provide picture labeling and journal writing activities	• Sort pictures and words by beginning sounds • Study word families containing a common vowel • Study beginning consonant blends and digraphs • Encourage invented spelling

Characteristics (late)	Reading and writing activities	Word study focus
• Spells initial and final consonants, some blends and digraphs • Spells phonetically • Omits most silent letters • Reads aloud and fingerpoints • Reads slowly word by word	• Read to students • Encourage invented spelling in independent writing, but students must be accountable for word features previously studied • Encourage more expansive writing and simple editing for high-frequency words	• Sort pictures and words by short vowel word families • Sort pictures and words by short vowel sounds and CVC patterns • Begin simple sound sorts for short and long vowels • Create a word bank of up to 200 unknown words

SOURCE: Adapted from Bear et al. (2000).

Students focus primarily on the alphabetic principle of matching sounds to letters in the letter-name alphabetic stage of development (Bear et al., 2000). Although students in this stage experiment with invented spellings, there is an order to this experimentation. Therefore, teachers should use their students' invented spellings to design word study instruction. A predictable pattern of student development may include using beginning consonants in writing and then adding vowels in stressed syllables. Thus, the teacher should begin by focusing word study on consonants and then on short vowels as students add vowels to their writing and spelling. Next, focus on long vowel patterns when students begin to use them. Keep in mind that although students follow a predictable developmental pattern, the sequence and pace may differ for individuals, particularly those with learning difficulties. Remember that when working with students whose primary language is not English that most other languages do not have as many consonants, consonant blends, or vowels as the English language (Bear et al., 2008). The following sections offer some suggestions for sequencing word study in the letter-name alphabetic stage.

Beginning Consonant Sounds. Although there is no particular order to teach beginning sounds, start with frequently occurring initial consonants (Bear et al., 2000). Make sure to choose consonants that differ clearly in how they look and also in how they sound. Chard and Osborn (1998) suggested teaching continuous sounds such as *s, m,* and *f* prior to teaching stop sounds such as *b, k,* and *p* because the continuous sounds are easier to pronounce. A continuous sound can be said for several seconds without distorting the sound, as compared to a stop sound that can be said only for an instant (Carnine, Silbert, & Kame'enui, 1997). Words beginning with a continuous sound (e.g., *sad*) are easier to sound out than words beginning with a stop sound (e.g., *pad*).

Final Consonant Sounds. When students have mastered initial consonant and phonemic segmentation, they likely will use this information to help them with final consonants (Bear et al., 2000). Note that final consonants also are covered when students study word families.

Initial Consonant Digraphs and Blends. Following the study of initial consonants, students are ready to learn about initial consonant digraphs and blends (Bear et al., 2000). Digraphs occur when two or more consonants are combined to produce a new sound. Begin with digraphs such as *ch, sh, th,* and *wh.* Then move to the three major groups of consonant blends: (a) *s*-blends, (b) *r*-blends, and (c) *l*-blends. Consonant blends are two or three consonants grouped together with each consonant retaining its own sound. The *s*-blends (*sk, sm, sn, st,* etc.) are the easiest to learn. *R*-blends include *br, cr, dr, fr, gr, pr,* and *tr,* while *l*-blends include *bl, cl, fl, gl, pl,* and *sl.*

Short Vowels. Word families are an easy and appealing way to introduce vowels (Bear et al., 2000). Once students are using short vowels consistently, they can compare short vowels in word sorts in which they compare the consonant-vowel-consonant (CVC) pattern using a variety of vowels. In the word family approach, students are introduced to the vowel and ending letter or letters following the vowel as a chunk or pattern (i.e., rime). The letter or letters preceding the vowel are the onset (you may wish to review the discussion of onsets and rimes in Chapter 2). Treiman (1985) found that segmenting words into onsets and rimes is an easier and more natural process for students as opposed to dividing words into individual phonemes. Bear et al. (2000) noted that it is not necessary to teach every word family thoroughly. Once students have been exposed to several word families, they probably will understand that words with the same sound likely will share the same rimes and spelling.

Once students work with word families easily and accurately, you will need to introduce short vowels in nonrhyming words that do not belong to word families (Bear et al., 2000). For example, the words *mad, flag,* and *track* do not rhyme and do not belong to the same word family. If these three words are written in onset and rime form they would appear as follows:

Onset	Rime
m	ad
fl	ag
tr	ack

If the same three words were presented as a CVC pattern, they would appear as

Consonant	Vowel	Consonant
m	a	d
fl	a	g
tr	a	ck

Note that the consonant letter combinations can be consonant blends (e.g., *tr*) or digraphs (e.g., *fl*).

When you introduce students to short vowel study, be sure to plan distinct contrasts such as short-*a* with short-*i* or short-*o* (Bear et al., 2000). Students are likely to confuse short-*e* with short-*a* or short-*i*. Teaching short vowels may take time and may not come easily for some students, particularly those with learning difficulties.

REFLECTIVE EXERCISE 3.1
SEQUENCE OF A DIRECT INSTRUCTION
READING PROGRAM

Although the aforementioned information serves as a basic guide for sequencing word study, you still may feel like you need more guidance to help your students with learning difficulties in reading. These struggling students often can benefit from intensive direct instruction in reading (Atkinson, Wilhite, Frey, & Williams, 2002) to help them recognize and say the appropriate letter-sound correspondences that constitute words. A well-known commercial direct instruction reading program is Reading Mastery (Engelmann & Bruner, 1995). Listed below is the sequence of sounds taught in the Reading Mastery I kit. Use the guidelines for sequencing that are listed prior to this exercise to see if you can determine why the sounds are sequenced as they are in this program. Keep in mind that various commercial reading programs may use different sequencings of sounds; thus, there is not just one way of appropriate sound sequencing that teachers should follow. Instead, use the guidelines for sequencing to help you plan logical sound sequencing with the phonics materials or curriculum that you use.

Letter	As in	Continuous or stop sound
a	and	Continuous
m	mat	Continuous
s	sat	Continuous
e	eat	Continuous
r	rat	Continuous
d	dad	Stop
f	fill	Continuous
i	if	Continuous
th	this	Continuous
t	top	Stop
n	nut	Continuous
c	cat	Stop
o	ox	Continuous
a	ate	Continuous
h	his	Stop
u	unde	Continuous

Letter	As in	Continuous or stop sound
g	got	Stop
l	let	Continuous
w	wet	Continuous
sh	she	Continuous
i	I	Continuous
k	kiss	Stop
o	over	Continuous
v	vet	Continuous
p	pet	Stop
ch	chat	Stop
e	end	Continuous
b	boy	Stop
ing	sing	Continuous
i	ice	Continuous
y	yes	Continuous
er	teacher	Continuous
x	fox	Stop
oo	moon	Continuous
j	jet	Stop
y	my	Continuous
wh	why	Stop
qu	quit	Stop
z	zoo	Continuous
u	use	Continuous

Strategy: Word Boxes

Word boxes are a modification of sound boxes by Elkonin (1973) and Clay's (1993) letterboxes (Schmidgall & Joseph, 2007). They are created by dividing a rectangle into the number of sections that correspond to the number of sounds heard in a word (Joseph, 2002). For example, a word that has three phonemes could be represented by a rectangle divided into three sections. Thus, the word *bug* is represented in Figure 3.1.

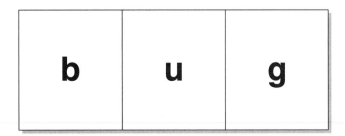

Figure 3.1   Word Box Example: Segmenting Sounds

Completing word boxes consists of three steps: (a) segmenting sounds, (b) matching letters to sounds, and (c) writing letters (Joseph, 2002). Teachers may help students to learn one step of completing word boxes over a span of several lessons by using words that are contained in students' speaking vocabulary, but that the students have not learned to read. When students have mastered the three steps, then they can be combined into one lesson. Word box phonics procedures are appropriate for whole class, small group, and peer buddy sessions. Word box activities contain some of the elements of teaching reading that Atkinson et al. (2002) suggested as important when teaching reading to students with learning disabilities: (a) integrating multisensory approaches instruction and (b) linking the teaching of reading and writing. Notice in the segmenting sounds activity that students see the letters and words (visual), hear the sounds (auditory), and touch (tactile) and move (kinesthetic) the magnetic counters to experience a multisensory approach. An additional tactile experience is included when students match the letters to sounds using magnetic letters. Kinesthetic learning and writing occurs when students write the letters in the spelling sounds segment.

Segmenting Sounds

Joseph (2002) suggested that a magnetic board, magnetic counters, and pictures representing target words could be used to help students with the segmenting sounds step. Pictures are used only if the word can be represented pictorially, as in Figure 3.2.

1. First, the teacher draws a rectangle on the magnetic board and divides the rectangle into the appropriate number of boxes for the targeted word.

2. The students are given the magnetic counters so that one counter is placed below each divided section of the rectangle.

3. The teacher models the segmenting sounds task by saying the word slowly and placing a counter in each section of the rectangle as the sound for that section is spoken.

4. Students place their counters in the respective rectangle sections of their individual magnetic boards or individual papers while the teacher says the targeted word slowly.

5. Finally, the students may articulate the targeted word while they place their counters in the respective rectangle sections of their individual magnetic boards or individual papers.

Matching Letters to Sounds

Follow the same procedures listed in Segmenting Sounds, except that students are given magnetic letters to place in the respective sections of the rectangle in place of the counters, as in Figure 3.3.

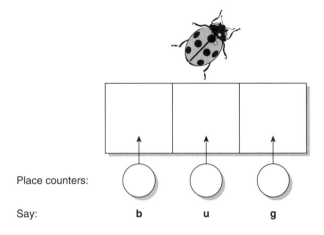

Figure 3.2   Word Box Example With Picture: Segmenting Sounds

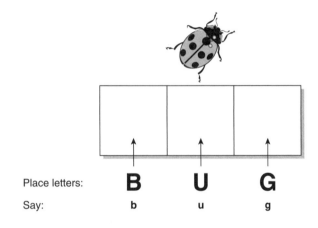

Figure 3.3   Word Box Example: Placing Magnetic Letters With Sounds

Spelling the Word

Follow the same procedure as in Matching Letters to Sounds, except students write the letters in the respective sections of the rectangle as they slowly say each sound (see Figure 3.4). Erasers can be used if students make an error.

When students demonstrate that they understand the one-to-one correspondence between letters and sounds by writing the letters in the rectangle sections, the teacher then can begin to take away some of the scaffolding or support (Joseph, 2002; see Figure 3.5). What once were solid vertical lines dividing the rectangle into connected boxes become dotted lines. Scaffolding provides the support that students with learning difficulties need and is removed gradually as the students begin to demonstrate that they are learning the skill (Larkin, 2001).

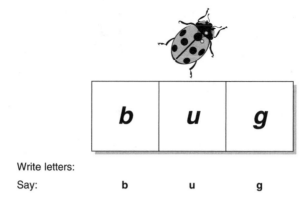

Write letters:

Say: b u g

Figure 3.4   Word Box Example: Writing Letters and Saying the Sounds (Spelling)

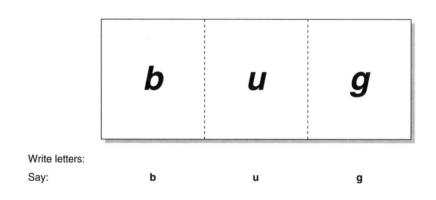

Write letters:

Say: b u g

Figure 3.5   Word Box With Dotted Lines (Scaffolding)

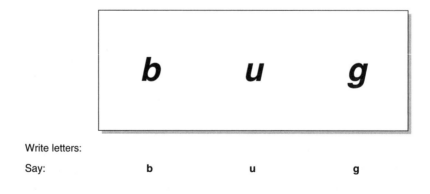

Write letters:

Say: b u g

Figure 3.6   Word Box With No Lines (Scaffolding Removed)

Finally, the dotted lines are removed to leave only the rectangle in which the students write the targeted word as the teacher says it (see Figure 3.6.). Be sure to give students as much practice time as they need with each step, prior to moving on to the next targeted word. Practicing all three steps helps students to learn the sounds in the word, match the letters to the sounds, and identify the letter sequence (i.e., spelling) of the word.

Research has shown that word boxes can help struggling students with their decoding skills. Schmidgall and Joseph (2007) found that a small sample of first graders increased the number of words read when they used word boxes as compared to traditional drill and practice. The traditional drill and practice did a better job of increasing the students' reading rate (Schmidgall & Joseph). Therefore, the combination of word boxes and traditional drill and practice can be powerful. Although reading fluency (i.e., accuracy and pace) is discussed in more detail in Chapter 4 of this book, it is important to note the importance of developing good decoding skills to promote accuracy and pace.

Devault and Joseph (2004) noted that word box instruction combined with repeated readings helped three high school students with severe reading delays improve their fluency on second and third grade level passages. These students had been identified in elementary school with either learning disabilities or mental retardation. Joseph (1998/1999) studied the impact of word box instruction on the decoding and spelling skills of six second through fourth grade students with learning disabilities. These students were mainstreamed into general education classrooms for particular subjects. For the study, the students received 20 minutes of individualized daily word box instruction for 21 sessions. The word box instruction was scaffolded. At first, the teacher placed the counters below the divided word box and demonstrated how to move the counters (and later magnetic letters) into the appropriate sections of the word box while articulating the corresponding sounds of the word. Later, students placed the counters while the teacher articulated the sounds of the word. Next, the roles were reversed so that the teacher moved the counters while the student articulated the sounds. Then, the student performed the task independently by moving the counters or magnetic letters into the word box while articulating the sounds of the word. Finally, the student wrote the letters of the word into the appropriate sections of the divided word box to correspond with the sounds in the word. Joseph (1998/1999) found that ". . . the word boxes approach was effective for improving and maintaining all students' word identification and spelling skills" (p. 351).

Although the aforementioned studies did not include large numbers of participants, the results are promising for the use of word box instruction for a variety of students either with or without disabilities who need assistance with their decoding skills. Additional ideas to help you scaffold reading instruction for students with learning difficulties when they have problems decoding a word are included in Teaching Tip 3.1.

TEACHING TIP 3.1

Analyzing Words Strategy

Students with learning differences need to know strategies for figuring out difficult words in their reading. Teachers may find it useful to think of possible prompts to help students learn these strategies for word analysis. These suggestions may help you to scaffold instruction to help students learn appropriate decoding strategies and use them independently.

Strategy	When used	Student self-question	Teacher prompt (if student has not learned or cannot remember self-question)
Pronounceable word part	Unknown word contains a part that the student can say (e.g., *am* in *champ*)	Is there a part of the word I can say?	Can you say any part of the word?
Analogy	Unknown word is like a word the student knows (e.g., *grain* is like *rain*)	Is the word like any word I know?	Is the word like any word that you know?
Sound by sound	Student cannot chunk word. Determines word sound by sound /s/-/p/ - /e/ - /l/ - /l/	Can I sound out the word?	Can you say the first sound, second sound, next sound, and so on?
Context	Student cannot use phonics clues, but can use context clues.	Can I read to the end of the sentence and see what would make sense?	Can you read to the end of the sentence and see what word would make sense?
Monitoring	Student checks to see if the word is a real word that makes sense.	Is this a real word? Does it sound right? Does it make sense?	Is this a real word? Does it sound right? Does it make sense?
Affirmation	Student's correct use of a strategy.	I used a strategy correctly to figure out a word I didn't know.	I liked how you used a part of the word that you knew to help you figure out the whole word.
Assessment	Teacher wants to determine strategies the student is using.	—	How did you figure out that word?
Starter	Student cannot use any of the strategies to decode an unknown word.	—	Could the word be _____?

SOURCE: Adapted from Gunning (2000, p. 96).

Strategy: Picture and Word Sorts

Sorting activities are excellent reinforcement activities to help students to learn word patterns and their associated sounds (Gunning, 2000). During word study activities such as sorting, students categorize words and pictures to illustrate similarities and differences among words (Bear et al., 2000). Younger students first will learn the beginning sounds of words. Later, they will examine vowel patterns, syllables, and affixes (i.e., prefixes and suffixes). Through sorting activities, students learn to make decisions about word sounds, patterns, meaning, and use.

Picture Sorts

Picture sorts can help students to make the letter-sound connections of words (Bear et al., 2000). For example, young students or students with learning difficulties who do not know all initial consonant sounds may be asked to sort picture cards according to initial consonant sounds. A multisensory approach enables students to see the pictures (visual), move the pictures (kinesthetic), and say the initial consonant sound and corresponding picture name as they are doing so (see Figure 3.7). *Bb = bird, ball, bat, book,* and *broom. Cc = cat, cake, candle, car,* and *clock. Dd = deer, dinosaur, doctor, duck,* and *dog.* Do you notice any of these words that could be problematic for some struggling readers? If students have not learned consonant blends or have difficulty saying stop sounds, then *broom* and *clock* may be problems. Likewise, the words beginning with *d* may be more difficult for students who have trouble with stop sounds. Be aware of potential problems such as these when selecting pictures and words for sorts. Be sure to provide students with learning difficulties the support they need to work successfully with these kinds of challenging tasks.

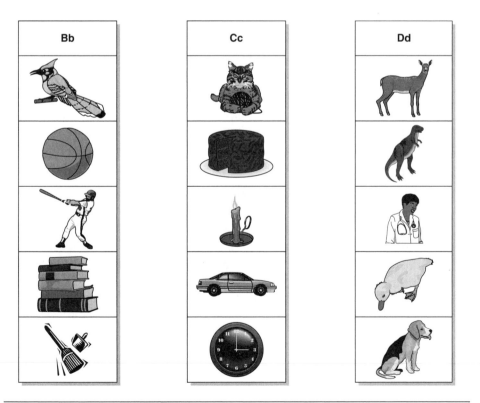

Figure 3.7   Picture Sort Example

Several important differences exist between picture sorting and commercial phonics programs (Bear et al., 2000).

Picture sorting	Commercial phonics program
Goes from known to unknown. Students pronounce the picture name and analyze the sounds as they sort through a stack of pictures.	Contains words that may be unknown to the students.
Uses analytic phonics—goes from the whole word to the word parts (i.e., onset and rime) and then to individual phonemes.	Uses synthetic phonics—goes from the individual phonemes to the whole word.
Determines similarities and differences among target features while using higher level thinking skills to make categorization judgments.	Involves rote memorization, isolated sound drills, or overreliance on rules that students may not understand.
Is efficient—students receive practice with several examples that they can study in a few minutes.	Is not efficient—students spend 10–20 minutes on a workbook activity that contains only a few examples.

 REFLECTIVE EXERCISE 3.2
IF YOU ARE USING A COMMERCIAL PHONICS PROGRAM, IS IT WORKING OR COULD IT USE SOME HELP?

As teachers, we need to be critical consumers of curricula and materials that may be available to us. Just because something is published commercially does not mean that it works for the students you are teaching. We need to determine if the commercial product is something of quality that includes research-based practices and is something that meets the needs of the students we are teaching. If you currently are using a commercial phonics program, review the comparison table between picture sorting and a commercial phonics program. Then, think about whether the commercial phonics program you are using or may consider using will work for your students. If the program contains most or all of the features listed in the commercial program column of the table, could your students benefit from adding some picture (or word) sorting as opposed to workbook activities? Are your students being exposed to whole words and then onset and rime prior to learning individual phonemes? Are your students spending more time memorizing than they are learning? If you answer yes to any of these questions, think about how you can incorporate picture or word sorting into your phonics instructional routine.

Word Sorts

The same process is used for word sorts as for picture sorts, with the main difference being that words rather than pictures are placed on the cards. Bear et al. (2000) indicated that familiar words should be used for word sorts and that word sorts work best for students who have a functional sight word vocabulary. Like in the word box procedures mentioned earlier in this chapter, Joseph (2002) recommended a three-step process for word sorts: (a) phonemic sorts, (b) word sorts, and (c) spelling sorts. Like the word box procedure, word sorts are appropriate phonics procedures for whole class, small group, and peer buddy sessions.

Phonemic Sorts

1. In phonemic sorts, the teacher prints category words on note cards for each student.

2. The teacher places the note cards horizontally on each student's desk and gives each student a colored plastic chip.

3. The teacher says a targeted word aloud and each student places a chip below the category word that sounds similar.

4. The teacher monitors students' responses and provides corrective feedback.

5. When the teacher says a new word, students are asked to move the chip to its place below the appropriate category word.

For example, if the three targeted categories of words were short-*e*, short-*a*, and short-*i*, each student would have the set of category cards shown in Figure 3.8. If the teacher first called the word *bad*, then *bed*, and finally *bid*, each student would move his or her chip in the order illustrated. If the teacher notices that some students with learning difficulties are not performing the sort successfully, then they may need extra practice working one-on-one with the teacher or in a small group. The students may need to watch closely as the teacher says the words. Then the students might see how the teacher's mouth moves differently as he or she makes the various sounds. Some students may need more practice hearing the words, so they can discriminate among the different short vowel sounds. At first glance, some struggling readers may think that all the words look and sound alike due to the same beginning and ending sounds. These students may need extra cues and teacher assistance to help them listen for the short vowel sound in the middle.

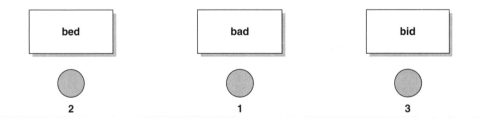

Figure 3.8   Short Vowel Phonemic Sort Example

Word Sorts

1. The teacher asks students to place the category word used in the phonemic sort near the top of their desks.

2. Each student has his or her own stack of words printed on note cards (prepared prior to the activity). The student places each card from his or her stack below the respective category word with the shared spelling pattern, as in Figure 3.9.

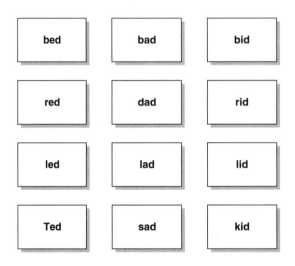

Figure 3.9   Short Vowel Word Sort Example

After all word cards are sorted, the student may read his or her words aloud. If the student has sorted a word incorrectly, he or she may check the incorrect word card against the category card to determine why the error occurred.

Spelling Sorts

1. Students are given or are asked to take out a sheet of paper and write the same category words from the phonemic sort and the word sort across the top.

2. Using the same set of words as in the word sort, the teacher says a word aloud while students write that word below the appropriate category word on the paper (Figure 3.10). The spoken word may share a similar sound or spelling pattern as the category word. This process continues until all words are presented.

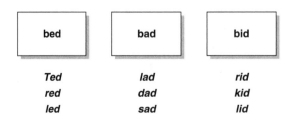

Figure 3.10   Short Vowel Spelling Sort Example

TEACHING TIP 3.2

Word Study Instruction Principles

1. *Determine what students use but confuse.* If students consistently make the same errors (e.g., leaving a vowel sound out of a word that needs it and adding an extra vowel to words that don't need it), take your cue from your students as to how they need assistance rather than trudging ahead with whatever happens to be in the curriculum.

2. *A step backward can be a step forward.* Build a firm foundation with what students already know and relate known information to the new task at hand. For example, be sure to compare and contrast new sound patterns to familiar ones.

3. *Select words that students can read.* If students are familiar with word pronunciations then they will have a better chance at performing word comparison activities (e.g., word sorts) and spelling the words.

4. *Compare example and nonexample words.* In order to define something, students need to be exposed to example words that fit into certain categories and nonexample words that do not fit into the categories. For example, if a student is confused as to when a word's spelling pattern contains the same double consonants and when it does not, the student should be presented with examples (e.g., planning, skipping) and nonexamples (e.g., cleaning, raining) of the same double consonant pattern.

5. *Use sound and sight for sorting.* Students need to have practice using both sound and sight for sorting. First, give students the opportunity to sort words by sound (e.g., soft *g*, hard *g*) and then ask them to sort by word pattern (e.g., *dge, ge, g*).

6. *Start with obvious contrasts.* When students are learning new information, they may become confused easily. Therefore, teachers should select target pictures or words that distinctively are different. For example, students who are learning initial consonant sounds easily could confuse *m* and *n* sounds. A better choice would be to compare the sound of *m* with the *s* sound. The idea is to move from general discriminations to more specific ones.

7. *Explain exceptions.* Instead of hiding exceptions, place them in a miscellaneous oddball category.

8. *Don't tell students spelling rules.* Students likely will memorize and forget spelling rules. Instead help them to compare and contrast word patterns. The teacher's challenge is to plan instruction to make word consistencies explicit.

9. *Aim for automaticity.* Although accuracy in sorting is important, it is not the only concern. In order to be proficient readers, writers, and spellers, students must acquire automaticity in recognizing and sorting patterns.

10. *Students find examples in meaningful texts.* Once students have had sorting practice they need to return to meaningful texts to locate other examples to add to the sorts. These hunts help students to extend their word analysis skills and acquire more difficult vocabulary.

The bottom line is that "in word study students examine, manipulate, and categorize words" (Bear et al., 2000, p. 70). Teachers are expected to create tasks that help students to focus on critical contrasts.

SOURCE: Adapted from Bear et al. (2000, pp. 67–70).

Like word boxes, research indicates that word sorts may help some struggling students with their word recognition and spelling. Joseph and Orlins (2005) provided a case study of how word sorts helped Sara, a second grader diagnosed with Attention Deficit Hyperactivity Disorder. She had difficulty identifying words that had more than three letters and received special education services. During baseline, Sara was given sets of words containing four letters such as *mold, bold, told, bank, rank, tank, rent, vent,* and *dent.* She was asked to read each word printed on an index card. During the word sort intervention, Sara was instructed to sort a set of ten words on index cards into three categories as specified by the instructor. Sara was given encouragement to correct mistakes she recognized when reading or sorting a word incorrectly. The instructor provided Sara with feedback for errors that she missed. Sara performed at a mastery level of 90% of words read correctly during two consecutive instructional conditions in contrast to her lower performance in baseline conditions. After the word sorts ended, Sara maintained her word recognition skills at 90% to 100% as measured by the maintenance probes.

Joseph and Orlins (2005) found that word sorts helped John, a third grader who had difficulty with spelling. The procedures for John were similar to those for Sara. He was given a set of words such as *coil, foil, boil, soil, broil, foul, loud, shout, route,* and *cloud.* During baseline conditions, John sometimes took six trials to reach mastery of a set of spelling words. Once John was instructed to sort words into two categories, encouraged to self-correct for any errors, and given feedback for words sorted incorrectly, he reached the 90% mastery level on two consecutive probes in three trials. Also, he increased the number of words spelled correctly. Joseph and Orlins suggested that teachers can teach reading and spelling while simultaneously using word sorts to assist students in making connections between reading and spelling.

A sample lesson for grades K–2 by Mills (2006) titled, "Word Sorts for Beginning and Struggling Readers," can be found at the ReadWriteThink Web site at http://www.readwritethink.org/lessons/lesson_view.asp?id=795. The focus of the lesson is to help students to identify word patterns and sort words into word families, practice reading words in the sort, and spell the same words. Instructions are provided for five 20- to 30-minute lessons.

 TEACHING TIP 3.3

Word Sort Categories

The following suggestions are just a few examples of categories that teachers can use in designing word sorts for their students. Be sure to determine which of these are most appropriate for students at particular developmental levels and which might be most beneficial for your students with learning difficulties.

Words with

- Consonant blends
- Prefixes

- No consonant blends
- No prefixes

- Suffixes
- Certain vowel sound
- One or two syllables
- Other words in them
- A designated word family

- No suffixes
- Without a certain vowel sound
- Three or more syllables
- No other words in them
- No designated word family

Words that

- Are nouns
- Express feelings
- You think are interesting

- Are not nouns
- Do not express feelings
- You do not think are interesting

SOURCE: Adapted from Rasinski and Padak (2001, p. 101).

Strategy: Making Words

In addition to sorting words activities, Cunningham and Cunningham (1992) suggested that students participate in making words activities. Making words activities are hands-on and allow students to discover letter-sound relationships and learn how to find word patterns. Students also learn that changing just one letter or letter sequence changes the whole word. The 15-minute making words activities consist of students individually being given some letters with which they are asked to make 12 to 15 words. Students with learning difficulties may do well to make about one-half that many words. Students begin with two-letter words and then continue on to three-letter, four-letter, five-letter, and longer words. Obviously, the teacher can adapt the making words activity to meet individual student needs with regard to number of words and word length. For example, students who are learning letter sounds for *a, m, s,* and *t* might make the following words: *a, as, at, mat, sat, Sam,* and *tam.* The final word of the day consists of a longer word that includes all the letters of the day, so the final word for our example would be *mast* (or possibly *tams* or *mats*). See Teaching Tip 3.4.

The research results are promising for the use of making words activities. Rasinski and Oswald (2005) studied the impact of a making words activity (Cunningham & Cunningham, 1992) on the decoding skills of second-grade students over five months. Students participated in the activity daily and made significant gains in decoding over peers who participated in a more traditional phonics program. Reutzel, Fawson, and Smith (2006) found that first-grade students who participated in a program where their parents were trained to help them with a type of making words program called *Words-to-Go* were able to read more words correctly than first grade peers who did not participate in the program. Also, the program participants spelled more words correctly than the program's nonparticipants. The participants also were able to write words with more accuracy from a dictated list than were their peers who did not participate in the program. During the making words lesson, students first write the vowels to be used in the lesson in one box and the consonants to be used in another box at the top of the page. Then the teacher gives the students clues to help them identify the other words to write in the remaining boxes on the page.

TEACHING TIP 3.4

Planning and Teaching a Making Words Lesson

Planning

1.   Choose the final word in the lesson, considering the number of vowels, students' interests, letter–sound patterns, and curriculum tie-ins.

2.   Make a list of shorter words that can be made using the letters of the final word.

3.   From this list, select 12–15 words that include (a) words that can be sorted by patterns, (b) little and big words, so the lesson is multilevel, (c) words that can be made using the same letters in different places (e.g., barn and bran) to emphasize correct sequencing of letters, (d) proper nouns to emphasize capitalization, and (e) words that most students have in their listening vocabularies.

4.   Write all the words on index cards ordering them from shortest to longest.

5.   Order the word cards further to emphasize that letter patterns and that changing position of letters makes different words.

6.   Store the cards in an envelope or plastic bag. Label the envelope or bag with the words in order and the patterns for the word sort.

Teaching

1.   Place large letter cards in a pocket chart or on the chalkboard ledge.

2.   Have a designated student give one letter to each student.

3.   As you hold up and name the letters on the large letter cards, have the children hold up their matching small letter cards.

4.   Write the numeral on the board designating the number of letters to be used to start making words (e.g., 2 or 3).

5.   Ask the first student who has the first word made correctly to make the same word with the large letter cards. Encourage any students who did not make the word correctly to fix their word when they see the correct version on the large letter cards.

6.   Have students continue making words as you change the number on the board to indicate the number of letters needed. Cue students to recognize whether they are just changing one letter, changing letters around, or using the letters to make words from scratch. Also, cue students to capitalize any proper names.

7.   Ask students if anyone has made a word containing all the letters. If so, congratulate them. If not, tell students to use all their letters to make the word _____.

8.   Once all words have been made, take the teacher's set of word cards and place them one at a time along the chalkboard ledge or in the pocket chart, making sure to place them in the same order in which the students made them. Ask the students to say and spell the words along with you. Use these words to point out word patterns and to guide sorting activities.

9.   To provide maximum generalization to reading and writing, have the students use the patterns they have sorted to spell a few new words dictated by the teacher.

NOTE: You may choose to do Steps 1–7 on one day and Steps 8–9 on the following day.
SOURCE: Adapted from Cunningham and Cunningham (1992, p. 108).

The final box is reserved for the challenge word that consists of all of the letters from the lesson.

Lisa Bayer (Aiken & Bayer, 2002) modified the making words strategy with her first-grade students. She gave the students a letter holder with the plastic letters *a, c, l, m, n, p, t.* The vowel, *a,* was colored differently from the remaining consonants. Lisa demonstrated the placement of the letters on the chalk ledge and asked the students to place their letters the same way in the letter holders and say the letters with her. The teacher then told the children that they were going to make the word *cap.* One student made the word for the class to see and the other students checked the word in their own letter holders. Lisa found that students were successful with the strategy even in the second week of school, particularly if the words made were connected to the story or poem the class read that week. She also found that the activity served as a review of letters and letter-sound correspondence for her students.

A sample lesson for grades K–2 by Olness (2007) titled, "Word Wizards: Students Making Words" can be found at the ReadWriteThink Web site at http://www.readwritethink.org/lessons/lesson_view.asp?id=150. The focus of this lesson is to help students to find word patterns in words, to see how changing one letter in a word can change the word, to make new words by moving letters from another word, and to use clues and phonics patterns to make words. Instructions are provided for 30-minute sessions as well as extensions and assessments.

Once students have learned basic word sorting and word making skills, they can hone and practice their skills further by performing some of the activities that are listed in Teaching Tip 3.5. Teachers will find these ideas easy to incorporate into their lessons to provide students with learning difficulties the extra practice that they may need.

 TEACHING TIP 3.5

Lesson Planning Ideas for Word Families

1. Word Family Wheel. Students may use the wheel individually or with a partner after they have had practice with word sorts. To make a word wheel, cut two six-inch circles from cardboard. Cut a wedge from the first circle and write the rime to the right of where the wedge was cut. On the second cardboard circle, write beginning sounds (onsets) that form words with that family. Space the word onsets evenly around the outside edge, so that only one onset will appear in the cut out window from the first circle. Place the first circle (with the cutout) on top of the second circle (with the onsets). Use a brass fastener to secure together in the center of the circles. Students can turn the top circle to learn new words in the same word family.

2. Flip Books. Flip books are similar to word family wheels in that they help students to learn a variety of words in the same family. Teachers or students may make flip books by placing each of several word onsets on individual index cards that have been cut in two (vertically). Then the rime portion of the word family is placed to the right of a whole index card. The word onset cards are stacked on top with the left edges of all the cards forming the spine of the book. The books can be stapled or secured near the left edge. Students can flip through the onset cards to identify different words in the same word family.

(Continued)

TEACHING TIP 3.5 (Continued)

3. Word Maker Cards. Index cards can be cut in half vertically for word maker cards. The onset portion of a word can be written on one cut card portion while the rime portion of the word can be written on the second cut card portion. Students have a variety of cards to place together to form new words. These cards can include initial consonants, blends, and digraphs as students become familiar with each. Students may use word maker cards to play a game with a buddy. Each student takes five cards from the deck, places them face up and tries to form one or two words. Then they take turns drawing from the deck. Whenever a student makes a word, he or she can draw two more cards. If the student cannot make a word, he or she may draw one more card. A variation is for students to use the word maker cards independently to create a word list of as many words as possible.

4. Roll the Die. On a cube write the rime for four contrasting word families. On one of the remaining sides write *lose a turn*, and on the other write *roll again*. Students take turns rolling the die. If the die shows a word family on the cube section facing up, then that student must identify a word from that family and record the word on a piece of paper or the dry-erase board. All students are responsible for keeping their own list. A word may be used only once. If the die lands on *lose a turn* or *roll again,* students follow those directions. The winner is the student who records the most words in the time allocated.

5. Go Fish. To make playing cards for word family go fish, turn index cards so that the longer portion of the card is vertical. Write a different complete word family word at the top of each card. The bottom portion of the cards will remain blank so that students can hold them like a hand of playing cards. Each player is dealt five cards and the remaining cards are placed face down on the table to serve as a pool from which cards can be drawn. After locating a particular card in his or her hand, the first player asks another to "Give me all your cards that rhyme with ___." For example, if the first player had the word card *bat* in her hand she might ask a particular player for all the cards that rhyme with *bat.* If the other player does not have the requested card(s), then the first player is told to "go fish" and draws a card from the "pond." A player's turn is over when a match cannot be made. The game continues until a player runs out of cards. Students may earn points if they are the first person to go out or if they have the most matching cards.

6. Modified Bingo. Modified bingo is a sorting activity in game format that may be played with three to five columns. The heading for each of the columns is a pattern word. Each row must contain words with the same pattern as the headings. Word cards are placed face down in the center of the table. A few wild cards may be included if desired. Players take turns selecting cards. The player reads the card selected and determines if it will fit on one of the squares on his or her game sheet. After placing a card on the game sheet, the player then must read all the cards that have been placed in that column. For example, a game sheet providing practice on short vowel families might look like the following:

cat	pet	sit	hot
hat	get	hit	pot
	wet		
	met		
	set		

SOURCE: Adapted from Bear et al. (2000, pp. 171–177) and Gunning (2000, pp. 87–88).

Strategy: Word Banks

As students study consonant sounds and begin to remember sight words that they can identify in isolation, they can form their own individual word banks (Bear et al., 2000). A word bank is an individual student's collection of words that he or she knows in isolation (Rasinski & Padak, 2001). Remember that the words are student chosen, not teacher chosen (Bear et al.). These words are written on small cards, collected over a period of time, and reviewed regularly. Cards containing forgotten words are discarded. Therefore, frequent review is crucial for students with learning difficulties who may forget learned words if they are not practiced often. A constantly diminishing word bank would be enough to discourage any struggling reader. Instead, regular review can help individual student word banks to increase. In the early alphabetic stage, word banks support students' increasing sight word knowledge and letter-sound correspondence knowledge. For students in the later alphabetic stage, their word bank words can be used in word sorts to determine similarities and differences in letters and sounds. Word banks may be used in conjunction with personal readers, which are individual student copies of selected passages that they can read independently or with little teacher assistance. Students may underline word bank entries found in their personal readers. This may be a helpful activity for struggling readers to ensure that they are identifying known words from their word banks in the context of stories. Entries in personal readers should be numbered and dated in order to use this information as an informal assessment of reading progress.

Research on the use of word banks to aid reading decoding skills is showing some promising results. Johnston (2000) found that beginning readers in first grade learned more words than when they used sentence strips although the use of sentence strips helped students learn more words than just reading and rereading books. After reading in context, the students each were given an unillustrated copy of the story to read and underline words they knew. After doing this for two days, the students read the story and reviewed the words in their individual word banks. When word banks were collected at the end of each week, students had three to eight words in their word banks. Johnston noted that when students place words in their word banks for longer than a week and teachers provide review during this time, it is a powerful way for students to learn decoding skills.

Kiley (2007) reported on the work of Tyner (2004) with the small group differentiated reading model that contains research-based strategies for beginning readers and recognizes the progression of stages for beginning reading. The progression of reading stages includes Emergent Reader, Beginning Reader, Fledgling Reader, Transitional Reader, and Independent Reader. The components of this model are Rereading, Word Bank, Word Study, Writing, and a New Read. The differentiation for the Word Bank component lies in the number of words and type of words targeted. For example, an Emergent Reader may focus on 10 sight words, a Beginning Reader on 50 sight words, and a Fledgling Reader on more than 100 sight words. A Transitional Reader and an Independent Reader may focus on specialized vocabulary or tricky words.

Word banks can either be individualized or group oriented. Borgia, Owles, and Beckler (2007) stated that word banks can be centered on a topic, theme, or unit of study. They suggested that students should be asked for words that they know related to the topic. The teacher also may add some key words. Definitions of words can be added to the back of word cards to turn the word bank into vocabulary study.

A sample lesson for Grades K–2 by Bouchard (2006) titled, "Word Study With Henry and Mudge" can be found at the ReadWriteThink Web site at http://www.readwritethink.org/lessons/lesson_view.asp?id=806. The focus of the lesson is to help students identify, read, and spell high-frequency words in a group word bank as well as to comprehend word structure by sorting and building words by spelling and phonemic patterns. Instructions are provided for six 30- to 40-minute lessons. See Teaching Tip 3.6 for suggestions about oddball high-frequency words.

TEACHING TIP 3.6

What to Do About Those Oddball High-Frequency Words?

Many high-frequency words do not have common spelling patterns but can be used in word sorts as oddballs (Bear et al., 2000). For example, the word said has the *ai* pattern, but is pronounced differently than paint, faint, and wait. The following are guidelines for the study of high-frequency words.

1. *Optional study.* The study of high-frequency words is optional and should not replace developmental word study for pattern words.

2. *Word selection.* Choose 6 to 10 words to study for one week of each grading period. Thus, if there are four grading periods, 24 to 40 words will be selected per year. The words may come from students' writing and the students may be involved in the selection.

3. *Develop routines.* Help students use a systematic way to examine and study the words carefully. This might include the following steps:

   a. *Introduce and discuss the words.* Students may copy the words from the board or be provided a copy of the words. Then the teacher can facilitate a discussion about each word, why it may be difficult to remember, and strategies for helping to remember the word.

   b. *Self-correct test method.* After students have written each word at least one time, they fold their papers to cover the list. The teacher says the words while the students write them. Then the students check their work and rewrite any misspelled words.

   c. *Self-study method.* Students study the words using the following steps:
       i. Look at and say the word.
       ii. Cover the word.
       iii. Write the word.
       iv. Check your work.
       v. Write the word again if you made a mistake.

   d. *Practice test.* As the teacher or a peer buddy says words, students spell aloud or write the words. Words are checked against a printed list or a chart in the room.

   e. *Final test.* The teacher calls the words and students write or spell them aloud. Once students have mastered the words on the final test, then they are responsible for them in the future. If any word continues to be a problem, it may reappear on future lists.

SOURCE: Adapted from Bear et al. (2000, pp. 196–197).

As students move to the within word pattern stage, teachers will notice that students' reading and writing become less labored in this fragile period of development (Bear et al., 2000). The following summarizes the characteristics, reading and writing activities, and word study focus for the within word pattern stage.

3. Within Word Pattern Stage

Characteristics	*Reading and writing activities*	*Word study focus*
• Spells most single-syllable short vowel words • Spells most beginning consonant digraphs and two-letter consonant blends • Reads silently with more expression and fluency • Can revise and edit	• Read to students • Plan self-selected silent reading • Encourage writing each day	• Sort words by long and short vowel sounds and by common long vowel patterns • Explore less common vowels and diphthongs (oi, ou, au, ow) • Review blends and digraphs

SOURCE: Adapted from Bear et al. (2000).

Strategy: Word Study Notebooks and Word Boxes

During the within word pattern stage, be sure to give students many opportunities to find reliable word patterns through word sorts and other activities (Bear et al., 2000). Word study notebooks will help students record routine word study activities and provide documentation of student progress with word study. Each spelling pattern will have a separate page. For example, in the section for the vowel *o*, there may be pages of short-*o* sounds, followed by pages of long-*o* sounds, then a page of CVVC (consonant-vowel-vowel-consonant) words, and finally a page of CVCe (consonant-vowel-consonant-silent-*e* words). You may find it useful to have students write about their thoughts as to why they chose a particular way to sort the words. This will help the student and teacher recognize what the student has learned about word patterns. These reflections may be contained in a reflection section of the student's word study notebook.

Keep in mind that students with learning difficulties may need extra support in the form of modeling and prompts to create and maintain an organized word study notebook. They may not know how to organize the information in a meaningful way, so be sure to show them examples of well organized and perhaps some unorganized word study notebooks. Focus some discussions on how easy it is to locate information in a well organized notebook as opposed to one that has papers placed in any direction. Periodic notebook checks may help reinforce the value of being organized as well as alert the teacher to potential problems that students may have in keeping their notebooks in order.

Students with learning difficulties also may need extra help in adding new words to their notebooks in the proper place. Using a variation of word boxes (see the explanation of word boxes under the letter-name alphabetic stage earlier in this chapter) and teacher cues to alert students to the particular word pattern being studied may be helpful. For example, if students were trying to determine if a word has a CVVC pattern, ask them to look at each letter of the word in the order that it appears and write the information down rather than trusting it to memory. If the word to be examined is *look,* then students might write

l	o	o	k
C	V	V	C

Yes, the word *look* fits the CVVC pattern. If the next word to be examined is *best,* then students might write

b	e	s	t
C	V	C	C

No, the word *best* does not fit the CVVC pattern because it has three consonants instead of two.

 **REFLECTIVE EXERCISE 3.3
USING WORD STUDY NOTEBOOKS
FOR STUDENTS AND TEACHERS**

You may want to reflect on using the information provided in this chapter for the letter-name alphabetic stage and the within word pattern stage, as well as the brief description of word study notebooks above to plan how you could incorporate student word study notebooks into your phonics instructional routine. What are some specific ways that students can use these notebooks? What are some specific ways that teachers can use these notebooks?

You should consider compiling a teacher version of the word study notebook that contains the originals of any word study activities that you provided for students. You can use sticky notes to jot down the date used as well as any changes or adaptations that might need to be made in the future or that would be helpful for students with learning difficulties having particular problems with the activity. As you accumulate new word study activities and information, be sure to keep this information organized in your notebook to correspond with your instructional plans for students. Don't let the notebook become a catchall of good ideas that never get used!

Strategy: Word Sorts

Students with learning difficulties who are functioning in the within word pattern stage will need practice sorting words by long and short vowel patterns, such as the long-*e* and short-*e* patterns seen in Figure 3.11. You may want to give the students a long-*e*/short-*e* study sheet in which they cut the rectangles apart to make the word cards to sort (adapted from Bear et al., 2000). Make sure that students with learning difficulties first have had practice with long-*e* sounds and short-*e* sounds separately before trying to discriminate between the two. Notice that the word sort contains some three-letter words to review from a previous sort (shown in the letter-name alphabetic stage) as well as new longer (four- and five-letter) words (Figure 3.12). It is important to tailor the number of words and kinds of words to sort to individual student needs. The sample word sort in Figures 3.11 and 3.12 contains 15 words, which likely will be plenty for many students with learning difficulties to sort and perhaps too many for others. You may want to provide envelopes that students can store their word sort materials in when they are finished with the activity. Each envelope can be labeled and stored in a folder or plastic sleeve in the student's word study notebook, where it will be available for future practice and review. See Teaching Tip 3.3 on word sort categories presented earlier in this chapter to glean additional ideas for word sorts.

Word study for English Language Learning should consist of comparing English language to the sounds of the student's primary language (Bear et al., 2008). There may be some differences in pronunciation, so some students may approach word sorting by sound differently than others. Once students have

Queen	e	Web
read	yes	jeep
met	beet	eat
led	meal	team
seen	bed	seat
red	jet	bell

Figure 3.11   Long-*e*/Short-*e* Study Sheet

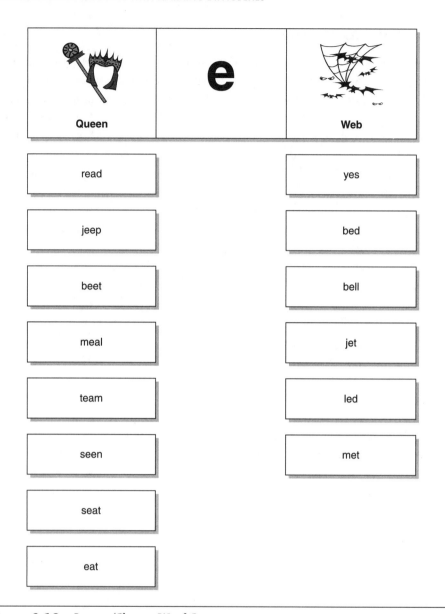

Queen	e	Web

read	yes
jeep	bed
beet	bell
meal	jet
team	led
seen	met
seat	
eat	

Figure 3.12   Long-*e*/Short-*e* Word Sort

focused on the word sounds, then they will examine word patterns. Teaching Tip 3.7 shows additional activities that can be used with many learners in the within word pattern stage.

 TEACHING TIP 3.7

Within Word Pattern Stage Activities

In addition to word sorts, the following are a few other word study activities that are suitable for students in the within word pattern stage.

   1. *Word Hunt.* Students may work independently or with a partner to examine familiar texts to find words that fit a particular pattern. For example, students may be asked to find all the

words that sound like the middle of the word *cake*. They write the words in their notebooks as the words are found. Then students may meet in small groups to read aloud the words they have found. Students are asked to look for words they could group together and discuss why they can be grouped together. The small group sharing gives an opportunity for students to find additional words they can add to their word study notebooks. A variation is to use a newspaper instead of familiar texts and to have students work in teams. For example, there may be an *ai* team, an *ay* team, and a CVCe team. Found words may be circled, highlighted, or written down and then shared.

2. Classic Card Game. Two to five players may participate in the classic card game, but three is optimal. Cards are made from index cards or tagboard. Known words representing the vowel patterns to be reviewed are written on the top of the cards in order for students to hold a hand of cards using the card bottoms. Each player is dealt seven cards. The dice are rolled to determine the first player. The first player places a card on the table, reads the word, and says the vowel pattern to be followed (e.g., *rain, ai*). The next player places a card on the table that contains the same vowel pattern and reads it. Players pass if they do not have a card to match the vowel pattern. Players forfeit a turn if they do not read their word correctly. The round continues until all players are out of the designated pattern (e.g., *ai*) for that round. The student who played the last pattern card begins the next round by choosing a card from his or her hand, placing it on the table, reading the word, and saying the vowel pattern to be followed. The object of the game is to be the first individual to play all cards in the hand.

3. Green Light! Red Light! A Sorting Game. This speed sorting game helps students to develop automaticity or fluency with long vowel patterns. The teacher or leader writes column pattern headings on the blackboard. The column headings for a long-*a* word study might consist of long-*a* CVCe, short-*a* CVC, long-*a* CVCC, and short-*a* CVCC. Then the teacher or leader writes numbers from 1 to 5 under the word sort headings to indicate how many examples are needed in a category. The total number of examples needed across all categories is five. If there are less than five categories, more than one random number may be placed under a category. For example, the numbers 1 and 4 may be placed under the long-*a* CVCC category to indicate that two examples must be located for that category. Each player faces the chalkboard and is dealt seven cards. The remaining cards (minimum of 10) are placed in the draw pile. To begin the game, the teacher or leader says "green light."

The object of the game is to be the first player to say "red light" when he or she has found all five examples. Other players then place their cards face down, while the player who said "red light" writes the words beside the numbers and reads the category headings and words aloud. Other players can challenge the word-sorting choices by pointing out any incorrect choices on the board and writing their own word(s) to substitute. The teacher or leader judges the accuracy of any challenges. One point is awarded to the players for each word that is correct. The teacher or leader may begin another round by writing a new set of numbers under the category headings. The winner is the player with the greatest number of points.

4. Scattergories. Scattergories is a game that is best suited for small groups of two to three students to help them generate words with particular patterns. Students and teacher can brainstorm five word patterns to be placed across the top of the game sheet. Then the teacher provides a random set of consonants and consonant blends that go down the left column of the game sheet (see the sample game sheet and a reproducible blank copy of the game sheet below). Then students are given 5 to 10 minutes to think of words that fit in the appropriate boxes. Only one word can go in each box. To encourage students to think of longer words, one point can be given for each letter in each correct word generated. Another variation is to encourage students to think of as many words as they can to fill each square. Give one point for each correct word generated.

SOURCE: Adapted from Bear et al. (2000, pp. 201–210) and Rasinski and Padak (2001, pp. 144–145).

Scattergories Game Sheet (Example)

Word families→ Consonants↓	at	it	ack	ick
b	bat	bit	back	brick
p	pat	pit	pack	pick
cl	clatter		clack	click
sl	slap	slit	slack	slick

SOURCE: Adapted from Rasinski and Padak (2001, pp. 144–145).

Scattergories Game Sheet

Word families→ Initial letters↓				

SOURCE: Adapted from several sources, including Bear et al. (2000, pp. 201–210) and Rasinski and Padak (2001, pp. 144–145).

**REFLECTIVE EXERCISE 3.4
MAKING WORDS STRATEGY**

Review the description and instructions for the making words strategy mentioned earlier in the letter-name alphabetic stage. Plan a making words activity that would be appropriate for your students who are in the within word pattern stage. Think about how many words would be appropriate for your students with learning difficulties. Is 12 to 15 too many or about right? Perhaps there are word lists in the reading curriculum or materials that you are using that could be adapted for use in a making words activity. You may want to include some three-letter words for review as well as some new four- or five-letter or longer words to challenge the students. The challenge for the teacher in preparing this activity is to create the final word of the day that uses all the letters that are in the other words.

After the within word pattern stage, students are in the intermediate stage of development where they can read a variety of texts including newspapers and magazines (Bear et al., 2000). During the intermediate stage, students should be expanding their reading interests and fine-tuning their reading strategies. Students at this level have increased word knowledge that helps them to read fluently and to read more sophisticated passages containing poly- or multisyllabic words. Thus, the focus of word study for this stage is on syllables and affixes (i.e., prefixes and suffixes).

4. Syllables and Affixes Stage

Characteristics	*Reading and writing activities*	*Word study focus*
• Spells most single-syllable words • Reads with good expression and fluency • Reads faster silently than orally • Writes sophisticated responses	• Plan read-alouds and literature discussions • Encourage self-selected or silent novel reading • Begin note taking and outlining skills • Explore reading and writing styles and genres	• Examine consonant doubling • Focus on unaccented syllables (*er, le*) • Link spelling and vocabulary studies (meaning and spelling) • Sort and study affixes (prefixes and suffixes)

SOURCE: Adapted from Bear et al. (2000).

Students without reading problems likely are to be in this stage from approximately Grades 3 to 8. Some of these students may be ready at Grade 5 to move on to the next and final stage, advanced derivational relations, while others need more time in the intermediate stage. Students with learning difficulties particularly may have difficulty with the intermediate syllables and affixes stage. Some may get stuck in this stage and others may never progress to this stage. Particular concepts to be learned during the syllables and affixes stage include (a) open and closed syllables, (b) accent, (c) other vowel patterns, and (d) base words and affixes. Open syllables end with a long vowel sound (e.g., *labor, reason*), while closed syllables end with a short vowel sound often closed by two consonants (e.g., *rabbit, racket)*. To determine whether a consonant should be doubled prior to adding a suffix such as -ing, consider whether the sound is long or short. If one is describing what a rabbit does, the base word is *hop* with a short-*o* sound and should be closed with two consonants to become *hopping*. If instead the base word is *hope*, which has a long-*o* sound, the syllable is open and is followed by a single consonant—*hope* becomes *hoping*.

English learners often have difficulty in the syllables and affixes stage because there are many things that may present conceptual difficulty for them (Bear et al., 2008). For example, verb forms may be constructed differently as compared to those in the student's primary language. Also, affixes and base words may not be as common in other languages as they are in English. Therefore, it is important to connect word study to the study of grammar and vocabulary, particularly for English learners in the syllables and affixes stage of development.

Tactic: Working With Homographs

Homographs are words that are spelled the same but have different pronunciations (Bear et al., 2000). These certainly can be confusing to students with learning difficulties. To help students understand the concept of accenting or emphasizing syllables in particular words, first have them examine the pronunciation of their own first name. For example, if the authors of this book examined the pronunciation of their own first names, they would discover that, for both, the first syllable of the first name is accentuated (William is pronounced WILLiam not willIAM, Martha is pronounced MARtha not marTHA).

Working with certain homographs also may be a fun way to help students with learning difficulties learn about accenting syllables (Bear et al., 2000). For example,

- I will give Cathy a PRESent for her graduation, not a presENT.
- Bob will reCORD a message on his answering machine, not RECord it.
- The baby is conTENT after being fed.
- The students will study the CONtent of the science lesson.

Learning Other Word Patterns

Students may not recognize a number of vowel patterns until the upper elementary years (Bear et al., 2000) and students with learning difficulties may find these especially difficult. Some examples of words with the same vowel sound but different spellings are

h*au*l, str*aw*, th*ou*ght

enj*oy*, embr*oi*der

m*ou*ntain, ch*ow*der

wint*er*, mot*or*, doll*ar*

nick*el*, midd*le*, met*al*

Strategy: Double Word Sort

Students with learning difficulties can benefit from doing a double word sort with confusing words such as the previously mentioned list that contains *au, aw, ou, ow, oy, oi, er, or, ar, el, le,* and *al* words. This list likely may contain too many different word patterns for a student with learning difficulties to tackle at one time, but selecting two to four of the combinations may be appropriate for these students. Notice below that students are given a word study sheet with *er, or,* and *ar* words. Make sure that you point out to students with learning difficulties that the words are not in proper order, but you would like for them to cut the word cards apart and sort them the first time according to the letter patterns of *er, or,* and *ar* that are written at the top of the sheet.

Word Study Sheet—*er, or, ar*

er	or	ar
winter	motor	dollar
scholar	teacher	player
dealer	collar	parlor
sailor	tailor	maker

After students have completed the first word sort by placing words under the appropriate *er, or,* and *ar* categories, have them sort the same words (without using the *er, or,* and *ar* labels) according to ending sound. You immediately recognize that all the words when sorted by ending sound will end up together because they have the same ending sound. Students with learning difficulties may not come to this conclusion unless they have the opportunity to use a variety of their senses to perform the second word sort.

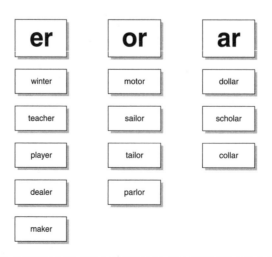

Word sort 1

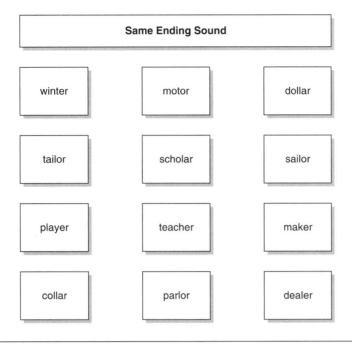

Same Ending Sound		
winter	motor	dollar
tailor	scholar	sailor
player	teacher	maker
collar	parlor	dealer

Word sort 2

For students to analyze unknown words in reading passages and to increase their vocabulary, knowledge of base and root words and affixes is helpful (Bear et al., 2000). Students still should be using their word study notebooks to record new words and word study activities that they complete as well as any reflections. At the intermediate stage, students usually can complete a good amount of individual and small group work. They should be able to use word study routines to help them become responsible for performing at their best. Choices for playing with words can be student selected or teacher selected. Note that students with learning difficulties may need extra cues and examples if they do not understand what they are supposed to do to perform the playing with words tasks. A review of key terms such as *base word, prefix,* and *suffix* may be helpful for these students prior to beginning the activities.

Tactic: Playing With Words

1. Select five words from a word list and circle the base word for each word.

2. When appropriate, make plurals for words on your list.

3. Select five words from a word list. For each word, make as many new words as possible by using the same letters.

4. Circle prefixes found in words on your list.

5. Underline suffixes found in words on your list.

6. Select three words on a word list and change at least one letter to make a new word.

7. When possible, add prefixes and suffixes to words on your list.

8. Sort your words according to subject areas (e.g., math, science, language, social studies).

9. Practice speed in word sorting.

10. Generate new lists of words with the same patterns.

Strategy: Analyzing Unfamiliar Words

In addition to using word study routines to play with words, students should be able to analyze unfamiliar words in context (Bear et al., 2000). Students with learning difficulties may find analyzing unfamiliar words difficult, but can benefit from learning and practicing a systematic strategy such as the following:

1. Examine a word for its parts.
   a. If it has a prefix, remove it first.
   b. If it has a suffix, remove it next.
   c. See if the base word is familiar or if you know another word that has the same base.
   d. Reassemble the word and think about the meaning of the base, prefix, or suffix if that meaning is known.

2. Look for familiar patterns and try to pronounce the syllables and the word.

3. Read the sentence containing the word to determine if meaning can be derived from the context or remainder of the sentence.

4. If you still do not know the word, use a dictionary.

5. Record the new word in your word study notebook.

See Teaching Tip 3.8 for additional activities for the syllables and affixes stage.

 TEACHING TIP 3.8

Syllables and Affixes Stage Activities

1. *Various sorts.*
   a. Plural word sorts (e.g., *s* and *es*)
   b. Compound word sorts (e.g., people—anyone, someone; things found outside—sunshine, campfire, airplane)
   c. Word endings (e.g., *ed* and *t*)
   d. Categories of word endings (e.g., no change, punching; double, bragging e-drop, trading)
   e. Base word and suffix or prefix sorts
   f. Confusing endings (e.g., *el* and *le*)
   g. Similar sounds but different spellings (e.g., *oi* and *oy*; *ou* and *ow*)

2. *Homograph concentration.* Prepare four sentence cards for each homograph (e.g., She had a tear in her jeans. I will *tear* the paper. A tear ran down the girl's cheek. The television program brought a *tear* to my eye). The sentence cards are shuffled and placed face down on the table. Players take turns turning over two sentence cards to try to find two homographs with the same pronunciation. If the two cards match, the player keeps them and gets another turn. If the two cards do not match, then they must be turned face down on the table. Each pair of sentence cards is worth 10 points and the object of the game is to reach 100 points.

SOURCE: Adapted from Bear et al. (2000, pp. 229–248).

5. Derivational Relations

Characteristics	Reading and writing activities	Word study focus
• Mastered high-frequency words • Makes errors on low-frequency multisyllabic words • Reads with good expression and fluency • Reads faster silently than orally • Writes sophisticated responses	• Include silent reading and writing, exploring various genres to accompany interests • Develop study skills • Focus on literary analysis	• Focus on words that students bring to word study from reading and writing • Link spelling and vocabulary studies (meaning and spelling) • Examine common and less common roots, prefixes, and suffixes • Study word histories in content areas

SOURCE: Adapted from Bear et al. (2000).

Students move from the intermediate stage (i.e., syllables and affixes stage) to a more advanced stage, referred to as the derivational relations stage (Bear et al., 2000). This advanced stage may occur about Grade 5 for some individuals, but may not occur until Grade 12 for others, and may not occur at all for some individuals with learning difficulties. For those students who do reach the derivational relations stage, many of the same instructional principles and activities listed for the intermediate stage also are appropriate for the advanced stage of word study. For example, at both stages students need to explore words actively and apply word knowledge to spelling, vocabulary development, and analyzing unknown words.

The particular word study concepts that students at the derivational relations stage need to learn are (a) the spelling-meaning connection, (b) Greek and Latin elements (i.e., word roots), and (c) word origins (Bear et al., 2000). Through the spelling-meaning connections, students learn to examine words that have related spellings and meanings. For example, students likely may forget to put the silent *n* in the word *condemn*. If students recognize that the word *condemn* is related to the word *condemnation*, they may be able to discover that the word *condemn* indeed ends with an *n* because they see the letter *n* in the word *condemnation*. Students have been exposed to base words to which affixes can be added. Now students are ready to explore word roots, particularly from Greek and Latin origins. Unlike base words that can stand alone, word roots cannot stand alone. If students learn the most common Greek and Latin word roots and how these elements are combined within words, then they will have powerful tools to continue vocabulary and spelling growth. Another powerful tool is etymology, or the study of word origins. Many words that have come from literature, mythology, and history provide important background knowledge to aid students' reading in content areas such as science, social studies, and math. See Teaching Tip 3.9 for additional activities for the derivational relations stage. Teaching Tip 3.10 provides suggestions for assessing decodability of text materials.

TEACHING TIP 3.9

Derivational Relations Stage Activities

1. *Various word sorts.*
   a. *sion* or *tion*
   b. *able* or *ible*
   c. *ence* or *ance*
   d. *ary, ery,* or *ory*
   e. Greek root word families (e.g., *diagram, monogram, telegram*)
   f. Categorize words with Greek and Latin roots. For example,

       i. Building and construction
          1. technology
          2. construct
          3. tractor

      ii. Government
          1. economy
          2. politics
          3. demagogue

     iii. Travel
          1. astronaut
          2. exodus

2. *Matching Greek or Latin word roots and definitions.* Place the word on one card and the definition on another. A word sort can be done with the card to match each word with its definition or a game of concentration can be played with the cards. See the directions for homograph concentration in Teaching Tip 3.8, Syllables and Affixes Stage Activities.

3. *Make root webs.* Students can make root webs for their word study notebooks, as in the following example.

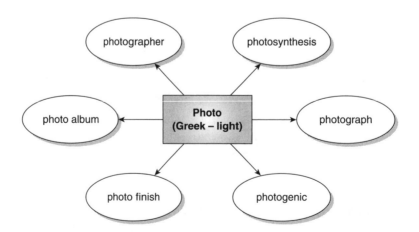

(Continued)

4. *Synonym and antonym continuum.* Students can be given word cards to arrange along a continuum. Students will need to explain why they arranged the cards in a particular order, as in the following example.

frigid	frozen	chilly	cool	tepid	balmy	warm	hot	boiling

SOURCE: Adapted from Bear et al. (2000, pp. 257–284).

REFLECTIVE EXERCISE 3.5
WORD ORIGINS

Teachers need to be role models for their students. Even older students can benefit from seeing their teachers model word study activities for lifelong learning. You probably have been modeling what good readers do by showing students that you enjoy reading to learn as well as reading for pleasure. Perhaps you could start by keeping your own word study notebook. An obvious section in your notebook would be unknown words (pronunciation, spelling, and meaning) that you encounter in your reading. Why not include another section of word origins?

For example, can you match the following word roots with their meanings?

phon (Greek)	to break, burst
auto (Greek)	writing
graph (Greek)	to look
spect (Latin)	sound
rupt (Latin)	to speak, say
dict (Latin)	self

If you still are having difficulty with some of these word roots, try to think of a word that you know that includes the word root. For example:

phon	*phono*graph
auto	*auto*matic
graph	dys*graphia*
spect	*in*spect
rupt	e*rupt*
dict	*dict*ate

Perhaps it has been a long day at school and you need help with one or two and would like to have the answers to put in your word study notebook. The following chart provides information on common word roots.

Word root	Origin	Meaning	Example word
phon	Greek	sound	*phon*ograph
auto	Greek	self	*auto*matic
graph	Greek	writing	dys*graph*ia
spect	Latin	to look	in*spect*
rupt	Latin	to break, burst	e*rupt*
dict	Latin	to speak, say	*dict*ate

This word origins reflective exercise can be used for your students when appropriate. Think of other word roots that you might include. A reproducible blank copy of a word root graphic organizer can be found on page 105.

 TEACHING TIP 3.10

Assessing Decodability of Text Materials

Much of this chapter has focused on providing students with developmentally appropriate activities to help them learn word patterns in order to decode unknown words. Last, but certainly not least important, is making sure that students have appropriate text materials to practice their decoding skills. Gunning (2003) has developed a list to help teachers select texts based on students' developmental levels.

_____ High-Frequency Word Level
Text can be read by using picture clues and knowing no more than 10 high-frequency words (e.g., *the, of, you, have, has, where*).

_____ Short Vowel Level
At least 10% of the words contain short vowels. At least 80% of the words contain short vowels or are high-frequency words.

_____ Long Vowel Level
At least 10% of the words contain long vowels. At least 80% of the words contain long vowels or short vowels, or are high-frequency words.

_____ Other Vowel Level
At least 10% of the words contain other vowels (e.g., *aw, oo, ow, oy*). At least 80% of the words contain other vowels or long or short vowels, or are high-frequency words.

_____ R Vowel Level
At least 10% of the words contain r vowels (e.g., *ar, air, er, ear, ir, or*). At least 80% of the words contain r vowels, long, short, or other vowels, or are high-frequency words.

_____ Multisyllabic Level
At least 10% of the words have more than one syllable.

SOURCE: Adapted from Gunning (2003, p. 185).

Word Root Graphic Organizer

Word root	Origin	Meaning	Example word	
phon	Greek	sound	phonograph	

RTI CASE STUDY FOR WORD ATTACK STRATEGIES

Ashley is a second grade student in Mrs. Green's class who exhibits above average listening comprehension skills, but struggles with reading decoding or word attack skills. When Mrs. Green reads a story aloud to her students and asks questions about the content, Ashley is the first to raise her hand and usually is able to provide a correct response. Mrs. Green is concerned that Ashley struggles to recognize words and word patterns when asked to read second grade level passages from the reading series required by the school district. When Mrs. Green asks Ashley to read aloud during small group reading time, she notices a difference in Ashley's demeanor. Ashley usually slides down in her chair or tries to hide behind another classmate because she does not want to read aloud. Ashley is embarrassed because she knows that she sometimes misses words such as *get*, *win*, and *sock*. Ashley knows all of the letters of the alphabet and most letter sounds, but she has difficulty blending the individual letter sounds to read words with the accuracy and pace expected of a typical second grader.

Mrs. Green administered the Dynamic Indicators of Basic Early Literacy Skills (DIBELS) Oral Reading Fluency (ORF) measure at the beginning of the school year. Ashley's ORF score of 35 placed her in the middle of the some risk category. See Figure 3.13 for Ashley's DIBELS Oral Reading Fluency Scores.

As Mrs. Green observed Ashley's difficulty with word attack skills during the first three weeks of school, she noted that Ashley was falling further and further behind many of her classmates in reading. Mrs. Green believed that Ashley could benefit from a tier one intervention. Although Mrs. Green found that most of her second grade students were progressing on target with their word attack skills, several others were struggling like Ashley.

Beginning of Year Months 1–3		Middle of Year Months 4–6		End of Year Months 7–10	
Scores/Status Second Grade	Ashley	Scores/Status Second Grade	Ashley	Scores/Status Second Grade	Ashley
ORF < 26 At risk		ORF < 52 At risk		ORF < 70 At risk	
26 <= ORF < 44 Some risk	36 Some risk	52 <= ORF < 68 Some risk	52 Some risk	70 <= ORF < 90 Some risk	?
ORF >= 44 Low risk		ORF >= 68 Low risk		ORF >= 90 Low risk	

Figure 3.13   Ashley's DIBELS Oral Reading Fluency (ORF) Assessment Scores

The next step for Mrs. Green was to contact the student support team at the school to ask their recommendations for supplemental strategies that could help Ashley to improve her word attack skills. The student support team introduced Mrs. Green to word sorts and loaned her a copy of *Words Their Way: Word Study for Phonics, Vocabulary, and Spelling Instruction* (Bear et al., 2008). As Mrs. Green began to read about word sorts in the book and to conduct Internet searches on the topic, she became excited because she believed that she could easily incorporate word sorting activities into her classroom reading instruction and could differentiate word sort activities for students like Ashley, characterized as being in the late part of the letter-name alphabetic stage. Mrs. Green determined that Ashley and other struggling students could practice word attack skills for at least 20 to 30 minutes daily while they were waiting for their group's turn at the reading table with Mrs. Green. Ms. Brown who served as a teacher assistant in Mrs. Green's room could work with Ashley and others on the word sorts.

First, Ashley's word sorts consisted of short vowel word families and later she was able to progress to long vowel patterns. Mrs. Green and Ms. Brown found the ReadWriteThink Web site at http://www.readwrite-think.org/ lessons/lesson_view.asp?id=795, supported by the International Reading Association (IRA) and the National Council of Teachers of English (NCTE), helpful in planning the word sort activities. On the Web site they found instructions for teacher modeling, partner word sorts where students could work with a peer, individual word sorts, and computer word sort practice. In addition, the Web site contained word sort assessments. Ms. Brown used the student evaluation sheet to record her observations of Ashley's progress with the word sort activities. She also used the word sort rubric to determine how Ashley did sorting and reading words independently. Mrs. Green decided to incorporate two of the extension activities found on the Web site to help Ashley with her word attack skills. After Ashley had learned many of the short vowel patterns, she looked forward to playing Word Family Bingo on Fridays to help her review what she had learned. In addition, Ashley liked the interactive Word Build & Bank, also found on the ReadWriteThink Web site. There she was able to create new word families and the computer would let her know if she made a wrong choice. Mrs. Green suggested that Ashley also keep a word bank on index cards so that she could continue to sort and review her words when she did not have access to a computer. When Ashley realized that working with words using word sorts could be fun, she did not mind taking home the word sort cards she created at school. Her mother agreed to work with Ashley on her word study for four 20-minute sessions a week. See Figure 3.14 for a summary of Ashley's tier one intervention.

Ashley responded positively to the tier one word attack strategy intervention that Mrs. Green implemented along with Ms. Brown in the second grade general education classroom. Ashley received favorable marks from Ms. Brown on the word sort rubric and indications of progress on the student evaluation sheet. Not only did Ashley's word bank grow larger, but Mrs. Green noticed that Ashley began recognizing her word bank words when she was reading aloud

Supplements to General Curriculum	Classroom Time (Facilitated by Paraprofessional)	Parental Assistance	Notes
Word Sorts	20 to 30 minutes daily		• Ashley's reading/ activity group = 5 students to 1 teacher or paraprofessional • In addition to DIBELS assessments 3 times per year and progress monitoring 2 times a month, the paraprofessional recorded progress data for all of the supplements.
Word Family Bingo (computer)	One 15-minute session on Fridays		
Word Build & Bank (computer)	Two 15-minute sessions per week		
Word Bank (index cards)	As new words were identified	Four 20-minute sessions per week	

Figure 3.14   Summary of Ashley's Tier One Intervention

during small group reading time. Although Ashley still did not volunteer to read aloud during this time, she no longer tried to avoid the reading task by hiding behind a peer.

Mrs. Green conducted progress monitoring two times a month on Ashley's ORF using DIBELS. See Figure 3.15 for Ashley's progress monitoring scores. Mrs. Green found that on the progress monitoring Ashley usually increased her ORF by approximately four to five words every two weeks or eight to ten words per month.

Mrs. Green noticed steady progress after Ashley began participating in the word sort and other supplemental activities. As scheduled for her entire class, Mrs. Green gave the DIBELS ORF during the middle of the year and Ashley's score had improved from a 36 at the beginning of the year to 52 by the beginning of month four and to 72 by the end of month six (See Figure 3.15). Ashley still is considered in the some risk category for ORF as she enters month seven of the school year because her assessment score is 72 (i.e., between 70 and 90). Although Mrs. Green remains concerned about Ashley, her conclusion is that Ashley is making substantial progress as a result of the tier one intervention. Mrs. Green believes that Ashley is likely to progress to the low risk category for Oral Reading Fluency by the end of the school year as a result of the word attack strategy intervention that she will continue implementing. The reason that Mrs. Green is making this prediction is based on the fact that Ashley is increasing her ORF by eight to ten words a month and has progressed to the low risk category by the end of the six-month segment in the school year. If Ashley continues to progress at the same rate of ORF until the end of her second grade year, she likely will surpass a score of 90, keeping her in the low risk category. The tier one supplements to the general curriculum appear to be working for Ashley.

Month	Number	Ashley's Scores	Plus or Minus Difference Between PM	Ashley's Status
2	1	36		26 <= ORF < 44 Some risk
2	2	41	+5	26 <= ORF < 44 Some risk
3	1	43	+2	26 <= ORF < 44 Some risk
3	2	47	+4	ORF >= 44 **Low risk**
4	1	52	+5	52 <= ORF < 68 Some risk
4	2	55	+3	52 <= ORF < 68 Some risk
5	1	59	+4	52 <= ORF < 68 Some risk
5	2	63	+5	52 <= ORF < 68 Some risk
6	1	67	+4	52 <= ORF < 68 Some risk
6	2	72	+5	ORF >= 68 **Low risk**

Figure 3.15   Ashley's DIBELS Oral Reading Fluency (ORF) Progress Monitoring (PM) Scores

CONCLUSION

This chapter has focused on a variety of word study strategies such as word boxes, analyzing words, picture sorts, word sorts, making words, word banks, and word study notebooks that can enhance phonics and word study instruction for students at a variety of developmental stages, especially those with learning difficulties. The authors hope that you will use a number of the individual student and class activities and games in your instructional plans to help your students become more proficient and independent at decoding unknown words and recognizing word patterns.

WHAT'S NEXT?

In the next chapter, you will find a discussion of sight word instruction as well as a number of strategies to help students with learning difficulties build their vocabulary and reading fluency. Students who have larger vocabularies likely will be more fluent and successful readers, and it is hoped they will discover that reading is pleasurable.

REFERENCES

Aiken, A. G., & Bayer, L. (2002). They love words. *Reading Teacher, 56*(1), 68–74.

Atkinson, T. S., Wilhite, K. L., Frey, L. M., & Williams, S. C. (2002). Reading instruction for the struggling reader: Implications for teachers of students with learning or emotional/behavioral disorders. *Preventing School Failure, 46,* 158–162.

Bear, D. R., Invernizzi, M., Templeton, S., & Johnston, F. (2000). *Words their way: Word study for phonics, vocabulary, and spelling instruction* (2nd ed.). Upper Saddle River, NJ: Prentice Hall.

Bear, D. R., Invernizzi, M., Templeton, S., & Johnston, F. (2008). *Words their way: Word study for phonics, vocabulary, and spelling instruction* (4th ed.). Upper Saddle River, NJ: Pearson Prentice Hall.

Bender, W. N., & Larkin, M. J. (2003). *Reading strategies for elementary students with learning difficulties.* Thousand Oaks, CA: Corwin Press.

Borgia, L., Owles, C., & Beckler, M. (2007). Terrific teaching tips. *Illinois Reading Council Journal, 35*(3), 29–32.

Bouchard, M. (2006). *Word study with* Henry and Mudge. Retrieved April 6, 2008, from http://www.readwritethink.org/lessons/lesson_view.asp?id=806.

Carnine, D. W., Silbert, J., & Kame'enui, E. J. (1997). *Direct instruction reading* (3rd ed.). Upper Saddle River, NJ: Merrill-Prentice Hall.

Chard, D. J., & Osborn, J. (1998). *Suggestions for examining phonics and decoding instruction in supplementary reading programs.* Austin, TX: Texas Education Agency.

Clay, M. (1993). *Reading recovery: A guidebook to teachers in training.* Portsmouth, NH: Heinemann.

Cunningham, P. M., & Cunningham, J. W. (1992). Making words: Enhancing the invented spelling-decoding connection. *The Reading Teacher, 46,* 106–115.

Cunningham, P. M., Hall, D., & Defee, M. (1998). Nonability grouped multilevel instruction: Eight years later. *The Reading Teacher, 51,* 652–664.

Devault, R., & Joseph, L. M. (2004). Repeated readings combined with word boxes phonics technique increases fluency levels of high school students with severe reading delays. *Preventing School Failure, 49*(1), 22–27.

Elkonin, D. B. (1973). U.S.S.R. In J. Downing (Ed.), *Comparative reading* (pp. 551–579). New York: Macmillan.

Engelmann, S., & Bruner, E. C. (1995). *Reading Mastery I* (Rainbow ed.). Worthington, OH: SRA Macmillan/McGraw-Hill.

Gunning, T. G. (2000). *Phonological awareness and primary phonics.* Needham Heights, MA: Allyn & Bacon.

Gunning, T. G. (2003). *Creating literacy instruction for all children.* Boston: Allyn & Bacon.

Johnston, F. R. (2000). Word learning in predictable text. *Journal of Educational Psychology, 92*(2), 248–255.

Joseph, L. M. (1998/1999). Word boxes help children with learning disabilities identify and spell words. *The Reading Teacher, 52*(4), 348–356.

Joseph, L. M. (2002). Helping children link sound to print: Phonics procedures for small-group or whole-class settings. *Intervention in School and Clinic, 37,* 217–221.

Joseph, L. M., & Orlins, A. (2005). Multiple uses of a word study technique. *Reading Improvement, 42*(2), 73–79.

Kiley, T. J. (2007). Research in reading. *Illinois Reading Council Journal, 35*(2), 72–75.

Larkin, M. J. (2001). Providing support for student independence through scaffolded instruction. *Teaching Exceptional Children, 34*(1), 30–34.

Merzenich, M. M., Jenkins, W. M., Johnston, P., Schreiner, C., Miller, S. L., & Tallal, P. (1996). Temporal processing deficits of language-learning impaired children ameliorated by training. *Science, 271,* 77–81.

Mills, N. (2006). *Word sorts for beginning and struggling readers.* Retrieved April 5, 2008, from http://www.readwritethink.org/lessons/lesson_view.asp?id=795.

Moats, L. C. (2000, October). *Whole language lives on: The illusion of "balanced" reading instruction.* Washington, DC: Thomas B. Fordham Foundation.

National Institute of Child Health and Development. (2000). *Teaching children to read: An evidence-based assessment of the scientific research literature on reading and its implications for reading instruction* (Report of the National Reading Panel). Retrieved January 18, 2003, from http://www.nichd.nih.gov/publications/nrp/smallbook.cfm.

Olness, R. L. (2007). *Word wizards: Students making words.* Retrieved April 6, 2008, from http://www.readwritethink.org/lessons/lesson_view.asp?id=150.

Rasinski, T., & Oswald, R. (2005). Making and writing words: Constructivist word learning in a second-grade classroom. *Reading & Writing Quarterly, 21,* 151–163.

Rasinski, T. V., & Padak, N. D. (2001). *From phonics to fluency: Effective teaching of decoding and reading fluency in the elementary school.* New York: Addison-Wesley Longman.

Reutzel, D. R., Fawson, P. C., & Smith, J. A. (2006). Words to go!: Evaluating a first-grade parent involvement program for "making" words at home. *Reading Research and Instruction, 45*(2), 119–159.

Schmidgall, M., & Joseph, L. M. (2007). Comparison of phonic analysis and whole-word-reading on first graders' cumulative words read and cumulative reading rate: An extension in examining instructional effectiveness and efficiency. *Psychology in the Schools, 44*(4), 319–332.

Sousa, D. A. (2001). *How the special needs brain learns.* Thousand Oaks, CA: Corwin Press.

Sousa, D. A. (2005). *How the brain learns to read.* Thousand Oaks, CA: Corwin Press.

Stein, J., Talcott, J., & Walsh, V. (2000). Controversy about the visual magnocellular deficit in developmental dyslexics. *Trends in Cognitive Sciences, 4,* 209–211.

Tallal, P., Miller, S. L., Bedi, G., Byma, G., Wang, X., Nagarajan, S., et al. (1996). Fast-element enhanced speech improves language comprehension in language-learning impaired children. *Science, 271,* 81–84.

Treiman, R. (1985). Onsets and rimes as units of spoken syllables: Evidence from children. *Journal of Educational Psychology, 77*(4), 417–427.

Tyner, B. (2004). *Small group reading instruction: A differentiated teaching model for beginning and struggling readers.* Newark, DE: International Reading Association.

Vacca, J. L., Vacca, R. T., Gove, M. K., Burkey, L., Lenhart, L. A., & McKeon, C. (2003). *Reading and learning to read* (5th ed.). Boston: Allyn & Bacon.

Wright, B. A., Bowen, R. W., & Zecker, S. G. (2000). Nonlinguistic perceptual deficits associated with reading and language disorders. *Current Opinion in Neurobiology, 10,* 482–486.

Strategies for Building Vocabulary and Reading Fluency

4

Strategies Presented in This Chapter Include

- ✓ Word Bank Activities
- ✓ Graphic Organizers
- ✓ Semantic Webs
- ✓ The Keyword Mnemonic Method
- ✓ IT FITS: A Learning Strategy
- ✓ Cloze Procedure
- ✓ Concept Circles
- ✓ RTI Case Study for Content Area Vocabulary
- ✓ The Repeated Readings Fluency Strategy
- ✓ *Read Naturally*: A Repeated Reading Curriculum
- ✓ Goal Setting Interventions to Enhance Fluency
- ✓ RTI Case Study for Reading Fluency

As children with learning difficulties learn to master phonemic manipulation, phonics, and initial word recognition skills, they begin to read more fluently. Thus, the early literacy skills discussed previously—phonemic manipulation and phonics instruction—are the building blocks for more advanced reading skills such as vocabulary development and fluency. Likewise vocabulary and reading fluency provide the basis for later success in reading comprehension. Further, skills in vocabulary acquisition and reading fluency become more important as children progress through school, and subsequent reading comprehension skills are highly dependent on both vocabulary and reading fluency (Davis, Lindo, & Compton, 2007; Foorman, 2007).

This transition from preliminary reading skills to more advanced skills results from differential brain processing. As a student's reading skills develop, many of the processes such as phoneme manipulation and decoding words become more automatic within the angular gyrus, the area of the brain associated with phonemic interpretation (Sousa, 2005). In short, as students develop automaticity in their decoding and word recognition skills, activity in the angular gyrus actually decreases, because that activity is now "automatic" to some degree, and this allows more of the brain's processing effort to focus on other more advanced areas of reading, such as comprehension of words, fluency, and ultimately comprehension of the text

This chapter builds on previous chapters, and examines both vocabulary development and reading fluency. Effective instructional strategies will be presented in each of these areas. Also, because each of these areas may be employed in documenting how a child responds to intervention in reading at various academic levels, several RTI case studies are presented.

BUILDING VOCABULARY ACROSS THE LIFE SPAN

Building vocabulary is a critical reading skill from early childhood and throughout the school years. For example, researchers have documented that wide gaps in overall vocabulary often exist as early as the preschool years; youngsters exposed to print-rich environments from their first year of life, have a much wider vocabulary than children with more limited language and vocabulary experiences (Coyne, McCoach, & Kapp, 2007). By Grade 2, some estimates suggest that variance in overall vocabulary may exceed 4,000 root words (Biemiller & Slonim, 2001). Thus, children from language and print-rich environments may have at least a listening (or receptive) vocabulary that exceeds vocabulary of other children by 4,000 words! Of course, this difference is quite likely to impact overall school achievement, and research has shown that this discrepancy in vocabulary does indeed get wider in later years, because limited vocabulary limits the overall positive impact of most school activities (Coyne et al., 2007).

In later years, vocabulary is even more important. For example, successful reading in the upper grades is highly dependent upon content specific vocabulary (Davis et al., 2007; Sousa, 2005). Further, building vocabulary is a lifelong task for most individuals, because advancement in many jobs involves learning vocabulary associated with those jobs. For this reason alone, skills in mastering vocabulary can facilitate success in life.

During the early years of life and the subsequent school years, vocabulary typically refers to one of four types, and each of these represents a progressively increasing mastery of vocabulary terms. These four types of vocabulary are as follows (National Institute of Child Health and Development [NICHD], 2000).

Listening vocabulary—words a child knows when he or she hears them

Speaking vocabulary—words a child uses in speaking

Reading vocabulary—words a child recognizes in print

Writing vocabulary—words a child uses in writing

The first two types of vocabulary relate to oral use of language, or oral vocabulary, whereas the last two types relate to print vocabulary. Thus, students experience and demonstrate use of the first two types of vocabulary prior to receiving formal instruction in school, whereas the latter two types of vocabulary typically are developed during the school years. However, there is more to vocabulary development than merely a jump from phonics into word lists. For example, Davis et al. (2007) suggested that the time a student is exposed to print in the early years influences his or her subsequent vocabulary and reading skill, and this suggests that teachers can do a number of things to enhance each type of vocabulary. Of course, teachers in the earliest years should read to their students, but more can be done. In particular, teachers from kindergarten up through the elementary grades should note for their class each time they obtain information from reading, thus making effective reading a desirable goal, and emphasizing the importance of print. Foil and Alber (2002) suggest that teachers employ a variety of methods to teach vocabulary, actively involve students, provide instruction that relates target vocabulary to other known words, and provide frequent instruction using new vocabulary terms in a variety of contexts. The National Reading Panel (NRP; Hall, 2000) was, perhaps, more succinct in stating that two things build vocabulary during the elementary years:

(a) Exposure to new words, their pronunciation, and their meaning, and

(b) Repetitive use of new words.

This chapter first will present a number of ways to build both oral and print vocabulary in the elementary and middle grades, and each strategy will address each of the fundamental requirements above. A discussion of vocabulary instruction and the importance of vocabulary is presented, along with suggestions to supplement the phoneme- and phonics-based decoding skills with sight vocabulary instructional skills. By combining sight-word recognition and phonemic decoding skills, students will be able to progress through ever more complicated reading content. Next, a variety of specific strategies that may be used to build and strengthen vocabulary are described. Finally, an RTI case study focused on vocabulary development in a middle school content class is presented.

THE IMPORTANCE OF VOCABULARY DEVELOPMENT

Research has documented that unless students develop and use a large vocabulary, they will not be successful in reading and many additional school endeavors (Coyne et al., 2007; Davis et al., 2007; NICHD, 2000). In fact, vocabulary instruction is one area of reading that takes on additional importance as a child progresses through school (Foorman, 2007). For example, children use the vocabulary terms that they have already mastered to decipher new words in their reading text, and a limited vocabulary can thus inhibit reading achievement overall (Davis et al., 2007; Sousa, 2005). Further, the National Reading Panel (NICHD, 2000) concluded that vocabulary instruction does lead to increased reading comprehension, and at a minimum it is quite clear that a limited vocabulary can impede reading success. Also, vocabulary development represents one measure of success in many middle and secondary school subjects, and an expanding vocabulary can lead to an increasing understanding of the fundamental constructs in many higher-level subject areas (Bender, 2008; Vacca & Vacca, 2002). Further, because content area learning in elementary, middle, and high school is extremely dependent upon mastery of subject-specific vocabulary terms, students who cannot learn new vocabulary will be severely impaired in their ability to understand the subject matter in these content area courses.

Upon reflection, teachers quickly realize that high levels of achievement in almost any subject area involve mastery of a set of vocabulary terms that are specific to that area. For example, when one hears any of the terms

> *vertebrates*
>
> *civil war*
>
> *asteroids*

one immediately thinks not only of the specific object or event referenced by the terms, but also of an entire field of study to which those vocabulary terms apply. Thus, when teachers consider the importance of vocabulary in every academic endeavor, it is readily apparent that students will need an array of skills that enable them to approach unknown vocabulary terms in the context of their reading and decipher these terms.

REFLECTIVE EXERCISE 4.1
REPORT ON NEW VOCABULARY INSTRUCTION

You may wish to review a variety of methods for learning new vocabulary, as described in the National Reading Panel study, *Teaching Children to Read* (NICHD, 2000). You can find this online at

www.nichd.nih.gov/publications/nrp/smallbook.cfm.

You may also consider the ongoing work of the National Reading Panel, at their Web site

www.nationalreadingpanel.org.

DO WE STILL NEED SIGHT-WORD APPROACHES FOR VOCABULARY INSTRUCTION?

While phoneme-based reading instruction coupled with phonics as presented in Chapters 2 and 3 is clearly the most effective instructional tactic for most children with learning difficulties (Kame'enui, Carnine, Dixon, Simmons & Coyne, 2002; NICHD, 2000), some children may require additional instruction that is not tied directly to letter-sound manipulation or phonics. In fact, some students may benefit from techniques that are not dependent exclusively on the alphabetic principle, but rather involve rote memory of whole words coupled with context clues to determine the meaning of new words. These nonalphabetic-principle techniques, taken together, may be thought of as sight-word instruction. That is, sight-word approaches would include rote memory of whole words, use of context clues to decode new words, and attempts to master instant word lists.

For many students with reading difficulties, a combination of reading decoding approaches seems to work best—approaches that involve both phonemic-based/letter-sound instruction and use of context clues to determine the meaning of unknown words. Also, we should note that some of the sight-word instructional techniques actually are more similar to the complex reading skills of advanced readers than are the letter-by-letter decoding skills described in Chapter 3. In fact, accomplished readers in the elementary and higher grades use context clues quite extensively in combination with phonics and word attack skills to decipher new words. Thus, there is some rationale for continuing to implement several instructional approaches that traditionally have been associated with sight-word instruction.

Further, because of the importance of vocabulary development in the later years of school, sight-word techniques and vocabulary development techniques that were originally associated exclusively with sight-word instruction in the primary grades now are being applied in various subject areas in the curriculum. For example, word bank activities and the use of context clues—techniques originally used to teach lower-level sight vocabulary in Grades 1 and 2—have seen a reemergence in higher grades and may assist many students in mastering vocabulary lists from social studies, math, or science in Grades 5, 6, or 7.

Vacca and Vacca (2002) noted an additional emphasis on vocabulary instruction. In the elementary grades, the introduction of vocabulary terms in a content area may be synonymous with an introduction to the fundamental concepts in that area. Thus, teachers across the elementary grade levels should become aware of these techniques and how they may be applied in content area classes from Grades 3 through 6. This chapter will present a variety of vocabulary strengthening techniques that originally were used in sight-word instruction that may be used in these grades.

Finally, a number of additional techniques that employ higher-order thinking skills also will assist in the development of vocabulary in elementary and middle school classes. Because of the strong correlation between a growing subject-specific vocabulary and comprehension in many subject areas (Vacca &

Vacca, 2002), a number of techniques that strengthen comprehension also may be used to strengthen vocabulary skills. These include techniques such as semantic webbing, semantic feature analysis, concept circles, and cloze procedures. This chapter will present this array of techniques for strengthening vocabulary skills among readers across the grade levels. First, a bit of history on sight-word instruction is necessary.

Sight-Word Instruction: A Brief History

Sight-word instruction was the reading method of choice for all students in the 19th century and the first one-half of the 20th century, and only gave way to phonics instruction from the 1960s through the 1980s. By the 1980s, most students in U.S. schools were taught to read using phonics for the first several years. Nevertheless, early reading scholars had identified certain words that seemed to do most of the work in the English language. Words such as *a, and, the, about, with, what, come,* and *to* account for a high percentage of words in almost every early reading text, and students were expected to master these words without sounding them out. These lists of lower-level, frequently used words were referred to as *instant words* or *sight words.* Mastery of these words at an early age was assumed to give students a reading advantage, and students became stronger readers if they mastered these words and could read them instantly. The term *automaticity* is sometimes used to represent the ability to read these instant words very quickly, with little conscious effort (i.e., automatically).

The sight-word approach involved sight memory of whole words, so that a student would be trained in instant recognition of these words. For example, in a sight-word approach, the word *cat* was taught as a whole, without breaking the word into the phonemes /c/a/t/ and without emphasizing these specific letter sounds. In many instances, words were taught by pairing them with pictures that represent them. Thus, in this version of sight-word instruction, paired associate learning was often employed (i.e., pairing two stimuli—word and picture—together very frequently, until both take on the meaning of the other). The student with reading difficulties would concentrate on mastery of the basic words used in English. Further, irregular words (i.e., words that do not follow the general rules for spelling or word formation; in the English language, these words account for approximately 15% of all words) were just as easy to master using this approach as words that were phonetically regular words.

Instruction in sight words resulted in a mastery of numerous words during the early months of instruction for students with and without reading difficulties. Also, sight-word instruction usually was paired with two additional teaching ideas: *configuration clues,* which involved drawing boxes around letters in words to concentrate on the shape of the word, and *context clues,* which involved using other text or pictures presented in the text to determine the meaning of new words. These techniques, along with a growing vocabulary of words that explicitly was taught, gave the student one method for deciphering new vocabulary terms in text. This also highlights the major advantage of this instructional approach. In short, the primary advantage of the sight-word instructional approach is the interdependence between sight-word instruction and the reading strategies applied by sophisticated readers in later years; sight-word readers were taught to read words as a whole—automatically—and that is how effective readers in later years most often read.

For example, attention to context clues is a skill that effective readers use at every grade level, and sight-word approaches tended to emphasize this skill much sooner than phonics-based reading approaches. Whereas phonics instruction involves taking large amounts of time to teach various letter sounds in isolation during the early grades, sight-word recognition involves practice in using the context of the vocabulary terms to determine meaning. Thus, students tended to learn a larger vocabulary sooner using a sight-word approach compared to an approach based exclusively on phonics.

Of course, we now understand that phoneme manipulation and phonics provide the best basis for later achievement in reading for almost all students (NICHD, 2000); still, there may sometimes be a need with some students with learning disabilities, for some sight instructional skills such as using text to cleverly decode the meaning of words.

 REFLECTIVE EXERCISE 4.2
HOW DO YOUR STUDENTS LEARN TO READ?

It may be interesting to review the basal reading series used by your school district and consider the points in the discussion above. Are most of the lesson activities addressed to phoneme and phonics instruction? Do you see examples of lessons in the reading series that attend to interpretation of new vocabulary terms in context? Are configuration lessons included in the text? How much is vocabulary development emphasized by the curriculum? Is your local school's reading curriculum a merger of phonemes and phonics and the sight-word approaches? Most reading curricula in schools today are, but not all. Use the questions above as a guide, and reflectively evaluate your school's basal reader.

HOW GOOD READERS READ

Have you ever driven a car to work and, as you turned into the parking lot, realized that you couldn't recall something about the route you took? If there are several similar routes, and you have been driving to the same job for quite a while, this feeling will not be unknown to you. Simply put, part of your brain was "driving," while you thought of other things, and when you got to work, you couldn't remember your route, or perhaps remember any specific corner, or if the light at that corner was green or red when you approached it.

In much the same way, effective readers in later years of school don't spend their reading time decoding words individually. While a part of their brain may be doing that, they very often are unconscious of it. Like the driver described above, effective readers read whole words or whole phrases within a sentence at a glance, without undue brain processing energy spent on decoding individual phonemic sounds. In fact, whole phrases may be read automatically; phrases such as "in the house" or "over the bridge" are read at a glance, without concentrating on either letter sounds or even individual words in the phrase. In fact, if one substituted "over the the bridge" in a story for the phrase "over the bridge," many sophisticated readers would not notice the additional word and would read the phrase as "over the bridge" simply because that was what the context suggested. Thus, their brain, by anticipating that phrase, simply supplied it as a whole phrase.

With the advent of the newly developed fMRI technologies, we now can see that process clearly. For experienced, successful readers, the sound-letter interpretation area (e.g., Wernicke's area) is working somewhat less than for less successful readers. The auditory discrimination areas in the brains of students with reading disabilities are working harder to decode the words in the text, whereas the more successful readers' brains are working harder in the language-processing area of the brain (i.e., Broca's area), which is more directly involved with comprehension of the reading passage. Thus, once automaticity with decoding letter sounds, words, and even phrases develops, the reading process within the brain itself has changed. Helping students make that transition from letter-by-letter reading to word- or phrase-level reading is the key to developing a successful reader, and that transition usually takes place during the first three years of formal schooling.

REFLECTIVE EXERCISE 4.3
HAVING STUDENTS THINK
ABOUT THEIR READING HABITS

How important is it for students to reflect on their reading? The examples of how good readers read (such as reading "over the the bridge" as "over the bridge") can provide a basis for your students to reflect on how they read whole phrases rather than individual words. You may wish to develop several additional examples of phrase reading, expose your class to these examples, and then lead a discussion in your class about developing habits of good readers such as reading entire phrases.

In this sense, sight-word strategies teach children with reading difficulties to read in the same way that more experienced readers read. In sight-word approaches, students learn to read words as a whole, and this eventually translates into reading whole phrases. In fact, this very similarity between sight-word instruction in Grades 1 and 2 and more sophisticated reading in later grades provides the basis for elementary teachers to investigate and use various sight-word instructional techniques with some students who may have extreme difficulty in phonemically based reading programs. As any veteran teacher can attest, no single rule for instruction applies for all students, and in particular for all students with learning disabilities.

LEARNING NEW VOCABULARY TERMS

The National Reading Panel report (NICHD, 2000) provides a wealth of information on vocabulary instruction. Specifically, children learn new vocabulary terms in one of two ways: indirectly or directly. Research has shown that students seem to learn much of their vocabulary terms indirectly, and historically reading researchers have recommended such indirect instruction for most vocabulary instruction in the lower grades. While spelling has traditionally been emphasized, in most cases, most students already knew the terms in most spelling lessons, and thus the emphasis was on spelling the terms and not instruction in unknown word meanings. Indirect vocabulary instruction takes place in many ways:

1. *Engaging in daily oral language exercises.* Conversations with others and hearing adults who use new and interesting words can provide a wealth of new vocabulary terms.

2. *Listening to adults read.* When adults read to children, the adult should use new vocabulary terms and point out the terms, perhaps even verbally quiz the children for a moment on the meaning of the term.

3. *Reading individually.* Students at every age should be encouraged to read to themselves outside of school time and also should be encouraged to ask questions about unknown words.

However, some researchers are challenging the assumption that vocabulary may be learned efficiently via such indirect methods. Coyne et al. (2007), for example, recently studied the impact of indirect vocabulary instruction versus more extended vocabulary instruction among students in kindergarten. In two separate studies, the researchers investigated the impact of vocabulary development, at three levels of instruction:

Incidental instruction—kindergarten children listened to a story that included three target words in context (students were then assessed on their learning of those words),

Embedded instruction—target words for which a definition was embedded within the reading, and

Extended instruction—in which additional instruction was provided for three other target words. This might include introducing definitions prior to reading, and encouraging students to listen for those target words.

These two studies demonstrated that the extended instruction was more effective than both incidental exposure to words and embedded instruction. The extended instruction also resulted in better learning of the target words and increased retention of the target words over time. While it is too early to tell if this and other research will result in more emphasis on vocabulary instruction in kindergarten and lower grades, it is interesting to contemplate this emerging research area, in an era when both vocabulary instruction, and early literacy skills are receiving so much national attention. It is at least possible that recommendations for increasing extended instruction in vocabulary in the earliest years of school might result from this line of recent research.

Although the question of early vocabulary instruction is, thus, still a matter of debate, vocabulary certainly will be taught in later years. When students reach their fourth and fifth grade years, they will be exposed to extended content vocabulary instruction in basic subjects such as history, science, and health. In those content classes, students typically would be taught some vocabulary terms directly. Specifically, terms that represent new and complex concepts that are not a part of the child's daily experience will necessitate direct instruction on the terms. Before reading a text involving new terminology, an introduction to the new terms can greatly assist students in understanding the text, as well as mastering the new vocabulary terms.

While research on vocabulary instruction for students with learning disabilities is fairly rare, it is clear from existing research that merely having struggling students utilize a dictionary is not sufficient to master new vocabulary terms (Bryant, Goodwin, Bryant, & Higgins, 2003). Rather, the NRP report suggests consistent, active engagement with the new vocabulary terms over a period of time to ensure mastery and long-term retention. This repeated exposure—sometimes referred to as distributed practice—will aid not only in learning the word, but in making the word a part of the student's spoken and written vocabulary, as well as his or her reading or listening vocabulary. Only when a student can use the new word in both speech and written products will the student have complete mastery of the new vocabulary term.

Finally, children should learn to master a set of vocabulary learning strategies such as using prefixes and suffixes, using the dictionary, or using context clues from the reading text itself to decipher new words (NICHD, 2000). With a set of strategies for working out the meaning of new vocabulary terms in text, a child will be prepared for classroom reading demands.

WORD RECOGNITION INSTRUCTION

Several of the strategies described here first were applied in the lower grades, but are equally effective for all elementary, middle school, and secondary grades in mastering the vocabulary associated with subject content courses (e.g., science, history, health). Teachers may wish to explore these strategies for vocabulary instruction in their classes.

Word Bank Instruction

Many teachers use a word bank in which five to ten unknown words are enclosed and used for a minimum of one instructional activity each day. Generally, the teacher begins by having the student read a sight-word list or a list of vocabulary terms from a content area. While the strategy description below presents this concept with a sight-word list in the lower grade levels for students with reading problems, teachers who wish to use this strategy for content area vocabulary instruction easily can adapt this strategy for their classes.

While the student with learning difficulties reads the list of terms, the teacher marks the errors and stops the child when ten words have been misread. A mark is made under the last word attempted, and that line is dated; the page is filed and will be used again as an informal vocabulary assessment measure. The ten unknown words are written on cardboard (or light paper stock) and become the student's word bank. The cards then can be placed in a word can. Any type of personal container will do; the first author used cardboard potato chip cans and had the junior high students decorate and personalize their individual word cans. While many teachers use word bank activities for teaching sight words in lower grades, the author had junior high students use word bank activities to learn vocabulary from the various junior high subject areas that were taught by other teachers in that departmentalized school! Thus, this is a great activity for today's inclusive classrooms, in which the special education teacher supports the student in mastery of the subject content terms. Daily word bank activities may include having a student with learning difficulties do the following:

- Write each word several times
- Read them to the teacher
- Look up the words in the dictionary
- Use them in sentences or paragraphs
- Locate them in a story

The critical aspect of the word bank tactic is that the student with learning difficulties must use each word in the word bank each day for one task or another. This directly addresses the second critical aspect of vocabulary instruction noted at the beginning of this chapter—frequency of use. For students with learning disabilities or reading difficulties of any kind, the importance of distributed practice on these vocabulary terms cannot be overemphasized. After about two weeks, the student with learning difficulties typically will be able to read these words with very little problem. At that point, the student should be praised and told to take the words home and share them with his or her parents. The word list should then be used again and another ten words selected for the word bank. For higher-grade students learning content area words, you may change words in the word bank as the units of instruction change in the inclusive class.

At the end of the year, students with learning difficulties will have learned a large number of new words. Further, the word list will have served as an informal assessment as well as a wonderful communication tool. The teacher will be able to show the parents the actual word list, which indicates specifically the vocabulary level of the student at the first of the year and the succeeding mastery of various groups of words throughout the year. Parents generally respond quite favorably to specific evidence of academic growth such as that represented by this word list. This seems much more concrete than the typical test scores that schools often share with parents. Teaching Tip 4.1 presents additional word bank activities that may be completed using these words.

TEACHING TIP 4.1

Activities for Word Bank Instruction

1. Look for words that have the same spelling.

2. Look for words that rhyme.

3. Look for words that may mean the same thing (i.e., synonyms).

4. Write words on cards and play a dominoes game by matching the first two or the last two letters of each word.

5. Categorize words by their type: nouns, pronouns, verbs, and so on.

6. Have groups of students write stories together using all their words.

Using Technologies to Teach Vocabulary

Computerized instructional technology offers an array of vocabulary instructional options for students with learning difficulties that did not exist only a decade ago (Bryant et al., 2003; Mastropieri, Scruggs, & Graetz, 2003). The NRP report (NICHD, 2000) suggested that computer technology can enhance vocabulary instruction for students with reading problems and every teacher should begin to explore applications of appropriate software for reading instruction.

For example, the use of hypertext functions allows a student reading a text to select (i.e., click on) a new, unknown vocabulary term in the text, and the software will present a definition of the term; in some cases illustrations and video demonstrations of the new term also are included. More sophisticated technologies will offer an audio pronunciation of the term. This is a highly effective vocabulary teaching tool, because the student has the information presented at the critical point at which he or she wishes to understand the term, to continue reading the text. Further, the student, in this context, does not have to stop his or her reading of the subject matter and "look up" the term in a dictionary—rather it is presented immediately, and in context. This in-context vocabulary instruction is thus not only more responsive to the needs of the student with learning difficulties, but also results in more effective vocabulary instruction than many traditional methods that present vocabulary terms out of context.

With this in mind, teachers should seek out software that presents vocabulary terms in this fashion. Further, today many reading texts are computerized, or come with options that allow for such technology-assisted reading. These curricula thus offer these vocabulary learning options for students with reading difficulties. Teachers may well experience a day in the near future when their basal reader is replaced by a basal reading computer disk, and teachers certainly should avail themselves of this new technology for vocabulary instruction as it becomes available. Today, many programs (though not basal reading programs) are available on the computer, and frequent use of programs that offer this hypertext function for vocabulary instruction will enhance the vocabulary development for many students with learning difficulties. Several reading programs that present vocabulary via instructional software are presented in the Resources section at the end of this book.

One additional application of technology for vocabulary instruction involves the use of video examples as anchors for the vocabulary instruction (Foil & Alber, 2002; Xin, Glaser, & Rieth, 1996). For example, when vocabulary is presented in terms of video examples, the video provides the situational context or the *anchor* for the new vocabulary term; this is referred to as *anchored instruction* or *situated cognition*. By providing video examples of an earthquake, for example, research has shown that students can master many more vocabulary terms dealing with that type of disaster than without the use of the video examples (Xin et al., 1996).

Of course, with the power of computer technology increasing, it is only a matter of time before full motion video is widely available in all classrooms, and the hypertext function described above, rather than presenting merely a definition of a word, will present that definition as well as a video example for the student with learning difficulties. Some software of this nature is available today, but the limits of computer technology on the user end (i.e., the computers in today's classrooms) usually prohibit wide application of this video instructional function. However, most researchers anticipate that this type of vocabulary instruction will be widely available in five years or so for all students with learning difficulties.

Edmark: A Sight Vocabulary Reading Program

The *Edmark* series of reading programs represent good examples of sight-word instructional curricula. These programs are available in both print and computerized versions. *Edmark* was designed to teach beginning reading and language development to nonreaders—students with learning disabilities and other reading problems. It is a highly structured program based on a whole-word approach to teaching sight-word recognition and comprehension. The original program, *Edmark Reading Program*, Print Level 1, taught 150 sight words, while other programs teach functional words, larger sight-word lists, and so on. Like many of the research-based programs, it uses a multimodality approach. Words are practiced in the context of stories with colorful full-page drawings that illustrate sentences. Language development is encouraged through planned introduction of words and development of sentence structures. Unlike many of the programs presented here, this program does not emphasize phoneme-based instruction or letter sounds, which is one reason we wished to present this program description. Rather, the emphasis is on mastery of whole words in context, and while this instructional approach is somewhat different from the current emphasis on phonemic- and phonics-based programs, research clearly has shown that this program works.

The *Edmark Reading Program* has been developed to fit a wide variety of student needs. Students with developmental or learning disabilities, preschool and kindergarten students who are deaf or lack vocabulary development and language awareness, students who are experiencing difficulty with phonetic-based approaches, or students for whom English is not their primary language may all benefit from this type of instruction. Lessons are presented in a direct instructional format with a one-on-one instructor for student lessons. This format allows teachers to make effective use of paraprofessionals and peer tutors. The program is available in several levels. Level 1 covers beginning skills:

- 150 words from the Dolch word list and basal readers
- Word endings: -s, -ing, and -ed
- Capitalization and punctuation skills
- Visual memory of words and sets of letters
- Left-to-right reading and tracking
- Thinking and discrimination skills
- Combined sentences for meaningful stories

Level 2 continues to practice the skills taught in Level 1. Skills then are built upon and extended to include

- 200 additional words from the Dolch word list
- Compound words
- Words, sentences, and phrases
- Vocabulary expansion
- Reading practice

The program is available in both a print version and a software version (www.riverdeep.net/edmark). Both of these include a teacher's guide with learning objectives, classroom activities, and research references. Review and test activities are completed at ten-word intervals throughout the program. A student record book is provided to assist in tracking student progress and may be used for developing objectives for individual education plans as well.

The *Edmark Reading Program* has received wide research support since it was first published in 1971, and much of this research is reviewed on its Web site. As one more recent example, Mayfield (2000) evaluated the effects of using the *Edmark Reading Program*, Level 1, to develop sight-word vocabulary in first graders who were at risk for reading failure. Three Title I schools in rural Louisiana were chosen to participate in the study. Teachers and principals identified a group of 62 first graders as at risk based on reading test scores and teacher observations. All 62 students were pretested and then were randomly assigned to either a control or an experimental group at each school. Experimental groups received 15 minutes per day of one-on-one tutoring in the *Edmark Reading Program* for the first semester of the school year. Six America Reads volunteers, who were also education majors at a local university, provided the tutoring. The tutors received two hours of training in the use of the *Edmark Reading Program*. The same volunteers read aloud to the control group for 15 minutes during the same time period. At the end of the semester all of the students were administered posttests by an independent examiner. The posttest included the same reading tests as the pretest. In addition, the students were asked to read aloud the 150 words taught in Level 1 of the reading program. Based on comparisons of the pretest and posttest results, Mayfield concluded that the *Edmark Reading Program* was successful in increasing the sight-word vocabulary and comprehension skills of the students. School administrators indicated in postintervention interviews that 25% of the experimental group participants achieved honor roll during the intervention period.

This is only one example of a direct instructional program for vocabulary instruction, and other programs are available. While research supports phonemic and phonics instruction for most students, teachers may find occasionally a student for whom a sight-word approach seems to work best, and the research on *Edmark* suggests that for those students with reading problems this may be an appropriate instructional choice.

DERIVING MEANING FROM VOCABULARY

Many experienced teachers have encountered students with reading difficulties who seem able to decode words and learn to pronounce new vocabulary terms, but never seem to comprehend the new terms as quickly as other students. Whereas the techniques reviewed above concentrated basically on word recognition, the following techniques address the issue of word comprehension in text, or a student's ability to derive meaning from words. In some of the strategies, correct pronunciation of the word is not addressed, because the skill is seen as less important than deriving meaning from the word in context for students with this type of learning difficulty. In other words, some of the following strategies emphasize reading vocabulary rather than speaking vocabulary. Still, numerous methods exist that address word comprehension at each elementary grade level. Some of these are useful for lower-level readers in the earlier grades, whereas other techniques may be used in Grades 4 through 7 or in subject content areas.

Graphic Organizers

Graphic organizers (GOs) assist students with learning difficulties in building vocabulary by presenting terms in a spatial relationship to other terms. This strategy addresses not only vocabulary development, but also concept development in a given unit of study (Bender, 1985; DiCecco & Gleason, 2002; Mastropieri et al., 2003). In the context of this chapter, we will discuss GOs as a vocabulary development tool, but in Chapter 6 these are presented again as a content area reading comprehension tool, and research has supported use of GOs for both purposes (Mastropieri et al., 2003).

Typically, a teacher will present a GO that encompasses a series of vocabulary terms representing the main concepts featured in a unit of study. A primary grade example is presented in Teaching Tip 4.2.

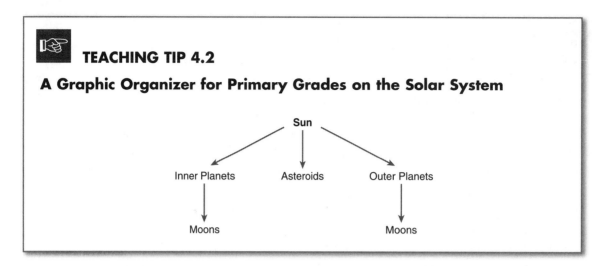

☞ **TEACHING TIP 4.2**

A Graphic Organizer for Primary Grades on the Solar System

This example of a graphic organizer shows—in graphic form—the basic structure of the solar system. The reading passage that this GO accompanies would indicate that the sun was the center of the solar system and that inner planets, outer planets, moons, and asteroids were objects within the solar system. The passage would indicate that the inner and outer planets are separated by the asteroid belt, which is why asteroids are presented between inner and outer planets. Further, the reading passage also would describe the fact that inner planets, outer planets, and asteroids travel around the sun, whereas moons travel around the inner and outer planets. Thus, in this simple GO, moons are pictured under inner and outer planets whereas all planets and asteroids are pictured under the sun. Although this GO presents merely the terms to be studied, other graphic organizers may present the vocabulary terms along with their definitions.

GOs may be developed along a variety of conceptual lines. For example, a whole-to-part GO demonstrates how a concept may be broken down or divided into component parts. Some GOs present a hierarchy of events or topics, such as the primary example above. Another type of GO involves a compare and contrast graphic representation. Yet another type of GO involves a timeline sequence of events. Finally combinations of various organizational concepts may be used, as in Teaching Tip 4.3, designed for the upper elementary grades.

In this teaching tip, a GO on the Civil War, a number of vocabulary terms are related to their definitions and to broader issues. These vocabulary terms include the following:

the Missouri Compromise	Abolition
states' rights	Emancipation Proclamation
Nineteenth Amendment	the Reconstruction period

TEACHING TIP 4.3

A Sample Graphic Organizer on Causes of the Civil War

THE CIVIL WAR

Root Causes

1. Economy based on agriculture in the South versus economy based on growing industry in the North

2. Growing number of western states and the desire to keep the number of slave states and nonslave states equal (Missouri Compromise)

3. Growing movement to free all slaves (abolition of slavery)

4. Confederate citizens' distrust of power of the federal government and belief in states' rights rather than federal government power

Immediate Causal Problems

1. The election of Lincoln—a man who was sympathetic to abolition of slavery

2. Firing of shots in South Carolina and South Carolina seceding from the Union

WAR IS FOUGHT BETWEEN 1861 AND 1865

1861 ⟶

Confederate Wins the First Two Years of the War

2 Battles of Bull Run

The Wilderness

Other Early Battles

1863 ⟶

The Turning Points

Vicksburg

Gettysburg

Emancipation Proclamation

1864–1865

Union Victories

Petersburg

Battle of Atlanta

Sherman's March to the Sea

Results of the War

1. Economy destroyed in the Confederate States after the war ends

2. Power of the federal government over the states established

3. All slaves in the United States freed (Emancipation Proclamation; Nineteenth Amendment)

4. Union moves to rebuild the Southern States—the Reconstruction period

Further, this GO is an effective teaching tool for a number of other reasons. Note that the causes are described as either root (i.e., basic) causes or as immediate causal problems. Whereas the root causes were ongoing disagreements between the South and the North, the immediate causal problems (i.e., the presenting causes) include the events that immediately preceded the outbreak of the war. This dualism can provide the basis for a good class discussion on this graphic organizer, which in turn offers students with learning difficulties the opportunity to use the vocabulary terms they are learning in a discussion of basic causes and precipitating causes. Recent research has shown that GOs assist students with learning disabilities in acquiring the skills needed for application of new knowledge better than instruction without graphic organizers (DiCecco & Gleason, 2002; Mastropieri et al., 2003).

Also, the concepts involved in studies of the Civil War are noted (i.e., causes, effects), and that information is coupled with a general timeline of the war itself. The variety of GO formats offers teachers the option of varying instruction based on the needs of the diverse students in the class. In developing a variety of curriculum supports for your students with learning difficulties, you may wish to use a simple GO organized exclusively around one organizing principle for some students with reading disabilities in your class, while you use a more complex GO, such as this Civil War example, for other students. This type of support during a reading assignment can assist students with learning difficulties in both vocabulary acquisition as well as comprehension of the material.

Also, a GO can assist children with learning difficulties in either the inclusive or the special education class setting. In the inclusive class, the special needs teacher may wish to work with a small group of students with learning difficulties and have that group jointly develop a GO for later use by all of the students in the class.

Note also that the GO on the Civil War pictures the timeline of the war in summative fashion (i.e., early Southern victories, turning points, later Union victories). Presenting these events, pictured in such a timeline fashion, makes this graphic organizer an effective memory tool for students with poor long-term memory (as demonstrated by many students with learning disabilities). All of these instructional advantages make this an effective teaching tool to emphasize the meaning of these vocabulary terms, as well as the general concepts related to this historical period. Here are several additional facts that are graphically represented, and these issues may serve as the basis for additional instruction after the reading assignment is completed.

1. The causes precede the event. Is that all it takes to be a cause? What makes one event a cause of another event in history? This is related to discussions of *historiography,* or the conceptual basis of historical study.

2. The results come after the war. Do these results become causes of problems later? Also, can we see evidence of unresolved issues from this war today in our society?

3. Who won most of the major battles in the first two years of the war? What evidence do we have that the Confederacy won? Who won the battle of Gettysburg? Did the Confederacy believe that their army lost that battle at the time?

4. What relationships do we see between the causes of the war and the results? Does this war end all discussion of these issues? Do we hear of the *states' rights* issue again in the history of race relations in the United States?

GOs may be developed in virtually any content field in the elementary grades and serve as one of the most effective methods for relating vocabulary to conceptual content in a fashion that is likely to enhance retention of the vocabulary terms among students with reading disabilities. There are a number of additional guidelines that teachers may use in developing GOs, as presented in Teaching Tip 4.4.

 TEACHING TIP 4.4

Developing Graphic Organizers

1. Select a portion of content, rich in vocabulary, which is critical to a student's understanding of the instructional unit. This material should allow for a logical pictorial depiction based on temporal, geographical, or causal relationships. In short, in order for a graphic organizer to work, there must be some logic as to the ordering of the items presented in the graph or picture to be developed.

2. Select an appropriate amount of information for your graphic organizer. Whereas some organizers may portray the entire unit (e.g., the graphic organizer in Teaching Tip 4.3 presents the basic information from a two- or three-week unit in history on the Civil War), other graphic organizers may present only a portion of the information or a selection of information from one portion of the unit of study. For example, the top portion of Causes of the Civil War may be used as a separate organizer, perhaps in a timeline sequence.

3. Select the broad topics to be presented first. This will assist you in delineating the scope of the graphic organizer. Put these down in some logical sequence.

4. Identify the points that should be presented under each of the broader points and place these on the chart.

5. Check the final organizer with the following questions and modify it if necessary.

    (a) Did I present the most important vocabulary terms and information?
    (b) Is the graphic presentation sensible and explainable to students?
    (c) Can I use this as both a prestudy organizer and a review organizer?
    (d) Should I develop an organizer with more (or less) information, broader in scope?

REFLECTIVE EXERCISE 4.4
STUDENTS DEVELOP GRAPHIC ORGANIZERS

Vacca and Vacca (2002) suggest using students to develop GOs. Consider the concept of scaffolded instruction as demonstrated in Chapter 1, and use that idea to develop a lesson plan for having students develop GOs in your classroom. What guidelines would you provide for students if you wanted to do this as a class activity? How could students with learning difficulties, working in groups, be used to check the work of other groups? Write down some guidelines for this type of assignment and consider using this idea in your class.

Semantic Webbing Strategy

Many students with learning disabilities and others with reading problems have difficulties that stem from difficulty in detecting the relationships between the concepts the vocabulary represents in the reading assignment. Further, those relationships often represent the basis of higher-order understandings. Thus, both the student's vocabulary and the student's sense of relationships between concepts may be weakened by poor word comprehension. The semantic web—sometimes referred to as either a semantic map or a webbing activity—can assist students in deriving meaning from words and in understanding the concepts those words represent (Bos, Mather, Silver-Pacuilla, & Narr, 2000; Bryant, Ugel, Thompson, & Hamff, 1999). This semantic web may be considered a highly specialized type of GO that is intended to present these relationships between different concepts.

A semantic web may be considered as a form of scaffold to bolster understanding among students with reading difficulties. The web presents a central word or phrase, located in the center of the page or chart, or on the dry-erase board for classroom use. The further development of the web involves having a group of students select other words that relate to the central word. These would then be presented in other locations on the page or the board, with the locations specifically selected to demonstrate the relationships between the words. A sample semantic web is presented in Teaching Tip 4.5.

In this semantic web, the word *galaxy* is presented as the central term. The names of items that make up a galaxy—galactic dust, stars, solar systems—are directly related to the central term. Perimeter arrows suggest that galactic dust is directly related to stars, as stars emerge from galactic dust, and solar systems relate to stars, as a star is the center of each solar system. Stars and solar systems are major components in galaxies, but planets, moons, and asteroids are more intimately related to solar systems than to galaxies, and thus are depicted as components of a solar system. In turn, the components of a solar system—sun/star, planets, moons, asteroids—are not directly related to galactic dust, because galactic dust forms stars first, and from some stars or double stars, solar systems emerge.

Additional terms and concepts also may be written on the board in separate circles and placed in proximity to each other as dictated by the underlying relationships between them. The emphasis in using the semantic web must be on meaningful relationships between the terms. Note how the text above explained the relationships depicted and why some items in the semantic web were not directly related to other items. This discussion exemplifies the type of discussion points the teacher may wish to make in the class during the semantic webbing activity. Teaching Tip 4.6 presents numerous ideas for developing semantic webs and using them in your class.

TEACHING TIP 4.5

A Semantic Web

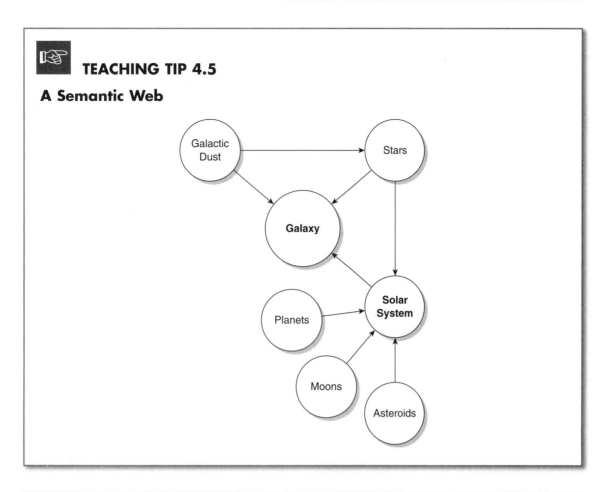

 TEACHING TIP 4.6

Using Semantic Webs

There are many variations teachers may use with the semantic web. Here are a few for you to consider.

1. You can use a semantic web for the key components of every chapter, as you begin a new unit. Leave the web posted in the room for the length of that unit.

2. Divide students into pairs and have each pair of students complete a semantic web on one portion of the chapter as you begin a new unit and then share the webs with the class.

3. Form groups of four or five students to develop a semantic web. Give each group of students the central word to begin the activity.

4. For some groups, provide the central word and a vocabulary list to be included. This provides a nice differentiated lesson for slower students.

5. Assign some students to develop an art project which presents a semantic web. In the example above, models of planets, suns, moons, and so on could be used or a collage of pictures could be obtained. The semantic web doesn't have to be words only!

6. Use a previously developed semantic web as the basis for review of the unit of study prior to the unit exam.

REFLECTIVE EXERCISE 4.5
USING KIDS TO DEVELOP SEMANTIC WEBS

Teachers may wish to consider using appropriate software to assist students with learning difficulties to develop semantic webs and/or other graphic organizers. This can be a wonderful reading activity for teaching vocabulary as well as the concepts described by the vocabulary. You may find a variety of appropriate software programs at www.inspiration.com

Semantic Feature Analysis (SFA)

Vacca and Vacca (2002) recommend a strategy for students with learning difficulties called semantic feature analysis (SFA), which relates vocabulary terms to prior knowledge and to each other. In the semantic webbing strategy described above, you may have noted how the relationships between the terms in the web were emphasized to assist the students in memorization of those terms. In semantic feature analysis, these relationships are again emphasized, in the context of likenesses and differences. In this strategy, a chart is developed and the characteristics on which terms are to be compared are listed down the side of the chart, while the terms themselves are listed across the top of the chart. The activity consists of having the students consider the terms at the top and how the characteristic or definitional aspect on the side applies to the vocabulary term. Students then indicate if that definitional aspect applies. This is illustrated in the sample in Teaching Tip 4.7. When finished, the student has a graphic depiction of the likenesses and differences between the new vocabulary terms.

 TEACHING TIP 4.7

A Sample Semantic Feature Analysis

Directions for the student: Each student should consider the vocabulary terms at the top of the page and ask if the characteristic listed on the left of the chart applies to that term. Mark each column in the SFA as true if the characteristic applies or false if it does not apply.

Types of Letters

	Personal letter	Business letter (block)	Business letter (standard)
1. The date and the closing are placed halfway across the page.			
2. The letter has no inside address.			
3. The opening and salutation are placed on the left margin.			
4. An inside address is used.			
5. All sections of the letter are placed on the left margin.			

In reviewing the SFA, teachers readily can see how this activity may be structured for classes or groups of objects in almost any subject area. Here are several additional examples of sets of terms for which an SFA may be useful.

1. In sixth grade geometry problems, the parallelogram, rectangle, rhombus, and square may be compared directly, because students often confuse these shapes and the characteristics associated with each.

2. In science classes, species and subspecies may be compared directly. Differentiating between these is often quite difficult for students with reading difficulties.

3. For a fifth grade earth physical sciences class, comparison of the different states of matter (e.g., liquid, solid, gas, plasma) using an SFA may be appropriate.

4. In studies of the solar system, several SFA diagrams on the different objects within the solar system would be useful (e.g., planets, moons, asteroids, comets, stars).

Seeing the characteristics associated with vocabulary terms with similar meanings portrayed in this fashion can enhance greatly the long-term memory of students with learning difficulties. Unlike the semantic webbing activity described above, in the SFA the similarities and differences between similar objects are directly highlighted. This can enhance understanding, because this type of pictorial representation is much easier for most students with reading difficulties to remember than merely the lists of characteristics associated with highly similar vocabulary terms. As a variation on this strategy, teachers may wish to provide a partially developed SFA to students with reading difficulties and have those students complete the SFA as they read a text passage. This strategy works in both the inclusive and the special education class settings.

A KEYWORD VOCABULARY DEVELOPMENT STRATEGY

Various researchers have presented the idea of using keywords and other similar mnemonic strategies to assist students with learning difficulties in learning new vocabulary terms (Foil & Alber, 2002; Mastropieri & Scruggs, 2002, pp. 133–136; Mastropieri et al., 2003). In using the keyword method, when a student with reading difficulties is presented with a new term, he or she thinks of a keyword or alternative term that will assist in remembering the new term. Foil and Alber (2002) present two examples suitable for students with reading difficulties:

Vocabulary term: *muck*

Keyword: *yuck*

In learning the term *muck,* a student might remember that it means "filth" by rhyming it with *yuck.* The student could then develop a picture in which the term was presented over a picture of a dirty horse stable.

Vocabulary term: *mumbo jumbo*

Keywords: *mum jum*

In learning the term *mumbo jumbo,* a student might remember that mumbo jumbo is a meaningless ritual by picturing *Mum* (i.e., Mom) in a *jum* (i.e., gym) shooting hoops. In using the keyword method, the student may visualize a cartoon of Mom shooting a basketball and think of how remote a possibility that is, thus reminding the student of the term *mumbo jumbo* and the definition, "meaningless ritual."

In using the keyword strategy, teachers can develop certain keywords for specific vocabulary terms, or teachers may use students to develop the keywords and pictures that go with them. Students with learning difficulties have benefited a great deal from using this type of strategy for vocabulary development as well as comprehension of new concepts (Mastropieri & Scruggs, 2002).

LEARNING STRATEGIES FOR VOCABULARY MASTERY

To extend this possibility, pairing this keyword concept with a learning strategy acronym that reminds students of the steps to use when confronted with a new vocabulary term can greatly assist students. A learning strategy is a series of steps that can assist a child in performing a specific task, such as learning a new vocabulary term. Most learning strategies are represented by acronyms in which the letters represent the various steps a child with a learning difficulty should perform.

King-Sears, Mercer, and Sindelar (1992) created the learning strategy acronym IT FITS for students with learning disabilities to learn new vocabulary terms. The steps (as represented by this acronym) that a student should perform when confronted with a new vocabulary term are as follows:

I   *Identify* the term (e.g., impecunious)

T   *Tell* the definition of the term (e.g., having no money)

F   *Find* a keyword for the term (e.g., penniless imp)

I   *Imagine* a picture of the keyword that represents the definition (e.g., an imp of a foolish boy, finding he has no money)

T   *Think* about the definition and the keyword

S   *Study* what you imagined until you know the definition

In visualizing a picture for this keyword, the student with a learning disability may imagine a foolish looking boy with both pants pockets turned out, finding no money. Of course, in using this keyword and learning strategy, students must practice the visualization aspect of the strategy numerous times. In fact, using teams of students to complete this strategy together can add to the benefits, since students with less skill in visualization can benefit from practice with students who visualize easily. Also, students must make certain to complete the final two steps above—thinking about the definition and studying the imagined picture—until they have mastered the vocabulary term. This strategy will work well in either an inclusive or a special education class setting.

A Vocabulary Card Strategy

Foil and Alber (2002) suggested the use of vocabulary cards to assist students with learning difficulties in learning new vocabulary terms presented in reading assignments. In using vocabulary cards, students would be encouraged to create picture cards to assist them in remembering the new vocabulary term and definition. The use of pictures can result in enhancing the memory of students with learning difficulties, because different brain areas are involved. Picture-based learning involves the visual cortex more than merely reading, and the spatial areas in the right hemisphere of the brain are more involved also. Thus, for students with learning difficulties, the brain will be more actively engaged in the reading process, and this will, in all likelihood, result in increased retention of new vocabulary terms, particularly when the students themselves create the picture cards.

Using pictures to teach words has received increasing attention and some curricula are available for this. The Web site www.vocabularycartoons.com presents a series of picture books and associated vocabulary terms, and many teachers have reported success in using these materials for students with reading difficulties. After you review the free sample materials, consider how you might use them in your class for students with reading problems.

A Cloze Reading Procedure

A cloze procedure can be used to emphasize the meaning of vocabulary terms in a particular unit of study for students with reading difficulties. This is one excellent way to emphasize the meaning of content terms in the upper elementary grades. A cloze procedure is a structured fill-in-the-blank activity that emphasizes word comprehension and use of context clues to decipher words (Vacca & Vacca, 2002). This strategy may be used from Grade 2 through Grade 6 or 7, in a variety of subject areas. An example emphasizing vocabulary from a social studies course is presented in Teaching Tip 4.8.

In using a cloze procedure, the semantic and syntactic clues embedded within the reading passage serve as an aid in the student's selection of the correct content term, which would then be used to fill in the blank. Inclusive class teachers can form a cloze procedure reading activity from almost any reading selection by deleting every seventh content word (i.e., omitting words such as *a, and,* and *the* from the count of words). In contrast, teachers may merely select a reading passage and choose random content words to replace with a blank line. Not only does this force the students to read the words, but this strategy

TEACHING TIP 4.8 (Continued)

A Sample Cloze Procedure for a Social Studies Unit

A _____ is the basis for most modern governments in the Western Hemisphere. In the United States the Constitution is divided into three _____ of government, and each has a separate function. The _____ makes laws, while the _____ enforces the laws. The _____ has the job of interpreting the application of the laws in specific instances. In addition to these separate functions, each branch of government has some _____ which allow it to exercise some control over the other branches of government. This system is called _____ . For example, in order for a bill to become a law, the legislature must vote on it, and the president must sign it. If the legislature passes a law that went against the _____ , the _____ branch could declare that law unconstitutional. Likewise, if the _____ decided not to sign a law, that is called a _____ and it effectively limits the power of the legislature. Of course, the _____ can override that veto with an overwhelming vote of support for the law.

Answer key for the 12 answers required above:

1. Constitution

2. branches

3. legislative

4. executive

5. judicial

6. checks

7. checks and balances

8. Constitution

9. judicial

10. executive or president

11. veto

12. legislative branch

also forces students with reading problems to attend to the content of the reading passage to interpret the context clues. Thus, comprehension becomes a factor that is emphasized. Of course, prior to use with students with reading disabilities, the newly prepared reading selection should be checked to ensure that the blanks may be completed by using the available clues. Finally, the cloze procedure activity can easily be modified for lower-functioning readers merely by providing a word bank or list of words from which the correct terms may be selected. These terms would then be matched to the particular blanks in the reading selection by the students.

REFLECTIVE EXERCISE 4.6
STUDENTS DEVELOP A CLOZE ACTIVITY

Could you use students with learning difficulties to develop cloze procedures to teach vocabulary? Alternatively, could you use a heterogeneous group of students to formulate an activity that then would be completed by the remainder of the class? Using a word processing system and a textbook with a chapter on the unit of study, you may give the group parameters such as which terms or concepts need to be embedded within the final reading selection. Having several groups working on different sections of the unit of study can generate a number of cloze procedure reading selections that may be used in subsequent years.

Concept Circles

Concept circles teach vocabulary in content areas through classification and presentation of relationships between the terms. This activity is useful for students with reading difficulties throughout the elementary grades, because it presents the conceptual basis of the relationships between terms. To develop a concept circle, one first presents a divided circle on a chart or on the dry-erase board. The teacher may divide a circle into quarters of a circle or fifths of a circle and place various terms in those separate sections. Students work in groups to describe the relationships between the ideas in each part of the circle in an effort to identify the specific concept represented (Vacca & Vacca, 2002). Students should make notes on their discussion of the concept in order to later summarize their discussion for the class. A sample concept circle is presented in Teaching Tip 4.9.

Teachers can make concept circles a more challenging task by placing in the sections of the circle a number of terms that relate to each other in a very specific way and one term that does not relate in the same fashion. This variation challenges the students to identify not only the concept, but also the term that does not fit. In this activity, various groups of students will complete the task in varying levels of complexity, and teachers often find that students can identify relationships (i.e., relevant concepts) that the teacher did not note prior to the assignment. Thus, this type of vocabulary instruction is most effective when students with learning difficulties are working in heterogeneous groups and the groups' thinking moves in different directions. The various groups should complete their thinking and discussions and present their results to the entire class.

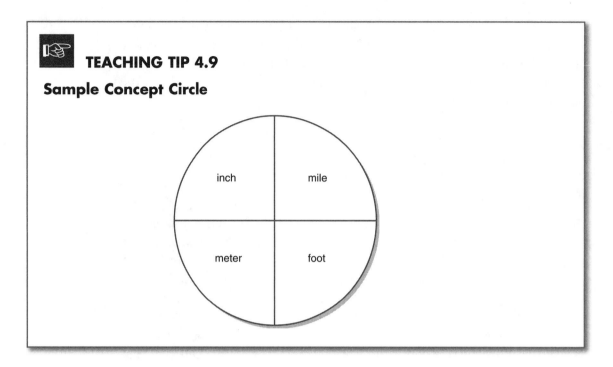

☞ **TEACHING TIP 4.9**

Sample Concept Circle

RTI CASE STUDY FOR CONTENT AREA VOCABULARY

The vocabulary instructional ideas presented previously are applicable from kindergarten up through the secondary grade levels, and as noted previously, many elementary, middle, and secondary teachers provide vocabulary instruction in content areas. However, envisioning an RTI for vocabulary acquisition in middle or higher-grade levels can be somewhat challenging. Here is an example of how instruction in content vocabulary may be considered as part of an RTI process to document eligibility of a student for learning disabilities services.

Ms. Crabtree teaches sixth grade American History, and was concerned with the academic skill of one of her students in her fifth period class; his name was Hinton. Hinton had transferred into the district just before the beginning of the school year. His school record indicated that he had very low grades (C's, D's, and F's), and had been retained in Grade 3. However, in spite of the fact that he was clearly struggling with academic work, he had never been considered for special education. Ms. Crabtree thought he might have a learning disability, as he struggled with reading in her class. In fact, his previous test scores indicated that his reading comprehension was quite low (around third grade). Further, in her class, during the first instructional unit—a two-week unit on the Colonial period in American history—he had a very difficult time mastering vocabulary for the class, and Ms. Crabtree thought his comprehension problems might stem from his lack of skill in mastering content vocabulary. Thus, Ms. Crabtree wanted to implement a content area vocabulary instruction intervention during the next instructional unit, a three-week unit on the

American Revolution. She also realized that such an intervention might become an initial intervention within a broader RTI process to document eligibility of Hinton for learning disabilities services, so she had to teach and repeatedly assess Hinton's performance in a manner consistent with the expectations of RTIs (e.g., repeated assessment over time).

Although most RTI procedures probably will be undertaken in lower grades, it is quite possible for this type of situation to develop—the need for an RTI procedure to document eligibility—for an older student. Bender and Shores (2007) provided a model for how such an RTI intervention might work in the upper grades, by implementation of a precision teaching instructional procedure. Efficacy of precision teaching has been repeatedly demonstrated, so this is a proven research strategy for teaching reading vocabulary, as well as instruction in many other reading areas (Bender & Shores). In precision teaching, instruction is provided directly on the appropriate content in a highly systematic fashion, and academic performance is monitored daily. Ms. Crabtree decided to implement an RTI tier one intervention, focused on learning content vocabulary in her history class using the precision teaching model.

In the next unit on the American Revolution, there were 15 main vocabulary terms identified for the unit, including terms such as *Declaration of Independence, Continental Congress, minuteman, Washington, Cornwallis, Concord Bridge, Bunker Hill, Yorktown, Articles of Confederation,* and *Constitution.* For each term, Ms. Crabtree selected a four- to six-word definition of that emphasized the definition and the importance of that term within the unit. She then developed a worksheet with those definitions presented in a fill-in-the-blank format in which students were expected to provide the correct term for the definition presented. This worksheet would be used each day during the unit, to assess progress in learning the relevant content vocabulary.

For instructional purposes, Ms. Crabtree also developed three graphic organizers, and all terms were included in at least one of these organizers. She then began instruction in the unit. Each day she would offer instruction as she would normally, while emphasizing the vocabulary terms and pointing out where each was found on one or more of the various graphic organizers. She introduced the graphic organizers systematically so that by the seventh day of instruction each GO had been introduced, though each organizer was not necessarily completed by then. She made a point of referring to the terms and to the graphic organizers regularly during all class activities, and of stressing the vocabulary terms.

While continuing to teach her group of 25 students in her general education fifth period class in a fairly traditional fashion, she did need to modify her instruction to monitor vocabulary mastery performance each day to complete an RTI for Hinton. Using the precision teaching worksheet on definitions, it was fairly easy to accomplish. She used the last ten minutes of the instructional period each day to have all students in the class complete the vocabulary worksheet described above. Thus, each day she conducted her lesson as she normally would, but she would terminate those activities with ten minutes left in the period. During that time, she would hand out a clean copy of the vocabulary worksheet to all students and instruct them to complete it. After five minutes or so of time to complete the worksheet, students were encouraged to exchange papers and cross check their answers, without changing those answers. Thus, this activity not only allowed Ms. Crabtree to monitor daily performance on Hinton's mastery of content vocabulary but also served as a reinforcer for all of the other students in the class on those vocabulary terms. Again, she used the same worksheet each day, and this drove home the students' understanding of the critically important terms in that unit of instruction; thus it was a very effective reinforcer for all students in the class.

Of course, in the early days of the unit, not all of the vocabulary had been introduced, so even the brightest students in the class were not expected to get all of the terms correct on the first several days. However, as the unit progressed and as the students did graphic organizers, and subsequently the same vocabulary worksheet each day, progress in mastery of the 15 vocabulary terms became obvious for most students in the class. Ms. Crabtree collected every student's worksheet each day. For students who mastered the terms on the worksheet within the first five or six days of the instructional unit, she developed additional, more challenging worksheets. However, the other students, including Hinton, continued to work on the same vocabulary-based worksheet, thus stressing mastery of the relevant vocabulary for all members of the class.

Finally, to generate daily progress monitoring data for Hinton, Ms. Crabtree charted the count of his correct answers each day. Thus, she had a daily performance monitoring record of his mastery of content vocabulary terms in her class. The chart of his performance is presented in Figure 4.1.

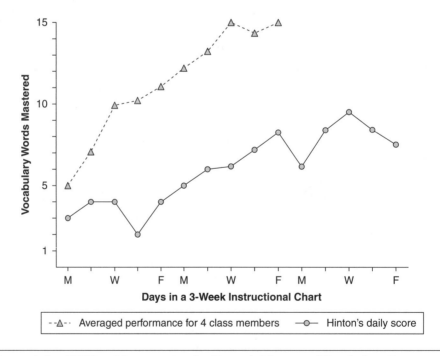

Figure 4.1   RTI Tier 1 Intervention for Hinton's Mastery of Vocabulary Terms

As this chart indicates, Hinton could learn vocabulary terms when they were systematically emphasized in this fashion. The chart presents Hinton's performance, as well as an indication of averaged performance of several average readers who also were in the class. In addition to noting some improvement by Hinton, Ms. Crabtree also noticed that charting Hinton's performance and comparing that to an average of performance from other class members did have the effect of motivating Hinton to try a bit harder. This can be one benefit of RTI, and teachers are encouraged to use this technique.

However, the data chart also shows that Hinton's progress was notably slower than other class members. The learning curve for the other students suggested that most students learned the 15 terms during the first eight to ten days of the unit. Even though Hinton mastered some of the terms, and did progress somewhat, this chart documents that his progress is considerably slower than would be expected. Further, this level of progress would probably not allow him to progress normally through the instruction in American History because in each successive unit he is quite likely to fall further behind. Based on these data, Ms. Crabtree contacted the student support team in the school concerning additional, more intensive instructional services for Hinton. Ultimately, additional interventions likewise showed very slow progress in Hinton's work, and he subsequently was placed in special education for learning disabilities.

It is important to note that, in this case, an eligibility determination was made, in part, based on these charted data from Ms. Crabtree's general education class on Hinton's slower development of vocabulary mastery. In this fashion, even a content area teacher in the upper grades may provide charted data for a tier one or a tier two intervention during the RTI process, and while this is likely to be quite rare, it may be expected of teachers at any grade level. Thus, teachers should be aware of these progress monitoring techniques that may be adapted to secondary content areas.

READING FLUENCY

As students progress in the reading skills previously described—phoneme manipulation, phonics, decoding, and vocabulary development—more emphasis is placed on reading words together and on extracting meaning from the written text (Archer, Gleason, & Vachon, 2003; Denton, Fletcher, Anthony, & Francis, 2006). As noted previously, good readers do not spend excessive time or brain energy in decoding words, but rather read entire words and even phrases together, with appropriate voice intonation, pauses for punctuation, and so on. These effective reading skills cumulatively are referred to as reading fluency.

Reading fluency provides a bridge between word recognition and subsequent reading comprehension, and is considered one of the more important aspects of early reading skill (Denton et al., 2006; Morgan & Sideridis, 2006; O'Connor, White, & Swanson, 2007; NICHD, 2000; Vandenberg, Boon, Fore, & Bender, 2008). When students do not have to concentrate so much energy on recognition and decoding of the terms in the reading, they can invest more energy in understanding the meaning of the reading passage. This differential investment of brain energy can be demonstrated in the areas of the brain that are highly active during the reading process (Sousa, 2005). If the brain of a student reading a particular passage tends to be more active in Broca's area (i.e., the language area that supplies meaning for the words read) than in the visual cortex or Wernicke's area (i.e., the areas that are first involved in visually detecting a stimulus letter and in internal phonemic recognition of the letter sound), that student is concentrating on the meaning of the reading and not on specific decoding efforts. The student would more than likely demonstrate very fluent reading skills on that particular passage.

Fluency in reading develops as a result of monitored reading practice—that is, having students read text that is relatively easy for them and monitoring the errors. In the discussion of reading fluency, the NRP (NICHD, 2000) recognized the following levels of text difficulty:

Independent level—Relatively easy text for the reader, with no more than approximately 1 in 20 words difficult for the reader (95% success)

Instructional level—Challenging but manageable text for the reader, with no more than approximately 1 in 10 words difficult for the reader (90% success)

Frustration level—Difficult text for the reader, with more than 1 in 10 words difficult for the reader (less than 90% success)

The NRP suggested that students should be able to correctly read 95% of the words in a reading passage (i.e., making errors on only 1 in 20 words) in order for the passage to assist the student in developing reading fluency (NICHD, 2000). Further, the various instructional strategies that the NRP identified as effective for developing reading fluency involve having someone monitor the oral reading of the student in one fashion or another. Thus, either self-monitoring or teacher-monitored oral reading can greatly assist students in building reading fluency (NICHD, 2000).

There is a surprising finding of the NRP (NICHD, 2000) related to current practice. The NRP found that there was a lack of support for silent reading programs as an effective reading instructional tactic. Students can benefit from reading aloud for someone, because a teacher, tutor, paraprofessional, or peer buddy can hear and correct the errors. However, in silent reading, there is no error correction procedure, and research has not documented the effectiveness of silent reading programs, such as the Silent Sustained Reading (SSR) or Drop Everything and Read (DEAR) programs. While these sustained silent reading programs are widely implemented around the nation, there seems to be little research evidence that demonstrated that these programs are effective in developing reading skills.

Rather than implementing these silent reading programs, the research supports carefully monitored repeated reading activities to build reading fluency, and a variety of tactics can be used to provide monitoring of the oral reading of students with reading problems (Archer et al., 2003; NICHD, 2000). These are tactics that should be employed by teachers who specialize in reading, but also by teachers teaching subject area content to students who are struggling in reading, since these tactics enhance not only reading fluency, but also comprehension overall. These include the following instructional tactics.

Student-Adult Reading	A student reads one-on-one with an adult. The adult reads the text first, providing a model for the student, and the student then reads the text until the reading becomes fluent—perhaps three or four times through the passage.
Choral Reading	In choral (or unison) reading, students read along as a group.
Tape-Assisted Reading	In tape-assisted reading, students read along as they hear a fluent reader read the book on audiotape. On the first reading, the student should follow along with the words and point to each word as it is read. Next, the student should read along with the tape several times.
Partner Reading	In partner reading, paired students take turns reading aloud to each other, and more fluent readers may be paired with less fluent readers. Each partner may provide assistance to the other.

The Repeated Readings Fluency Strategy

You may have noticed that each of the reading strategies mentioned above involved repeated readings of the same passage until fluency was achieved. Simply stated, one of the most effective ways to increase reading fluency among students with reading difficulties is repeated reading (Denton et al., 2006; Morgan & Sideridis, 2006; O'Connor et al., 2007; Vandenberg et al., 2008; Welsch, 2007). This strategy involves having the student repeatedly read the same passage between three and five times to achieve fluency in the passage as well as learn any specialized vocabulary terms that may be included in the passage. In many examples in the research on repeated reading, the struggling reader reads with a reading fluency model, that may be the teacher, a partner reader, or a computer program that presents a model of fluent reading. From the model, the struggling reader will pick up the correct habits of phrasing in reading, use of punctuation, and word timing. In inclusive classes, the special needs teacher, or perhaps a peer buddy, should be assigned to read with the student and to monitor these repeated readings for students with learning difficulties.

In using a repeated readings strategy, the reading passages have generally been presented at the independent level for the student; that is, a student should be able to read a minimum of 95% of the words correctly initially. The student should be expected to repeatedly read the passage until he or she reaches a criteria of 100% correct on the words in the reading passage. Help with unknown vocabulary words should be offered, either by the teacher or by a peer buddy.

Research on the use of repeated readings has documented that this strategy increases reading fluency for students with reading disabilities in both the elementary grades and secondary grades (Denton et al., 2006; Mastropieri, Leinart, & Scruggs, 1999; NICHD, 2000; Vandenberg et al., 2008). However, research is ongoing in this area. For example, one question involves whether it is more effective to use simpler materials or grade appropriate materials in a repeated reading intervention. Welsch (2007) recently studied that question, by using both easier reading passages and passages written at the instructional level, as recommended in most of the literature. His results indicated that for three of the four children in his study, the repeated reading with easier materials offered the best instructional results over time; for the fourth student the repeated readings at the instructional level was most effective.

Clearly research of this nature will continue to appear relative to how to best implement a repeated reading intervention. For now, teachers should consider implementing repeated readings to enhance fluency for struggling readers, and various guidelines for such implementation have been provided (Mastropieri et al., 1999). These guidelines are presented in Teaching Tip 4.10.

 TEACHING TIP 4.10

Ten Steps for Implementing a Repeated Reading Tactic

1. The teacher should explain to the student how reading practice will help the student read more fluently and understand the content vocabulary better. This tactic typically will lead to less embarrassment in inclusive classes for many students with reading problems. Further, most students with reading problems will be highly motivated to use this tactic, if it is presented in this fashion.

2. The teacher and each student should select an appropriate reading rate goal, and each goal should be stated in terms of words read correctly per minute.

3. Based on the reading instructional level for each individual student (i.e., the reading level at which the student accurately reads a minimum of 90% of the words correctly), the teacher and the student should select reading passages for use in the repeated reading tactic.

4. The teacher should calculate the reading rates for each student. Divide the number of words a child reads correctly in a reading selection by the number of minutes or seconds it takes to read the section.

5. The teacher also should teach students how to calculate, record, and interpret their own reading rates.

6. Tell the students to choose a story that interests them and practice reading the story or reading selection alone, or with a buddy if you wish to use the buddy system. Students should read the story a minimum of three times. If reading the story alone, students should jot down each vocabulary term that they need help with, and between each reading, the teacher or a peer buddy should review those words with the student.

7. Students should be encouraged to ask for help when needed in pronouncing words during the first three readings. This will assist them in learning the new vocabulary terms.

8. After practicing three times, the student should read the story again, as fast as possible, while using a stopwatch or clock with a second hand to time him- or herself.

9. After the final reading the student should record the time on a graph.

10. The student should be encouraged to compare that performance with the reading rate goal set earlier and also with previous performance.

Read Naturally: A Repeated Reading Curriculum

Read Naturally is a recently developed reading curriculum based on repeated reading of brief stories (typically 100 to 200 words) written at a variety of grade levels (Ihnot, Mastoff, Gavin, & Hendrickson, 2001; see the Web site at www.read naturally.com). This program is receiving much attention across the nation and in Canada, since emphasis on reading fluency is increasing at the same time that teachers note a need for scientifically validated reading curriculum for use in RTI procedures. The curriculum has received considerable research support in the brief time since publication (Denton et al., 2006; Hasbrouck, Ihnot, & Rogers, 1999). Also, a new Spanish version of this repeated reading curriculum is currently in development (see the Web site mentioned above).

The program is designed to enhance both reading fluency and reading comprehension by presenting a safe, structured, and highly motivating opportunity for struggling readers to engage in brief reading stories on a variety of interesting topics. The program includes a variety of research-based strategies for improving fluency, such as teacher modeling, goal setting, repeated readings, and daily or weekly progress monitoring. Implementation of *Read Naturally* involves the student reading the same passage multiple times. Initially, a teacher would listen to a student read a story at the student's instructional level. The teacher would mark oral reading errors, and note the time the student began and ended the passage. The teacher then would calculate the number of words read correctly per minute for that initial read-through of the passage. This initial reading is referred to as the "cold timing." Based on this correct per minute reading score, the teacher and the student should jointly set a goal for how quickly the student should read the passage by the end of the instructional period.

Next, the student would re-read the same passage several times, which may be facilitated in a number of ways. In some cases, the teacher may chorally read the passage along with the student, thus modeling fluent reading. Alternatively, the student may read the passage one or more times chorally, accompanied by an audio version of the story passage presented on the computer. Once the student feels he or she has reached proficiency, the student and teacher would again go through the story with the student reading, and the teacher again noting the time, and words read correctly. This is referred to as the "hot timing." In almost every case, the student's hot timing will represent an improvement above the cold timing, and students may then be reinforced for their improvement.

While one might well expect repeatedly reading the same passage will enhance fluency on that passage, the research has shown that such repeated readings is also quite likely to enhance fluency on text to which the student has not been exposed (Denton et al., 2006; O'Connor et al., 2007; Vandenberg et al., 2008). *Read Naturally* has received research support as an effective instructional reading fluency curriculum. Further, it is quite useful in RTI procedures, given the emphasis on daily performance monitoring.

Goal Setting Interventions to Enhance Fluency

While much of the recent reading fluency research has focused on repeated readings, some research has suggested that having students set specific individual goals for their reading fluency is highly effective. Morgan and Sideridis (2006) reported an analysis of literature on reading fluency interventions that suggested goal setting might be more effective than other types of interventions in terms of long-term growth of reading fluency. The RTI case study described below presents an example of a goal setting intervention coupled with a repeated readings curriculum.

When one considers the motivational aspects of having students set specific goals, the impact of goal setting interventions makes sense. Particularly for older students, having a stated goal toward which a student strives daily can greatly impact his or her learning. In particular, coupling such a stated goal with daily reading activities, and carefully monitoring the child's reading fluency performance can be very effective. In fact, Morgan and Sideridis (2006) note that the goal setting strategies they reviewed typically included charting a child's performance over time (generally daily or weekly charts were generated), and sharing that charted data with the child to help the student set meaningful goals. Again, sharing charted daily or weekly performance monitoring data on a student's performance with that student can be one of the most effective motivational strategies available to teachers and should be encouraged; in fact, the RTI mandate stresses such use of charted performance monitoring data. Further, note that the *Read Naturally* curriculum described above included this element of goal setting, by stressing the use of charted data to document for the student how he or she was progressing.

RTI CASE STUDY FOR READING FLUENCY

Thomas is a third grader who has consistently struggled in reading. In Mr. Acre's third grade class, students use a basal reading book for reading instruction, and Mr. Acre has noted that Thomas is having problems in both fluency and comprehension. While Thomas has never been identified as having a learning disability, Mr. Acre did note that his reading grades had never been higher than below average. He suspected that Thomas might have a learning disability, and he wanted to see if a tier one intervention, providing supplemental, more intensive instruction than the basal instruction would alleviate Thomas's reading difficulty. Mr. Acre requested some guidance from the student support team in his building, specifically soliciting their recommendations for a supplemental reading curriculum that focused on reading fluency, because Mr. Acre was convinced that if the reading fluency problem could be addressed, Thomas's reading comprehension problems would also be alleviated somewhat.

The student support team recommended that Mr. Acre implement the *Read Naturally* curriculum described above in the general education class over the next grading period (a period of six weeks). Of course, Mr. Acre was concerned about how long the individualized instruction might take, since the *Read Naturally* curriculum requires the teacher to do a "cold timing" (i.e., a count of words read correctly per minute) and a "hot timing" for each instructional period. What was Mr. Acre to do with the remainder of his third grade class while he worked with Thomas? Of course, this is a major concern that every general education teacher will confront when determining how to develop and implement a tier one intervention in the general education class.

In considering that problem with the student support team, two things became apparent. First, it only takes about two or three minutes to do each timing, and in between those timings, the student is engaged in choral reading with a reading fluency model presented by a computer program. Therefore, Mr. Acre would be free to teach and interact with the rest of the class during that time. This is a very important advantage of using a supplemental reading curricula that is technology based such as *Read Naturally* or other computerized supplemental curricula presented in this book; simply put, these technology-based interventions require less teacher time to implement during the RTI process. This is one reason that a variety of these research-supported interventions are presented in this text.

Next, on two mornings each week—Monday and Wednesday—Mr. Acre had the services of a special education teacher in his inclusive class, so that Mr. Acre could work with Thomas, while that co-teacher led instruction for others in the class. Implementing an RTI procedure at a time when the general education teacher is supported by the inclusion teacher also helps alleviate the time concerns. Based on these factors, and with the assistance of the student support team, Mr. Acre decided that he would be able to work with Thomas a minimum of three days per week (Monday, Wednesday, and Friday) using the *Read Naturally* curriculum. Also, prior to the project, Mr. Acre held a meeting with Thomas and determined that Thomas's goal was to reach 50 correct words per minute. The two then discussed Thomas's performance at least once per week.

The data from the cold timings for that six-week tier one intervention are presented in Figure 4.2. Remember that a "cold timing" is a measure of words read correctly per minute (typically referred to as "words per minute," or wpm) on material that the child has not previously read. Thus, this is the best overall measure to address the effectiveness of the reading fluency intervention over time.

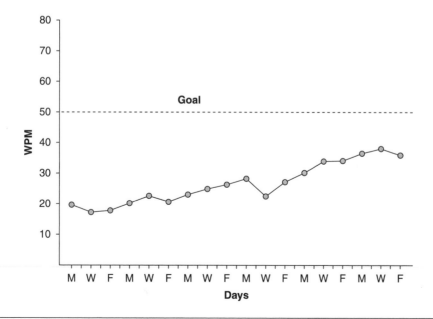

Figure 4.2   Thomas's Reading Fluency—Tier 1 Intervention

As these data indicate, this intervention resulted in a slight improvement in reading fluency over the six weeks, but increases in fluency as shown here are very minor, and would not be expected to result in reading success over the long term. In short, while these data showed that Thomas is improving slightly—that is, he was responding to instruction in a limited fashion—these data also suggest that he was moving forward at such a slow pace that he would continue to fall behind his classmates. Thus, when Mr. Acre presented this data chart to the student support team, it was determined that a second, more intensive intervention tier was needed for Thomas, to assist him in catching up with his classmates.

In discussing this problem with the team, the school reading teacher, Ms. Lovorn, indicated that she could take Thomas into a small group of five students that she worked with each day from 10:15 to 11:00 a.m. Thus, the second intervention would be more intensive than the first, since it involved daily supplemental repeated readings, that lasted for a longer period of time each day over the next six-week grading period.

While different tiers of interventions in the RTI process typically will involve implementation of instruction from different curricula, a change in curricula between intervention tiers is not mandated by federal regulations. What is expected is a more intensive intervention in each successive tier of instruction. In this case, Ms. Lovorn used the *Read Naturally* curriculum in her morning reading group, and the student support team decided to continue with that same curriculum, while presenting Thomas with a much more intensive intervention in terms of exposure time each week. Also, Thomas's performance would be monitored daily during this tier two intervention. The team agreed that Ms. Lovorn should work with Thomas daily each week for the next six-week grading period, while monitoring his reading fluency using the cold timing results each day as his measure of progress. She was urged to chart those data, and then present the results of that tier two intervention to the team. Data for that six-week grading period are presented in Figure 4.3.

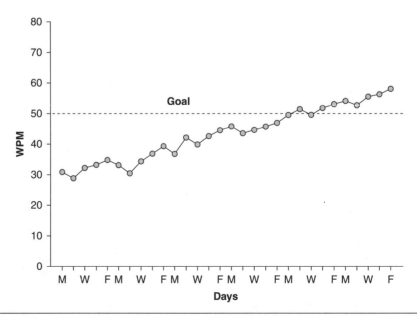

Figure 4.3   Thomas's Reading Fluency—Tier 2 Intervention

As these data show, the more intensive intervention resulted in a very significant increase in Thomas's reading fluency. Ms. Lovorn presented these data to the student support team and indicated that the second tier intervention was working well enough that Thomas had a very good chance of "catching up" to his classmates by the end of the year. Thus, in this case the second intervention demonstrated that Thomas would and did respond to effective instruction when the instruction was intense enough. Therefore, there was no need to consider him further for placement in special education based on a learning disability.

However, the team did determine that the intensive supplemental intervention should be continued throughout the remainder of the school year, since that level of intensity was required to assist Thomas in his reading progress. The team requested that Ms. Lovorn continue to work with Thomas daily, and monitor his performance daily in the same fashion, to assure his continued progress. Further, the team in this case decided to review those data for the remainder of the academic year at the end of school, and then make any additional recommendations that might be necessary for the next year, to assure Thomas's continuing progress in reading.

In this RTI case study, several things are apparent. First, even when a tier one intervention doesn't result in appropriate progress, it is quite often the case that a tier two intervention will; this results from increased intensity of instruction in each succeeding tier. Next, educators must realize that when an intervention tier does result in appropriate academic progress, that tier of intervention should be continued long enough to help the student catch up to his or her peers. At that point, a successful intervention has been identified, and even though the eligibility question is settled (i.e., the student should not be considered learning disabled because he or she responded to effective intervention), the successful intervention must continue to alleviate the ongoing academic problems. In most cases, such longer-term interventions will continue to be monitored under the purview of the student support team as in the example above.

CONCLUSION

This chapter has presented a series of strategies for increasing vocabulary and reading fluency for students with reading difficulties in both early reading and during the later elementary years. The importance of exposure to new vocabulary terms, and the students' pronunciation of vocabulary development, was discussed and emphasis was placed on learning several techniques for increasing vocabulary. Several of these strategies represent ideas used in kindergarten and first grade that can also be applied in the upper elementary grades to help students with learning difficulties master vocabulary terms.

Next, vocabulary development was presented as a critical reading skill, since in almost every elementary school subject, a specialized vocabulary is used to represent the foundational concepts and constructs. Thus, having a limited ability to learn vocabulary can limit severely one's comprehension in virtually every subject area. A series of strategies has been described, including using graphic organizers, semantic webbing, SFAs, keyword learning strategies, cloze procedures, and concept circles. Using one or more of these strategies to strengthen vocabulary in each unit of study will result in increased variation of instruction and in increased academic progress for students with reading difficulties, as well as every other student in the class. These strategies should enable teachers in virtually every elementary grade to invest time in vocabulary development, while strengthening their students' understanding of the complex constructs involved in the lessons.

Finally, several strategies were presented to assist students with reading disabilities to develop reading fluency during the elementary years. Strategies include monitored reading practice, repeated readings strategies, the *Read Naturally* curriculum, and goal setting strategies. With an emphasis on reading fluency as aggressive vocabulary development, most students in the elementary grades will progress nicely in their reading endeavors.

WHAT'S NEXT?

As readers become more sophisticated, the emphases in reading instruction change, as do the techniques and brain capacities involved in reading. From approximately Grade 3 onward, the focus of a great deal of reading instruction is not on developing reading skills themselves, but on developing comprehension of the content covered by the reading. The next chapter focuses on a variety of strategies to facilitate content comprehension in Grades 3 through 7.

REFERENCES

Archer, A. L., Gleason, M. M., & Vachon, V. L. (2003). Decoding and fluency: Foundation skills for struggling older readers. *Learning Disability Quarterly, 26*(2), 89–102.

Bender, W. N. (1985). Strategies for helping the mainstreamed student in secondary social studies classes. *The Social Studies, 76,* 269–271.

Bender, W. N., & Shores, C. (2007). *Response to intervention: A practical guide for every teacher.* Thousand Oaks, CA: Corwin Press.

Bender, W. N. (2008). *Differentiating instruction for students with learning disabilities* (2nd ed.). Thousand Oaks, CA: Corwin Press.

Biemiller, A., & Slonim, N. (2001). Estimating root word vocabulary growth in normative and advantaged populations: Evidence for a common sequence of vocabulary acquisition. *Journal of Educational Psychology, 93,* 498–520.

Bos, C. S., Mather, N., Silver-Pacuilla, H., & Narr, R. F. (2000). Learning to teach early literacy skills collaboratively. *Teaching Exceptional Children, 32*(5), 38–45.

Bryant, D. P., Goodwin, M., Bryant, B. R., & Higgins, K. (2003). Vocabulary instruction for students with learning disabilities: A review of the research. *Learning Disability Quarterly, 26*(2) 117–128.

Bryant, D. P., Ugel, N., Thompson, S., & Hamff, A. (1999). Instructional strategies for content-area reading instruction. *Intervention in School and Clinic, 34*(5), 293–302.

Coyne, M. D., McCoach, D. B., & Kapp, S. (2007). Vocabulary intervention for kindergarten students: Comparing extended instruction to embedded instruction and incidental exposure. *Learning Disability Quarterly, 30*(2), 74–88.

Davis, G. N., Lindo, E. J., & Compton, D. L. (2007). Children at risk for reading failure: Constructing an early screening measure. *Teaching Exceptional Children, 39*(5), 32–39.

Denton, C. A., Fletcher, J. M., Anthony, J. L., & Francis, D. J. (2006). An evaluation of intensive intervention for students with persistent reading difficulties. *Journal of Learning Disabilities, 39*(5), 447–486.

DiCecco, V. M., & Gleason, M. M. (2002). Using graphic organizers to attain relational knowledge from expository text. *Journal of Learning Disabilities, 35,* 306–320.

Foil, C. R., & Alber, S. R. (2002). Fun and effective ways to build your students' vocabulary. *Intervention in School and Clinic, 37*(3), 131–139.

Foorman, B. R. (2007). Primary prevention in classroom reading instruction. *Teaching Exceptional Children, 39*(5), 24–31.

Hall, S. L. (2000). *Report of the National Reading Panel: Teaching children to read.* Retrieved January 20, 2003, from http://www.ldonline.org.

Hasbrouck, J. E., Ihnot, C., & Rogers, G. (1999). Read Naturally: A strategy to increase oral reading fluency. *Reading Research and Instruction, 39,* 27–38.

Ihnot, C., Mastoff, J., Gavin, J., & Hendrickson, L. (2001). *Read Naturally.* St. Paul, MN: Read Naturally.

Kame'enui, E. J., Carnine, D. W., Dixon, R. C., Simmons, D. C., & Coyne, M. D. (2002). *Effective teaching strategies that accommodate diverse learners* (2nd ed.). Upper Saddle River, NJ: Merrill-Prentice Hall.

King-Sears, M. E., Mercer, C. D., & Sindelar, P. T. (1992). Towards independence with keyword mnemonics: A strategy for science vocabulary instruction. *Remedial and Special Education, 13,* 22–23.

Mastropieri, M. A., Leinart, A., & Scruggs, T. E. (1999). Strategies to increase reading fluency. *Intervention in School and Clinic, 34*(5), 278–283.

Mastropieri, M. A., & Scruggs, T. E. (2002). *Effective instruction for special education.* Austin, TX: ProEd.

Mastropieri, M. A., Scruggs, T. E., & Graetz, J. E. (2003). Reading comprehension instruction for secondary students: Challenges for struggling students and teachers. *Learning Disability Quarterly, 26*(2), 103–116.

Mayfield, L. G. (2000, November). *The effects of structured one-on-one tutoring in sight word recognition of first grade students at risk for reading failure.* Paper presented at the Mid-South Educational Research Association Annual Meeting, Bowling Green, KY.

Morgan, P. L., & Sideridis, G. D. (2006). Contrasting the effectiveness of fluency interventions for students with or at risk for learning disabilities: A multilevel random coefficient modeling meta-analysis. *Learning Disabilities Research, 21*(4), 191–210.

National Institute of Child Health and Development. (2000). *Teaching children to read: An evidence-based assessment of the scientific research literature on reading and its implications for reading instruction* (Report of the National Reading Panel). Retrieved May 23, 2002, from http://www.nichd.nih.gov/publications/nrp/findings.cfm.

O'Connor, R. E., White, A., & Swanson, H. L. (2007). Repeated reading versus continuous reading: Influences on reading fluency and comprehension. *Exceptional Children, 74*(1), 31–46.

Sousa, D. A. (2005). *How the brain learns to read.* Thousand Oaks, CA: Corwin Press.

Vacca, R. T., & Vacca, J. A. L. (2002). *Content area reading: Literacy and learning across the curriculum.* Boston: Allyn & Bacon.

Vandenberg, A., Boon, R., Fore, C., & Bender, W. N. (2008). The effects of repeated readings on the fluency and comprehension for high school students with learning disabilities. *Learning Disabilities: A Multidisciplinary Journal, 15*(1), 18–27.

Welsch, R. G. (2007). Using experimental analysis to determine interventions for reading fluency and recalls of students with learning disabilities. *Learning Disability Quarterly, 30*(2), 115–130.

Xin, F., Glaser, C. W., & Rieth, H. (1996). Multimedia reading: Using anchored instruction and video technology in vocabulary lessons. *Teaching Exceptional Children, 29*(2), 45–49.

Gaining 5
Meaning
From Reading

Strategies Presented in This Chapter Include

✓ Story Grammar

✓ Student Think-Alouds

✓ Question Answering

✓ Gist Summaries

✓ Improvisational Drama

✓ Coop-Dis-Q (Cooperative Discussion and Questioning)

✓ Collaborative Strategic Reading

✓ Bibliotherapy

✓ RTI Case Study for Gaining Meaning From Reading

READING COMPREHENSION AND THE BRAIN

The ultimate goal of reading is to develop children's ability to gain meaning from text or to comprehend what they have read. The National Reading Panel (NRP) indicated that one gains meaning from text when engaged in "intentional, problem solving thinking processes" (NICHD, 2000, p. 14). To enhance text comprehension, readers need to relate actively the ideas contained in print to their own background knowledge and then construct mental representations in their memory. This active engagement is one cornerstone of the brain compatible instruction research described previously. As noted in Sousa's

(2001) model of reading described in Chapter 1, when an individual encounters a word in text, several things must happen for meaning to be associated with that word. First, the word is recorded in the visual cortex and then decoded by the angular gyrus to separate the word into its basic sounds or phonemes. Then the word is identified by activation in Broca's area. Finally, the brain's vocabulary store, reasoning, concept formation abilities, and activity in Wernicke's area combine to give meaning to the word. Thus, all parts of the brain must process information accurately in order for appropriate meaning to be attributed to the word.

Students who have learning difficulties may process information differently and thus struggle with reading comprehension. Some of these students may have difficulty with input or receiving the information (i.e., the students struggle to get information into the brain). Others get the information into the brain, but then have processing problems once the information is there. Still others get the information into the brain and process it appropriately, but have problems with output or expressing the information in oral or written form. Sousa (2001, p. 94) indicated that students with learning difficulties might manifest deficits in reading comprehension in the following ways:

- Do not understand the words used in the text
- Do not have adequate background information about text information
- Are not familiar with semantic and syntactic structures that help predict relationships between words
- Are not knowledgeable about writing conventions (e.g., humor, explanation, dialogue)
- Cannot read between the lines to infer meaning
- Have difficulty remembering information

The NRP further noted that reading comprehension could be improved by the explicit teaching of specific cognitive strategies (NICHD, 2000). The strategies enable struggling readers to "reason strategically" when barriers to their understanding arise (NICHD, p. 14). One key to the success of these strategies is teacher demonstration or modeling of the strategies for the students until the students can perform the strategies independently. Teacher demonstration and modeling are part of the scaffolding process discussed in Chapter 3. Thus, students receive more support when they are learning new or difficult information and as they begin to show mastery of the information, the support gradually is removed. Scaffolded instruction can be beneficial to all students, but especially is crucial for students with learning difficulties.

The NRP conducted an extensive literature review of studies published since 1980 in which they identified seven categories of text comprehension instruction that are supported by research (NICHD, 2000, p. 15):

- *Comprehension monitoring*, where readers learn how to be aware of their understanding of the material
- *Cooperative learning*, where students learn reading strategies together
- *Use of graphic and semantic organizers (including story maps)*, where readers make graphic representations of the material to assist comprehension

- *Question answering,* where readers answer questions posed by the teacher and receive immediate feedback
- *Question generation,* where readers ask themselves questions about various aspects of the story
- *Story structure,* where students are taught to use the structure of the story as a means of helping them recall story content to answer questions about what they have read
- *Summarization,* where readers are taught to integrate ideas and generalize from the text information

Evidence from the NRP's literature analysis suggests that reading comprehension strategies should be taught in combination as a "multiple strategy method" (NICHD, 2000, p. 15). Younger students with learning difficulties may benefit from learning the various substrategy routines and then later combining them into a multiple strategy.

This chapter will present an array of reading comprehension strategies for elementary through middle grades. Each of these strategies includes several of the seven levels of text comprehension instruction supported by the NRP. Teachers may use this chapter by reading it from beginning to end or by selecting one or two strategies and reading only about these. After a brief introduction, the following topics will be addressed for each strategy: (a) What is this strategy? (b) Why use this strategy? and (c) How can teachers use this strategy? The sections detailing how teachers and students can use the strategies are divided into the following subheadings: (a) advance preparation, (b) before reading, (c) during reading, (d) after reading, and (e) follow-up activities. Many of the strategies discussed in this chapter are presented as being used with a whole class, but can be adapted easily for use with small groups or individuals. Also, the strategies are presented when all class members are reading the same passages. If the intent is to promote listening comprehension, then it may be likely that students with diverse reading abilities can all hone their listening comprehension skills by hearing the same passage read aloud. If, instead, the intent is for students to practice comprehension skills from silent reading, then reading passages will need to be selected to meet individual student needs. Once again, the strategies presented are flexible enough to be adapted for students' various abilities.

 **REFLECTIVE EXERCISE 5.1
SELECTING NEW COMPREHENSION TACTICS**

Review the list of comprehension tactics from the NRP and make notes on the tactics already in use in your class. Be sure to distinguish between tactics that are built into the text and curriculum and tactics that you initiate. Based on this, which additional tactics would you like to try? Also, visit the Reading Lady Web site (http://www.read inglady.com/index.php?module=pagemaster&PAGE_user_op=view_ page&PAGE_id=13) to find printable posters (e.g., asking questions, visualizing, repairing comprehension) to supplement your comprehension lessons.

You can use any of the following strategies and tactics to help students with learning difficulties learn and practice comprehension skills and to help you evaluate their comprehension mastery. As appropriate, try to incorporate various types of comprehension practice into the strategies. Some students will need to focus on *literal* comprehension, such as lessons in story context, sequence of story events, main ideas, and essential details. Others are ready for *inferential comprehension,* in which they determine cause and effect, predict events, and express characters' perspectives. Still others are ready for *critical comprehension* activities such as demonstrating moral or aesthetic concerns, analyzing the author's intent, or providing evidence of literature appreciation (Choate, Enright, Miller, Poteet, & Rakes, 1995). Students with learning difficulties may struggle with literal comprehension as well as find the abstract nature of inferential and critical comprehension tasks quite challenging.

 TEACHING TIP 5.1

Teaching Reading Comprehension Strategies

Begin by teaching one or two strategies at a time. Introduce new strategies only when strategies taught earlier are well established. Teach strategies to students in context where they are expected to practice reading comprehension, not as a separate part of the curriculum.

1. Start with materials at easier reading levels to ensure initial success. Then assist students using the same comprehension strategy with more difficult materials.

2. Individualize instruction by deciding (a) what strategy will be most beneficial to a particular group of students, (b) what type of self-regulatory procedure is appropriate for each student, and (c) the manner in which feedback should be given to the student to monitor his or her progress in using the strategy and in reading comprehension.

3. Scaffold instruction by fading instructional supports (e.g., prompting) as students demonstrate competency in using the strategy. This may be difficult to do because students may be unsure if they are using the strategy correctly for a while.

4. Students with learning and reading disabilities must be taught explicitly to generalize strategies or to be able to apply them in a variety of settings. Teachers can help students to generalize learned strategies by showing students how to monitor their progress.

SOURCE: Adapted from Swanson and DeLaPaz (1998).

STORY GRAMMAR

Struggling readers and students with learning difficulties may have difficulty with reading comprehension because they do not understand the structure of the story. They cannot identify the main character(s) of the story or the plot. They may not know how the character(s) feel about a particular problem or story event. These readers may be able to identify isolated details about a story, but often the details they can identify may be interesting trivia rather than ideas essential to the story. Story grammar reflects story structure just as English grammar reflects language structure (Hagood, 1997).

What Is Story Grammar?

Story grammar is a cognitive structure that aids the comprehension of simple stories (Hagood, 1997) by identifying story elements and their temporal and causal relationships (Montague & Graves, 1993). It provides a set of rules to identify the important story ideas and a method for analyzing stories into their meaningful parts. Story grammar can help struggling readers to become efficient readers by establishing a framework to keep track of important component parts in the story. These parts often consist of (a) a setting, (b) a problem experienced by the main character(s), and (c) the events that occur as the main character(s) attempt to solve a problem (Hagood).

Why Use Story Grammar?

Hagood (1997) noted that story grammar strategies can help elementary students improve their reading and writing skills, particularly those students who are low achievers or have learning disabilities. Gardill and Jitendra (1999) found that direct instruction in story mapping improved the reading comprehension of middle school students with learning disabilities. When teachers provide detailed and explicit instruction as well as repetitive experiences of analyzing and manipulating story grammar, it helps students to internalize a story's structure (Hagood). The internalization of a distinct organizational structure aids both the reading comprehension and the writing of narrative stories.

There are a variety of story grammar strategies from which teachers may choose, including (a) self-questioning, (b) story maps, (c) comparing and contrasting similar stories, and (d) manipulating story grammar elements (Hagood, 1997). These strategies can be used as part of the regular curriculum, making sure that students receive explicit instruction (e.g., teacher modeling, teacher guidance, and repetition; Gambrell & Chasen, 1991). Hagood noted that story grammar strategies such as these could help teachers to meet students' individual needs. In self-questioning, students learn to use a set of standard questions to guide story reading to help them identify the important story elements. Students with learning difficulties may need a more concrete structure such as a pictorial story map to help them to visually recognize and organize key story elements. A story map helps students establish relationships between their background knowledge and the reading passage by focusing on the text structure (Hagood). Idol and Croll (1987) indicated that students who use a story map during reading could improve their ability to categorize relevant information. Davis (1994) found that third graders who used a prereading story mapping procedure improved both their literal and their inferential comprehension. Hagood noted that book discussions such as comparing two books on similar topics help students to grow as readers and learners. Idol and Croll also indicated that students can internalize elements of story grammar through writing and drawing. The levels of comprehension instruction included in story grammar are (a) cooperative learning, (b) graphic and semantic organizers, (c) question answering, (d) question generation, and (e) story structure.

How Can Teachers Use Story Grammar?

Four tactics for using story grammar will be discussed: (a) self-questioning, (b) story maps, (c) analyzing and comparing elements of similar stories, and (d) manipulating story grammar elements.

Self-Questioning

Advance Preparation. The teacher will select a familiar story to read aloud to the students and write questions such as the following on the board (Hagood, 1997):

1. What is this story about?

2. Where does this story take place?

3. What is the problem in this story?

4. What happens while the main character in this story is trying to solve the problem?

5. How is the problem solved?

6. How does the main character in this story feel about the solution?

Before Reading. You should introduce the students to the story and to the questions on the board. Be sure to appeal to both visual and auditory learners by writing the questions on the board and reading the questions aloud. You can let students know that they will read the story to enjoy it as well as to answer the questions on the board, thus establishing a purpose for reading. You will need to indicate that the questions will help them to identify and remember important information about the story. Such explicit statements help students with learning difficulties to understand the purpose of the task and focus on the teacher's expectations.

During Reading. You should read the story aloud and model answering the questions while you are reading. The teacher shows students how a good reader refers to the questions while reading to determine if any important information can be gleaned to help answer the questions. You will need to scaffold the amount of assistance you provide to students in this phase. Once students seem to understand how to proceed with self-questioning, you then can have them read a story aloud and attempt to answer the questions. Finally, students should read silently and independently answer the story questions. This scaffolding or gradually turning responsibility for self-questioning during reading over to the students may take several lessons. You should not take away assistance until you are sure that students will be successful with less assistance from you. The teacher always should be available to provide support when needed. Students with learning difficulties may need more help than others.

After Reading. You will need to reinforce the idea that self-questioning during reading is a strategy that good readers use to help them learn and remember important information about the story (i.e., main character(s), setting, and plot or problem solution). You will indicate, too, that focusing on the questions prior to and during reading may reduce the amount of effort later in trying to answer the questions. This particularly may be appealing to students with learning difficulties who might put forth a great deal of time and effort, but make little progress because they likely will use ineffective and inefficient strategies unless they are taught better strategies.

Follow-Up Activities. Once students are familiar with the typical questions that they should ask themselves while reading each story, you can have them generate additional questions that may help them learn important information about other familiar stories. This activity will help them to follow a basic story grammar structure, but also to vary it when appropriate.

Note, however, that although this story grammar strategy as presented is used with whole class instruction, it may be adapted for use with small groups or individuals. Students with learning difficulties may benefit from working with a partner or in a small group to generate and discuss answers to the questions. These students need to be exposed to the kind of thinking that "good readers" do.

Story Maps

Advance Preparation. Often story parts or elements are organized into a graphic organizer called a story map. The teacher will prepare the story map to be used in the lesson. Hagood (1997) suggested listing the following headings on the story map: (a) characters, (b) setting, (c) problem, (d) events, (e) solution, and (f) how do the characters feel about the solution? The Web site http://content.scholastic.com/browse/article.jsp?id=2994 provides a printable version of a story map graphic organizer suitable for elementary students. A lesson using a story map along with a rubric for evaluating students' completed story maps can be found at http://www.educationworld.com/a_tsl/archives/01-1/lesson0019.shtml. A more advanced story map is located at http://www.interventioncentral.org/htmdocs/interventions/rdngcompr/storymap.php.

Before Reading. You will need to show the students a copy of the story map that will be used in the lesson and discuss each element on the map. Students with learning difficulties need to be exposed to "whole to part to whole." In other words, they need to be given an overview about the story map (i.e., the whole), given a demonstration of the parts in detail, and finally shown how the parts relate to each other to form the story map (i.e., the whole).

During Reading. You can model using a story map as you read the story aloud (Hagood, 1997). Reading the story aloud enables all students to hone their listening skills and eliminates the pressure for students with learning difficulties who are not fluent readers. You should follow a similar scaffolding procedure as listed for the self-questioning strategy. That is, gradually turn over responsibility for using the story map as students are ready to accept this responsibility. Once you have modeled using a story map, you will guide the students using a story map while either you or they read a story aloud. You may want to work with students who are struggling in a small group to read the story aloud, before asking them to do so individually. You must make sure to stop students at specific points in the story for them to identify the element that has just been read. If students give incorrect responses, then you should provide feedback to guide them to the correct response. Sometimes students with learning difficulties believe that task completion is the only objective of the lesson. By stopping a lesson at specific points in the story to identify and discuss story elements, students can learn that the task involves certain critical steps along the way. Finally, when students are ready, you can have them complete the story maps independently during silent reading. Your goal should be to eventually phase out the story maps without decreasing students' level of comprehension (Hagood). Keep in mind that reducing the scaffolding or support may take several lessons and some students may continue to need more support than others. Some students with learning difficulties may find that the visual representations that story maps provide are something they need to aid story comprehension.

After Reading. Some students may benefit from reviewing their completed story maps. Review may help them to see how all the story elements are tied together

---

☞ **TEACHING TIP 5.2**

Questions to Prompt Discussion and Aid Story Map Completion

To help students focus on why something happened rather than what happened:
> Why did _____ act in this way?
> What was _____ thinking when this occurred?
> What did _____ want at this point?
> How does _____ feel now?

To help students consider the character's perspective rather than their own:
> Is that the way you would have felt?
> In what way is _____ different from you?
> Since _____ is different in this way, how do you think he felt?
> Let me reread some of the parts that may help us understand why _____ might respond differently than you would.

To help students focus on the story as a whole rather than just one particular part of the story:
> What else might _____ be thinking? Be feeling?
> Think about what's happened in the story so far that clues us in to other feelings that _____ might be having.
> What about the part where _____ did ___ and ___ in the beginning?
> What does that tell you about what she or he might be thinking now?

To help students focus on other perspectives rather than just one character's perspective:
> We mentioned (character 1), what about (character 2)? How was he or she feeling?
> What did (character 1) believe that (character 2) was thinking/feeling/wanting?
> What did (character 2) believe that (character 1) was thinking/feeling/wanting?
> When (character 1) did that, how did he or she think that (character 2) would react?
> What was (character 2) believing about (character 1) when he or she did that?

SOURCE: Adapted from Emery (1996, p. 539).

to form the big picture of the story. The review may help them to avoid getting lost in the trees (i.e., focusing too much attention to details and losing sight of the main ideas) as students with learning difficulties may have a tendency to do.

Follow-Up Activities. Once students have learned to use story grammar to aid their reading, you should teach them how to use it to increase their writing skills. Some students have trouble organizing narrative stories that they create (Hagood, 1997). When they are shown how to organize their ideas into writing for a specific audience, students likely will gain greater appreciation for all stories and receive pleasure from engaging in the writing process.

Another variation on the use of story maps is to include characters' perspectives. Stein and Levine (1990) stated that nine- to eleven-year-old readers focus more on *what* occurs in the story rather than *why* the particular things are occurring. Also, even young children respond to story characters using knowledge of their own culture and familiarities (Emery, 1996). Readers who are seven to eleven years old consider the main character's perspective rather than recognizing multiple perspectives and relationships. Story maps with character perspectives can help students understand why things happened in the story and how characters may have perspectives different from their own (Emery, 1996). A reproducible blank chart shown on page 164 will help students focus on multiple perspectives in stories. Feel free to copy this chart for use in your class.

Still another variation in using the story map is cooperative story mapping. Mathes and Fuchs (1997) suggested that heterogeneous groups of three to five students working together using a story map could improve their reading comprehension in a learning environment where all students are placed in roles of academic value. Prerequisite skills for cooperative story mapping include familiarity with story grammar elements, knowledge of how to map a story, and knowledge of how to work in a cooperative group. Note that students with learning difficulties can benefit from explicit instruction in how to work in cooperative groups prior to working in small groups with their peers. Similar to traditional story mapping, students read and review (or skim) the same story. Then they complete the story map in their groups. Each student serves as a leader for one story element such as main character or setting and one major event. Student 1 may be the leader for the main character and the first major event while Student 2 is the leader for the setting and the second major event, and so on. Although leadership roles change weekly, the leader responsibilities remain constant. Mathes and Fuchs (1997) stated that all students are taught the following leader routine:

1. *Tell.* The leader tells the answer for a specific story part and presents evidence in support of his or her answer.

2. *Ask.* The leader asks other students in the group to share their answer. All must present evidence to support their answers.

3. *Discuss.* The leader guides group members to discuss the story part and ensures that, in each instance, they attempt to reach consensus. When the group cannot agree, the leader has final say.

4. *Record.* The leader records the group's answer.

5. *Report.* The leader reports the group's answer for the story part.

Focusing on Multiple Perspectives

Character 1's Perspective	Story Event	Character 2's Perspective

TEACHING TIP 5.3

Facilitating Student Discussion After Completion of Story Map

Mathes and Fuchs (1997) made the following suggestions to help the teachers to facilitate student discussion following groups' completion of the story map.

1. Ask members of a cooperative group to report their answer, restate the answer, and then ask if another group has a different response.

2. Discuss disagreements in a nonjudgmental fashion so students feel comfortable about sharing opinions.

3. Encourage the class to discuss conflicting answers using the text as evidence.

4. Ask why some answers may be better than others, providing help when necessary.

5. Lead students to agreement using the term *our answer* to provide the class with a sense of collaboration and ownership.

6. Review why story elements are important and how they are related to each other in the course of discussion.

7. Discuss the four major events as one unit of common elements listed in a correct basic sequence.

Comparing and Contrasting Similar Stories

Advance Preparation. The teacher should make sure that students are familiar with the different kinds of story elements. Helping your students work through the self-questioning and story map strategies mentioned previously will give them exposure to story elements prior to trying to analyze and compare them. You will prepare a comparison table that includes the five story elements being discussed (i.e., characters, setting, problem, events, solution). Feel free to reproduce the blank comparison table on page 166 for use in your class. Hagood (1997) stated that the table provides an advance organizer for the activity. You also might like to visit http://www.readwritethink.org/lesson_images/ lesson275/ compcon_chart.pdf for a compare and contrast graphic organizer that could be used to compare and contrast similar stories. A Venn diagram found at http://www.eduplace.com/graphicorganizer/pdf/venn.pdf would be suitable for younger students to compare and contrast similar stories.

Before Reading. Show the students a copy of the graphic organizer that will be used for the activity and talk about the kind of information that they will need to find during the reading of the story.

During Reading. To expedite the activity, you may want to read one or both of the stories aloud to the class and ask them to listen for key story elements. Hagood

Comparison Chart for Comparing and Analyzing Story Grammar Elements

Story	Characters	Setting	Problem	Events	Solution

(1997) suggested reading a book such as *The Egyptian Cinderella* (Climo, 1989) to compare with the traditional *Cinderella* story. You can model how to fill in the graphic organizer showing the comparison of the two stories. Students can help you complete the graphic organizer as they discuss the similarities and differences of the stories.

After Reading. Like with story maps, some students may benefit from reviewing the completed comparison table. Review may help them to see how stories can be alike and different at the same time.

Follow-Up Activities. Once the teacher and students have worked together to complete the comparison graphic organizer of two stories and students appear to be comfortable with this activity, then some of the scaffolding or teacher support can be removed. You may choose to read new stories to the students, have them read the stories independently, or have them work in small groups to read the stories for comparison. Then either ask the students to form groups or designate teacher-selected small groups to complete the comparison graphic organizer. Make sure that students understand what they are being asked to do. Another form of scaffolding that might be provided is to gradually move the students when appropriate into comparing books that are less concrete (Hagood, 1997). Students with learning difficulties may have difficulty with abstract ideas, so they may need a lot of support when working with books that are less concrete. Also, you might try using a different format for comparison such as a Venn diagram, an example of which can be found at www.teachervision.com/lesson-plans/lesson-2281.html.

Manipulating Story Grammar Elements

Advance Preparation. To make sure that students are familiar with the different kinds of story elements, you may want to help them work through the self-questioning or story map strategies mentioned above prior to trying to manipulate the story grammar elements.

Before Reading. Inform students of their assigned task after reading or reviewing a familiar story. If students know in advance what they will be asked to do, they can pay attention to important story points and be thinking about how they might like to change an element of the story by drawing, retelling, or rewriting it. This is a crucial step in scaffolding instruction for students with learning difficulties. Since they may need more time to process information, letting them know the teacher's expectations in advance gives them the extra time needed to process information quickly.

During Reading. You will re-read or review a familiar story. Students or the teacher may do the re-reading. Although students may be familiar with the story, re-reading or reviewing it may help them to have key points fresh in their minds and to recall some important information that they may have forgotten otherwise. An additional benefit for students with learning difficulties is that re-reading a familiar story enables them to boost their reading confidence level and work on fluency.

After Reading. You will need to make sure that students understand the task that they are to perform. For example, Hagood (1997) suggested that you ask students to rewrite the traditional story of *Goldilocks and the Three Bears* by changing the setting to Alaska or letting students choose a new setting for the story. Story redrawing, retelling, or rewriting enables students to activate their background knowledge and tap into their imaginations. If a student recently had taken a trip to another state or had seen a movie filmed in a different region of the United States from where the student lived, then the student may be able to incorporate some of his or her new knowledge about geography with the familiar story. As with any new task that a teacher asks students to perform, you will need to model how to do the task. Hagood noted that the teacher modeling might include making story adjustments such as giving Goldilocks a heavy coat and hat to wear in Alaska. Also, Goldilocks may have been lost due to a snowstorm, and the three bears may have been polar bears that lived in an igloo.

Follow-Up Activities. Once students have practiced changing one story element, then the teacher and students can experiment with changing others such as the characters (Hagood, 1997). Give your students opportunities to share their versions of the stories with their peers in order to compare and contrast how they manipulated various story grammar elements. Such sharing can encourage students with learning difficulties to take risks with their learning. Students will be exposed to different kinds of thinking and reasoning as they share how they manipulated story grammar elements.

Research supports the use of story maps and story grammar for elementary students (cf. Baumann & Bergeron, 1993; Idol, 1987; Schmitt & O'Brien, 1986). Dymock (2007) stated that story comprehension is a critical academic skill in the early grades. Students who learn narrative text structure in Grade 1 have a foundation to help them comprehend more complex narrative text in later elementary and in secondary grades.

Foley (2000) explored psychological theories employed in story mapping. Feature analysis is a pattern-recognition theory in which visual configurations such as letters and words can be identified because their features are compared to lists of features that the individual has stored in memory. Signal detection is another type of pattern-recognition theory in which an individual scans a large amount of information to locate a particular piece of information. The individual must be vigilant when looking for the piece of information and ignore the irrelevant information. Schema theory involves connecting new information with existing knowledge. Metacognitive theory refers to thinking about one's thinking. All of these theories are present in story mapping tasks. The student completing a story map must be vigilant in scanning (i.e., signal detection) a large amount of information (i.e., the story) to find a particular piece of information (e.g., the setting) while ignoring the irrelevant information. To find the pertinent piece of information, the student must examine the critical features of the information (i.e., feature analysis) while comparing new information with known information (i.e., schema theory) and being aware of what he or she is thinking (i.e., metacognition).

What prompted Foley's (2000) exploration of theories that support story mapping was the fact that she noticed that many of her first grade students' story maps were similar in their responses. She had expected her students' story maps to somewhat reflect their diverse home environments and experiences. She concluded that when creating story maps, students or readers follow particular procedures that reduce stories to elements (i.e., parts) and then the elements are put back together to form the completed story map (i.e., the whole). Foley concluded that story maps help students to identify the author's presumed intentions, but may not allow for the students' individual responses to the work.

To extend Foley's (2000) thinking, the authors of this book note that story mapping can provide the much-needed structure for students with learning difficulties to comprehend stories and passages that they read. When the intent is for students to provide their own responses to what they have read, artwork, poetry, and other projects that encourage individual responses may be warranted. Explicit instruction may be needed to help some students to comprehend narrative text (Smolkin & Donovan, 2002). Dymock (2007) noted that teachers can help students to understand the structure of narrative text.

Boulineau, Fore, Hagan-Burke, and Burke (2004) conducted a descriptive study replicating the use of story mapping with six third and fourth grade students with learning disabilities. They found that each participant's correct identification of story-grammar elements increased using a story map intervention. Before reading the story, the teacher showed the students a story-map transparency and taught them each story-grammar element individually. The teacher questioned the students about each story-grammar element, summarized each element, and led students in a discussion of each element. Instruction took place and then students read parts of the story aloud. Finally, students independently prepared their story maps. This intervention occurred daily until students were able to complete a story map achieving 90% accuracy for three consecutive sessions. At that point, story-grammar instruction was discontinued. Maintenance procedures were implemented. Students continued to take turns reading passages. The teacher encouraged students to think about story-grammar elements and visualize the story map. Then students completed a blank story map independently. The researchers found that students were able to maintain their use of the story-mapping procedure even when instruction was terminated. The researchers stated that these results were achieved using a small number of students with learning disabilities in the study. Also, they noted that the students were not given any time limitations for completing their story maps.

Fink (2008) indicated that knowing story elements helps students to understand what is occurring in a book or novel and when they are more involved with the story they pay more attention to the details. She published a lesson plan found at the Web site http://www.readwritethink.org/lessons/lesson_view.asp?id=236, in which students in Grades 3–5 prepare a story map through the use of a comic strip. In two 50-minute sessions, students work independently and as a group to read a text and analyze it, find the story elements in the text, create a six-frame comic strip based on the story elements, and reflect on the text. Fink noted that the product that the students create can be an alternative to a book report.

STUDENT THINK-ALOUDS OR INFERENCING SUBSTRATEGIES

One reading comprehension strategy that will help students with comprehension monitoring is student think-alouds. Teachers have been encouraged whenever possible to share their thinking with their students in order for students to learn new information and to have good thinking procedures modeled for them. Wilhelm (2001) exposed his students to teacher think-alouds (i.e., teachers sharing their expertise), and then he expected his students to adopt the teacher's strategy and apply it to their own reading. He created a chart to help students practice thinking on their own. Students were instructed to check off when they practiced particular substrategies, to make comments to share their thoughts, and to set goals for future strategy practice. A blank reproducible chart on student inferencing substrategies is provided on page 171 for you to copy and use in your classroom.

Although Wilhelm (2001) did not suggest having students put the date on their strategy checklists, this would provide the student and teacher with a running record of what reading comprehension strategies students are using and what goals they are setting. Completing strategy sheets such as this one helps students to monitor their own comprehension. As noted by Manning (2002), readers of any age need to be aware when they are not creating meaning while reading. Self-monitoring helps students to select and use appropriate strategies for improving their comprehension. Comprehension monitoring was one of the seven critical categories of text comprehension instruction mentioned by the NRP (NICHD, 2000). The think-aloud strategy and inferencing substrategy can be used to enhance other strategies mentioned in this chapter.

Block and Israel (2004) described think-aloud as what good readers do throughout the reading process. In other words, think-aloud occurs before, during, and after reading. They suggested 12 think-aloud strategies that have been used to help students in Grades K–5. The first think-aloud strategy is overview the text. The teacher selects a book that he or she has enjoyed and shares with students why the book and topic was attractive. Next, the teacher can guide the students through the think-aloud process using a book that the class will be reading silently. The second think-aloud strategy is look for important information. The teacher can share his or her thinking about looking for clues and key ideas. Next the teacher guides the students through the process of looking for important information. As students demonstrate that they can find important information, then the teacher can gradually remove some of the support or scaffolding that is no longer needed.

The other think-aloud strategies that Block and Israel (2004) suggested to help students include: connect to an author's big idea, activate relevant knowledge, put myself in the book, revise prior knowledge and predict, recognize an author's writing style, determine word meanings, ask questions, notice novelty in text, relate the book to my life, and anticipate use of knowledge. Once students have been taught the 12 think-aloud strategies, then they can participate in games using the strategies. For example, Block and Israel included a picture flashcard to represent each of the think-aloud strategies. The teacher can hold

Student Inferencing Substrategies

Name _____ Date _____

Story _____ Author _____

Inferencing substrategies	Did I do it?	Comments	Goal
Accessing background and connecting it to reading			
Making predictions about future actions			
Filling gaps in the story			
Adding things together to see connections			
Elaborating beyond the story			
Asking "what if?" questions			
Visualizing			

SOURCE: Adapted from Wilhelm (2001).

up one of the flash cards and ask students to share their thinking when they perform the strategy indicated on the flashcard. Then the teacher can ask one or two of the students to perform the think-aloud strategy while reading a few pages of text to the class. Students also can work in pairs while reading. When a student performs one of the think-aloud strategies, he or she holds up the flashcard indicating that strategy for his or her partner to see. Another aid to help students with the think-aloud strategies is to prepare bookmarks for them. Block and Israel suggested the following strategies to include on the bookmarks:

First few pages

- Overview a text
- Look for important information
- Connect to an author's big idea
- Activate relevant knowledge
- Put myself in the book

As you read

- Revise prior knowledge and predict
- Recognize an author's writing style
- Determine word meanings
- Ask questions

After having read for a while

- Notice novelty in the text
- Relate the book to my life
- Anticipate use of knowledge

Oster (2001) noted that think-alouds not only improve students' comprehension, but also their discussion skills and their enjoyment of literature. In addition, the learners accept responsibility for whether they are making meaning from what is read and become aware of whether a particular strategy is or is not working at any given time. Oster modeled the think-aloud strategy for her students by listing on the chalkboard some things that good readers may notice (e.g., important information, facts about characters or the story, predictions, questions, and personal reactions). Next, Oster demonstrated the think-aloud strategy while reading a short story. Then she led the students in a discussion about the comments she made to help her understand the story. Next, students read a paragraph as a class and Oster asked them to share their think-aloud comments. Then Oster paired students to use the think-aloud strategy on the next two paragraphs. They wrote their think-aloud comments to minimize the noise in the room. Then students read individually and wrote down their think-aloud comments. The next day's discussion was centered on the students' think-aloud comments from the previous day.

A sample lesson by Henry (2005) for using think-alouds to improve reading comprehension for students in Grades 6–8 can be found at http://www.readwritethink.org/lessons/lesson_view.asp?id=139. The lesson can be completed in two 45-minute sessions. The focus is for students to practice using the think-aloud strategy, share their interactions with texts, relate the newly learned text information with their background knowledge, respond in various ways to text reading, and to determine their level of understanding about what they read.

QUESTION ANSWERING

For students to be able to answer questions about what they are reading, they need to determine how they will obtain the information being asked of them. Raphael (1982) identified four types of questioning strategies that students should learn: (a) right there, (b) think and search, (c) author and me, and (d) on my own (p. 378). Casteel, Isom, and Jordan (2000) used these strategies to prepare an answering questions strategy reference card to remind students of possible ways to obtain an answer to a question about the material they are reading. A reproducible modified version of that reference card is provided on page 174 for you to use in your classroom.

Both the right there and the think and search strategies require locating literal information (Casteel et al., 2000). For example, right there and think and search questions might include, "How was the main character described in the story?" and "Where did the story take place?" The author and me strategy requires students to infer or evaluate the answer based on the author's ideas and their own background knowledge. For example, "Why did the main character have trouble communicating how he or she felt about the problem?" The on my own strategy gives students an opportunity to answer questions based on their own knowledge such as opinion questions. An example of an on my own question is, "What do you think that the old man could do to help the boy with his problem?" Students with learning difficulties may have more success with locating literal information, although they might need to be taught explicit strategies for finding the information. Work with individuals or small groups of struggling students to help them learn how to respond to author and me type questions. They may need many teacher prompts to guide their thinking through this process. Perhaps if students learn the cues for opinion questions (e.g., what do you think, how do you feel, in your opinion), then they will recognize that they need to share their own thinking. The question answering strategy may be used in conjunction with other strategies covered in this chapter. Also, it may be helpful to review the information on question-answer relationships located in Chapter 6.

GIST SUMMARIES

Gist summaries encourage students to use single sentences to summarize information contained in single paragraphs (Swanson & DeLaPaz, 1998). To teach students how to create a gist summary, model for them how to restate information using the fewest number of words possible. Begin by having students

Answering Questions
How do I do it?

Right There

   I can find the answer in one place in the book.

Think and Search

   I can find the answer in the book, but all of the answer won't be in the same place.

Author and Me

   I have to use what the author wrote and what I know to answer the question. I have to "read between the lines."

On My Own

   I can answer the questions by using what I already know about the topic.

SOURCE: Adapted from Casteel, Isom, and Jordan (2000).

summarize two sentences of text using 15 words or less. Then make the task more difficult until students are able to summarize an entire paragraph using 15 words or less. Provide students with guidance and feedback in order for them to learn to retell only the most crucial information. You may want to help students set goals (e.g., the maximum number of words to use in one sentence when creating a gist summary). The gist summaries strategy may be used along with other strategies mentioned in this chapter. In fact, gist is one of the strategies used in collaborative strategic reading, which will be discussed later in this chapter.

A sample lesson by Gray (2007) on using gist can be found at http://www.readwritethink.org/lessons/lesson_view.asp?id=290. The lesson is for Grades 6–8 and can be completed in five to seven 30-minute sessions. In the lesson, students learn and practice gist to help them summarize information and then they apply the gist strategy to help them with their reading assignments in various content areas.

IMPROVISATIONAL DRAMA

Students who have learning difficulties and struggle with reading may be reluctant to participate in classroom reading activities because they dislike reading and fear failing in front of their peers (Stanfa & O'Shea, 1998). They may either withdraw or misbehave to disguise their inability to read. Improvisational drama may be the key to help some students take the risk and read. Kelin (2007) noted that drama strategies can help students to better understand and appreciate a story. Some of the drama activities may take place prior to reading the story and some later. Students can even provide their own interpretations of characters and story events.

What Is Improvisational Drama?

Improvisational drama, as defined by the Children's Theatre Association of America in 1975, enables participants to imagine, act out, and reflect upon human experiences (Dupont, 1992). This strategy combines high involvement and movement, both of which are supported in the emerging research on how the brain learns and supports the learning style of students who need to be active. Improvisational drama differs from theatre drama in that it is process centered and theatre drama is audience centered. Improvisational forms include dramatic play, pantomime, puppet shows, and story dramatization (Stanfa & O'Shea, 1998).

Why Use Improvisational Drama?

Struggling readers may not feel confident about their reading skills and may welcome dramatic activities as a safe place to share perspectives and ideas (Stanfa & O'Shea, 1998). Improvisational drama also can aid students' generalization, help them apply knowledge, and transfer information learned in one setting to other situations and settings (Stanfa & O'Shea). Through drama, students may be required to use language in several ways: (a) explain or instruct; (b) argue, defend, or persuade; or (c) plan or project. The language becomes part of the situation and encourages group interaction. Key to the success of improvisational drama is structured reflection to deepen readers' thinking, challenge assumptions, and provide opportunities for self-assessment of learning.

In a meta-analysis of dramatic activities studies, Wagner (1988) concluded that drama could improve reading comprehension through language growth, improve self-confidence and self-concept, and aid behavior and cooperation. Bidwell (1990) noted that drama (a) activates prior knowledge and requires the readers to involve themselves in the reading, (b) encourages readers to use metacognitive strategies to locate information and analyze situations, and (c) provides immediate teacher feedback in order for readers to check their understanding. At least two levels of comprehension instruction are included in improvisational drama: (a) cooperative learning, and (b) question generation.

How Can Teachers Use Improvisational Drama?

Advance Preparation. Teachers should select reading objectives for a topic and plan the improvisational drama using appropriate reading selections (Stanfa & O'Shea, 1998). The drama may explore issues, themes, events, characters, or settings. You should plan the dramatic context with the following features: (a) opportunities for effective engagement of the readers in the story, materials, or lesson; (b) open-ended context to provide room for reader contributions; and (c) a level of tension or uncertainty (O'Neill, Lambert, Linnell, & Warr-Wood, 1976). You can plan your role as to how you will guide and support the readers through questioning, challenging, organizing, and focusing on pertinent text details (Stanfa & O'Shea). Props can be used, but are not essential. If you would like for your students to use props or to decide if they would like to use props, make sure that a selection of props is available. You might ask students ahead of time if they would like to bring some appropriate props from home.

Before Reading. You should talk with students to give them an advance organizer to help them understand the purpose of the reading lesson, how the lesson will proceed, and what is expected of them during and after the lesson. If students are not familiar with improvisational drama, you will need to introduce them to the concept and be sure to set parameters for the lesson. For example, you may tell students that, "We will begin reading the story together, but instead of stopping and discussing the story events, we will stop and act out the story." You must make sure that each student has a part so that everyone will participate.

Determine whether students will volunteer for character roles or whether the teacher will assign the roles. If you would like for students to "get into a character" to later act out how that character thinks, feels, and behaves, then make character role selections or assignments known prior to reading. If students are to assume a character role during reading, they may feel more comfortable having an opportunity to preread their parts one-on-one with the teacher or a peer buddy prior to whole class reading. To help students prepare to be a particular character, you may want to have them complete a character map using the printable form for Grades 3–8 found at www.teachervision.com/tv/printables/087628411X_218.pdf.

During Reading. The entire class may read the story orally together or students who are able to read the story independently may wish to do so silently, while the teacher works individually or in a small group with students who prefer having teacher assistance. You may wish to point out critical features or events as the story is being read to help the students later prepare their dramatizations. You can encourage students to ask questions to aid their understanding. If they become lost in one section of the story, then the remainder may not make sense to them. The improvisational dramatization may occur at various teacher-selected points during the story reading or it may be postponed until the class has read the story. You should keep in mind that some students with learning difficulties may not be able to remember the entire story and would do better working with small portions of it and then putting the big picture together.

After Reading. For improvisational drama, the during reading and after reading activities may be the same or different. If you are stopping the story at various points and asking students to provide the dramatization for each of those points, then the dramatization in itself, student responses to teacher queries, and student reflections may provide evidence that students have comprehended the intended material. For some stories, the teacher may deem that after reading dramatization is more appropriate. Either way, note that story drama does not have to consist of literal interpretations only. Instead, the dramatization may be used to explore interesting issues, create new story events or endings, or help students read between the lines to tease out implicit information. This particularly may be helpful for students with learning difficulties who may have difficulty with inferential information.

Follow-Up Activities. Follow-up activities might include additional dramatizations to provide variations on a theme. For example, if the story contained historical characters, the students may want to create a modern-day version. Or the students may want to change the setting for the story (e.g., from a rural area to the city or from Mexico to the United States). Another version may be to add new characters such as famous people or to substitute school or community leaders for original story characters. Writing prior to dramatization may aid student organization of ideas (Stanfa & O'Shea, 1998), especially for students with learning difficulties. You may ask older students (Grade 3 or 4 and up) to write a script for the new version and younger students (Grades K through 2 or 3) to dictate a script to the teacher or into an audiotape recorder. Older students may work in small groups to create additional dramatizations. Writing can be an appropriate follow-up activity to dramatization to ensure students' understanding and also may serve as an assessment piece (Stanfa & O'Shea). Drawing may be an appropriate means for younger students to show their understanding of the dramatization.

COOPERATIVE DISCUSSION AND QUESTIONING (COOP-DIS-Q)

Struggling readers can benefit by working with others to make meaning of a story or novel. Working with others in a risk-free environment emphasizes the importance of sharing and that two or more heads can be better than one. Students may feel more comfortable sharing with peers in small groups as opposed to the entire class.

What Is Coop-Dis-Q?

Coop-Dis-Q was developed by incorporating the elements of cooperative learning, discussion, and questioning into one strategy (Gauthier, 2001). The premise is that the combined strengths of each element will create a synergistic instructional effect. The strategy was field-tested in a fifth grade classroom after a novel had been read to the whole class and resulted in the students taking active roles to aid their comprehension and to assume responsibility for decision making. The students participating in the field-testing generated robust discussion and minigroups were eager to share their information with each other.

Why Use Coop-Dis-Q?

A combination of cooperative learning, group discussions, and questioning tactics results in enhancing each tactic. According to Johnson, Johnson, and Holubec (1994), cooperative learning helps students maximize their learning through the use of small instructional groups. Brown, Collins, and Duguid (1989) noted that cooperative learning can help students recognize that many roles often are needed to solve authentic problems and also help them identify ineffective problem-solving strategies.

Gambrell (1996) stated that group discussions strengthen students' recall and understanding of text material read. Alvermann, Dillon, and O'Brien (1987) cautioned that the teacher must provide explicit instruction, modeling, and numerous practice opportunities for effective discussion to occur. If the teacher demonstrates respect for students' ideas and perspectives, then the students will be more likely to participate in classroom discussions. Discussion activities can enhance interpersonal communication skills and social interactions, which are precursors to cognitive growth (Rogoff, 1990; Vygotsky, 1978).

Questioning is an instructional facilitator that can aid reading comprehension (Strother, 1989). Questions help students make meaning from text because they are guided with choices to accept or reject. Evaluative questioning can assist the teacher in determining the amount and type of comprehension acquired by the student. Rosenblatt (1982) suggested that questions that are a representative mixture of instructional, evaluative (i.e., informative, expository), and aesthetic (i.e., feelings) are the most effective way to develop students' multidimensional comprehension.

Although Coop-Dis-Q is new and only field-tested, the separate elements of cooperative learning, discussion, and questioning have literature support. The levels of comprehension instruction included in Coop-Dis-Q are (a) cooperative learning, (b) question answering, (c) question generation, and (d) summarization.

How Can Teachers Use Coop-Dis-Q?

Advance Preparation. The teacher should decide if the groups of six students should be heterogeneous or homogeneous in order to accomplish the lesson objectives (Gauthier, 2001). Students with learning difficulties likely can benefit from being in a heterogeneous group where they can see a variety of good thinking styles being modeled by their peers. Then you should determine the composition of each group. You might wish to field-test the strategy with one group to help you become familiar with it. To prepare a set of questions, determine elements that are important for students to glean from the reading. You will need to make sure that the questions address literal, inferential, and critical comprehension as well as integrate instructional, evaluative, and aesthetic aspects. For example, a fifth grade teacher used some of the following questions after reading the book *Summer of the Monkeys* (Rawls, 1976) to her students (Gauthier, 2001). Notice that the types of questions are indicated in parentheses.

- Did the first part of the book interest you enough to make you want to keep listening? Why? (instructional, evaluative, aesthetic)
- What were the names of the two main characters who were children? (literal, evaluative)
- What was the financial or money situation in the Lee family? At what point in the book did you first think this? (inferential, evaluative)
- What was the first point in the story when you didn't understand something? Why did you think you didn't understand it? Did you ask the teacher to re-read or explain? (literal/critical, instructional/evaluative, efferent/aesthetic; Gauthier, 2001, p. 219)

You will need to make sure that the questions are contained on a single sheet of paper and that each student will be able to have a copy of the questions. Also, you can cut one question sheet into strips containing one question per strip.

Before Reading. The teacher in Gauthier's (2001) study chose to read a book aloud to the class prior to implementing the Coop-Dis-Q reading comprehension strategy. If you plan to proceed in the same manner, then a brief preview of the book with the class would suffice to help the students activate their background knowledge. You might ask your students questions about the title, book cover, and any beginning illustrations to help them make predictions about the book's story events. Students with learning difficulties may need extra teacher cues to help them tap into their background knowledge and use available information (e.g., story pictures, graphic organizers, title, topic headings) to make predictions. Let them know it is okay to take a risk making predictions, even if we later learn that the predictions are incorrect.

During Reading. You will need to instruct your students to listen carefully as you read the book aloud to the class. Students should show you that they are listening by having their eyes on you and by leaning slightly forward in their seats.

After Reading. After the story reading is completed, you should initiate a general discussion with your students on the text that was read (Gauthier, 2001). As soon as possible, you can gradually turn over responsibility for the discussion to the students. When the discussion is completed, you will present the students with the sheet of questions you have prepared. The questions should be contained on one sheet of paper with a copy available for each student. A duplicate set of questions will appear on cut strips of paper with one question per strip. Next, you will divide the students into groups of three to give all students opportunity for discussion. The questions are to be divided equally among the triads.

You should ask each triad of students to work on its designated questions (Gauthier, 2001). Provide each group with a copy of the text and give it as much space as possible away from the other groups to minimize distractions. Then you will ask the groups to select a recorder to write the group's responses to the questions. Encourage the groups to respect the comments of all group members and to add additional questions if necessary to address important points. Next, you will ask two triads who had different questions to answer to become a new discussion group of six students (Gauthier). Ask the two original triad groups to present their answers to their new group of six. You should ask each original triad group if it generated any new questions to be added to the list. As teacher, you will moderate the discussion, model appropriate discussion practices, and make sure the discussion includes any new questions that either group added to the list. Coop-Dis-Q is considered complete when all questions have been answered and all topics of discussion have been addressed adequately.

Follow-Up Activities. Coop-Dis-Q is an intensive reading comprehension activity and may not require any follow-up. If you think that students continue to struggle with the main ideas and essential details of the story read, then you may want to plan an individual or group follow-up activity such as creating a picture book to accompany the text or completing a graphic organizer to summarize key events and ideas. You may add another comprehension strategy such as improvisational drama to give students more comprehension practice.

COLLABORATIVE STRATEGIC READING (CSR)

Some students with learning difficulties may struggle with reading comprehension because it requires their attention to several things at one time. Teaching students a single strategy may help them to tackle only one aspect of comprehension. Instead, teaching them a process that involves several related strategies may give students that extra boost toward becoming good comprehenders.

What Is CSR?

Collaborative strategic reading is an instructional framework that can help students to understand all texts that they read. In CSR, students are taught four comprehension strategies to use with all texts (Liang & Dole, 2006). CSR helps students to improve their reading comprehension, increase their vocabulary, and work cooperatively with peers. CSR is an instructional approach for multilevel classrooms that has been used successfully by teachers who teach heterogeneous intermediate grade classes (Klingner & Vaughn, 1998). As part of the CSR Plan for Strategic Reading, students learn four strategies that take them through the before, during, and after reading stages. Preview is the before reading strategy, click and clunk and get the gist are the during reading strategies, while wrap-up is the after reading strategy. The before and after reading strategies in CSR are used only once, but the during reading strategies can be used many times.

Why Use CSR?

The four CSR strategies are based on the previous research of Palincsar and Brown (1984) and Pressley, Brown, El-Dinary, and Afflerbach (1995), for example (Vaughn, Klingner, & Bryant, 2001). The click and clunk strategy of CSR can help struggling readers to monitor their understanding when they read. It helps them to notice when they understand and when they fail to understand (Klingner & Vaughn, 1998). CSR can be used with expository and narrative text and is compatible with a variety of reading programs (e.g., literature-based instruction, basal reading programs, and balanced reading approaches). Teachers who have used CSR indicate that it aids not only reading comprehension, but also study skills (Vaughn & Klingner, 1999). Klingner and Vaughn (1998) noted that students participating in CSR improved their scores on reading achievement tests. The levels of comprehension instruction included in CSR are (a) comprehension monitoring, (b) cooperative learning, (c) graphic and semantic organizers, (d) question answering, (e) question generation, and (f) story structure (implied).

How Can Teachers Use CSR?

Advance Preparation. Students need to be taught the CSR strategies and be given opportunities for strategy practice prior to being expected to perform the strategies. Initially, the teacher will model, role play, and use think-alouds to teach the four CSR strategies: preview, click and clunk, get the gist, and wrap-up. Then you will need to provide teacher-facilitated activities to help the students practice each of the strategies (Klingner & Vaughn, 1998). If you prefer to have teacher-selected groups of heterogeneous students, then you should determine student grouping arrangements prior to beginning the strategy.

Before Reading. Preview is used once prior to reading the text selection for the entire lesson. In preview, students will have two to three minutes to learn as much as they can about the passage they will read. They will activate their background knowledge about the passage topic and will make predictions about what they will learn. In addition, previewing helps to activate student interest and engagement in reading. You might use movie previews as an analogy to help students understand the concept of previewing. Klingner and Vaughn (1998, p. 33) suggested the following questions to help students determine what they learn from movie previews:

- Do you learn who is going to be in the movie?
- Do you learn during what historical period the movie will take place?
- Do you learn whether you might like the movie?
- Do you have questions about what more you would like to know about the movie?

Students should look at headings, boldface type, pictures, tables, and graphs to help them determine what they know about the topic and what they will learn. You will need to remind students that, just like movie previews, they will have only a short period of time (i.e., two to three minutes) to discuss their background knowledge and predictions. A fifth grade teacher in an inclusion class used a five-minute structured preview strategy. She gave her students a minute and a half to write their background knowledge in their CSR learning logs, one minute to share their responses with other students, a minute and a half to write their predictions of what they may learn, and another minute to share their ideas with peers (Klingner & Vaughn, 1998).

During Reading. You must teach students the click and clunk strategy to help them monitor their reading comprehension and identify when they have difficulty understanding. Students click (comprehension clicks into place) and clunk (comprehension breaks down) while they read each passage section. Click indicates that the reader is progressing smoothly through the text, while clunk indicates a problem such as an unknown word meaning. Be sure to ask students if they have clunks regarding the passage section just read. In turn, students will expect the teacher to ask this question as they read various passage sections. By having a procedure where students are encouraged to let the teacher know when they encounter problems, students with learning difficulties feel more comfortable admitting that they are struggling. When students encounter a clunk, they can select a fix-up strategy. Each fix-up strategy may be printed on clunk cards (flashcards) to serve as a visual reminder (Klingner & Vaughn, 1998, p. 34):

- Reread the sentence without the word. Think about what information is provided that would help you understand the meaning of the word.
- Reread the sentence with the clunk and the sentences before or after the clunk looking for clues.
- Look for a prefix or suffix in the word.
- Break the word apart and look for smaller words you know.

The second during reading strategy is get the gist, which helps students to state in their own words the most important information from the passage read. This aids student understanding and memory of information learned. You can prompt students to identify the most important person, place, or thing in the passage read and to restate it in their own words. Remind students to state the gist in as few words as possible to convey the essential meaning. Klingner and Vaughn (1998) described one teacher who asked her students to write the most important person, place, or thing from the passage. Then she asked individual students to share their responses. The remainder of the class commented as to which responses they liked and why. Finally, the teacher asked students individually or in pairs to write the passage's gist and to solicit their peers' comments as to the gist's effectiveness.

After Reading. Wrap-up is used after reading the entire lesson text and helps students to generate questions and answers about the learned material (Klingner

& Vaughn, 1998). The intent is to help students know, understand, and remember what they read. The five W's (i.e., who, what, when, where, and why) and an H (i.e., how) are question starters that students may use to formulate their questions. A graphic organizer can be found at http://www.teachervision .fen.com/creative-writing/graphic-organizers/43066.html and may help students with learning difficulties to record this essential information. You can ask students to place themselves in the role of a teacher who is making test questions to find out if students understood what they read. Then you can give other students the opportunity to answer the questions. If no one can answer a question, it might mean that the question needs more clarification. You should teach students to ask different kinds of questions: (a) questions in which the answer is stated explicitly in the information read, and (b) questions in which the answer is in the student's head rather than in the passage read. Make sure that students ask some questions that involve higher-level thinking skills as opposed to only information recall. One teacher shared with her students that asking "Why do you think that?" can help every question become an even better question (Klingner & Vaughn, p. 35). Some of the following question stems may help students to generate higher-level questions:

- How were _____ and _____ the same? Different?
- What do you think would happen if _____?
- What do you think caused _____ to happen?
- What other solutions can you think of for the problem of _____?
- What might have prevented the problem of _____ from happening?
- What are the strengths (or weaknesses) of_____? (Klingner & Vaughn, 1998, p. 35)

Students review by recording the most important ideas from the day's reading lesson in their CSR learning logs. These logs enable students to keep track of important information as they learn it and provide a launch pad for follow-up activities. Students can record information in their learning logs while applying every strategy or only for some of the strategies (e.g., recording clunks and key ideas).

When students become proficient at applying the comprehension strategies through teacher-directed instruction, they will need to learn cooperative group roles to perform during CSR. Students should have an opportunity to perform different roles; therefore, they should rotate roles regularly. Each role should come with a cue sheet to help students know the responsibilities for their role and to help them stay focused. A cue sheet particularly is important for students with learning difficulties who either may not remember or may not understand their roles. Teachers can take the opportunity to go over the cue sheets the first few times the strategy is used to make sure that everyone understands his or her role. Some of the roles may include the following (Klingner & Vaughn, 1998, p. 35):

- *Leader.* Tells students what to read and what strategy to apply. Asks for teacher assistance when needed.
- *Clunk Expert.* Uses clunk cards to remind students of the steps in the clunking strategy when they are struggling with a difficult word or concept.

- *Announcer.* Asks group members to read or share an idea and makes sure that everyone in the group has an opportunity to participate.
- *Encourager.* Gives feedback by praising positive behaviors and encouraging all to participate in discussions and help each other. Also evaluates the group collaboration and makes suggestions for improvement.
- *Reporter.* Reports to the class the main ideas learned from the group and a favorite question generated.
- *Timekeeper.* Sets the timer and informs the class when a new portion of CSR should begin.

You will need to monitor students as they begin working in their cooperative roles by clarifying difficult words, modeling strategies and positive attitudes, and encouraging all students to participate.

Follow-Up Activities. These activities can reinforce important vocabulary words and ideas students have encountered in the reading assignment. Reviewing important vocabulary words and ideas can help students with learning difficulties to summarize and remember key information. Each group might be assigned or asked to choose different follow-up activities in which they will share their final products with the entire class. Klingner and Vaughn (1998) suggested that a different group might prepare each of the following: (a) semantic map, (b) mnemonic devices, (c) clunk concentration, (d) Venn diagram, and (e) theme pictures.

As compared with other instructional frameworks, CSR takes a medium amount of teacher preparation (Liang & Dole, 2006). As with teaching any new strategy, the teacher is heavily involved in introducing CSR to his or her students. It is taught to the whole class and the teacher uses modeling and think-alouds to show students how to use each of the four comprehension strategies in CSR. As the students begin working in groups, the teacher's role is monitoring and providing the scaffolding or support as needed. As students become more proficient using the strategies, then less teacher assistance may be needed. Students use different texts, but repeat the same four CSR strategies with each text (Liang & Dole).

Research on CSR is promising. For more than eight years, Klingner, Vaughn, and colleagues have studied the effects of CSR in elementary and middle school classrooms (Klingner, Vaughn, Arguelles, Hughes, & Leftwich, 2004). A variety of students including those who are English Language Learners and students with learning disabilities participated in the studies. Overall gains in reading comprehension and "improved strategic discourse in groups" (p. 292) are associated with CSR. Klingner et al. studied the implementation of CSR in five intervention and five control classrooms in five schools. Intervention teachers attended a CSR professional development and were given support following the workshop. The overwhelming majority of the students were Hispanic with limited English proficiency. The students in the CSR classrooms performed significantly better in reading comprehension than their peers in the control classrooms. Eleven out of twelve teacher case studies showed the student gains in reading comprehension were related to the quality of CSR implementation.

A sample lesson, titled "Scaffolding Comprehension Strategies Using Graphic Organizers," can be found at http://www.readwritethink.org/lessons/lesson_view.asp?id=95. In this lesson plan, Ruckdeschel (2007) introduces students in Grades 6–8 to CSR in three to four 45-minute sessions. As students learn CSR, they use graphic organizers to record information, verbalize their thinking by applying think-aloud strategies, as well as use self-monitoring and self-correction strategies

BIBLIOTHERAPY

One reason that students with learning difficulties may have difficulty understanding and remembering what they read is that they cannot identify with the characters or events in the story. Sridhar and Vaughn (2000) advocate the use of bibliotherapy for all students to enhance not only their reading comprehension, but also their self-concept and behavior.

What Is Bibliotherapy?

Originally, bibliotherapy was intended to help students deal with problems or stressful situations (e.g., visiting the doctor, dealing with the death of a loved one or pet, or attending a new school). Students were given books to read that had a therapeutic intent (Cornett & Cornett, 1980). To achieve the therapeutic effect, the reader must (a) *identify* with the story's main character and events, (b) *experience catharsis*, which involves becoming emotionally involved with the main character and situation, and (c) *develop insight* by analyzing the main character and his or her way of dealing with the situation (Afolayan, 1992). Based on these activities, the students could become involved intimately with the story content.

Why Use Bibliotherapy?

Low-achieving students as well as students with learning disabilities often have reading comprehension problems and difficulty with social relationships (Hager & Vaughn, 1995). Peer rejection, poor social skills, and low self-esteem are some of the social consequences of low academic achievement (Sridhar & Vaughn, 2000). Research has shown that bibliotherapy positively impacts reading readiness, achievement, and self-concept (Afolayan, 1992; Bauer & Balius, 1995; Borders & Paisley, 1992; Myracle, 1995). This strategy is flexible enough to be used in a general education setting or a resource room with a single student or a group of students. Several levels of comprehension instruction are included in bibliotherapy: (a) comprehension monitoring, (b) question answering, (c) cooperative learning, and (d) summarization.

How Can Teachers Use Bibliotherapy?

Advance Preparation. Teachers should select an appropriate book for the student(s) by matching the book to the problem. For example, the book *Shelley: The*

Hyperactive Turtle (Moss, 1989) would be appropriate for students who have difficulty remaining in their seats, listening to directions, and making friends (Sridhar & Vaughn, 2000). Make sure that the book also is selected for its developmental and reading-level appropriateness (Pardeck, 1995).

Before Reading. A prereading strategy is intended to help the students focus on the story topic and access background knowledge related to the story. The teacher should share with the student(s) the book's general theme and some of the things that the main character does. For example, Shelley does not remain in his seat during class. Further, he talks often without first raising his hand. You should ask the students questions to help them talk about how someone like the main character might feel in those situations. Also, guide the student(s) to make predictions about the story's content based on their prior knowledge (Sridhar & Vaughn, 2000).

During Reading. You may not want to wait until after reading the entire story to begin asking the students questions about its content. By asking questions, you can help the students, especially those with learning difficulties, to summarize key information in the story and to eliminate trivial details. Sridhar and Vaughn (2000, p. 76) suggested the following questions to ask about Shelley:

- Why do you think Shelley got out of his seat?
- How do you think Shelley felt?
- Does that mean he is bad?
- What do you think Shelley can do now?
- What has happened so far?
- What did Shelley do before he got out of his seat?

Also, it is important to ask questions to help students identify with the main character (Sridhar & Vaughn, 2000, p. 76):

- Has that ever happened to you?
- What would you do if you were Shelley?

After Reading. To help the students synthesize key information from the story and apply it to their own life situations, you may initiate a discussion. If the entire class has read the story, then you might divide the class into small groups of three or four students. Each group works collaboratively to suggest ideas that could be helpful to Shelley (Sridhar & Vaughn, 2000). Then each group can retell the story to the entire class and share its ideas about Shelley's feelings and how Shelley and others could improve the situation. The story retelling or verbal reconstruction of the reading helps students focus on the big picture of the story and provides a comprehension framework. Encourage students to interact with each other during the retellings and idea sharing by elaborating on another student's summary, providing an opinion about someone's interpretations, or asking questions. The teacher's role is to scaffold or provide support for students by restating or elaborating on their verbal contributions (Rosenshine & Meister, 1994).

Follow-Up Activities. Ouzts (1991) noted that follow-up activities should focus on the fundamental process of identification, catharsis, and insight. You might want to provide follow-up activities geared to the students' age and interest levels. Students of all ages may enjoy recreating the story through original art or computer clip art. Likewise, students of all ages may welcome the chance to recreate the story through drama. Perhaps the students would like to provide a new ending or a sequel to the story based on their discussions and conclusions after reading the story. They may use art, computer clip art, or drama to do so, or may choose to use a desktop publishing computer program to develop their own books. Activities such as these give students a choice and allow students with learning difficulties to capitalize on their strengths.

 REFLECTIVE EXERCISE 5.2
LOOKING FOR APPROPRIATE STORIES?

If you are looking for stories that might be used for bibliotherapy activities in your classroom, go to http://www.best-childrens-books.com/bibliotherapy.html or http://falcon.jmu.edu/~ramseyil/bibliotherapy.htm, which provide suggestions for using bibliotherapy and lists of books for students of various ages.

RTI CASE STUDY FOR GAINING MEANING FROM READING

Bill is a third grade student in Mr. Taylor's class. Mr. Taylor noticed immediately that Bill's favorite subject was math because it seemed to be easy for him and he was successful in it. With regard to reading, Bill did not mind reading aloud as long as the teacher did not ask him any questions about what he had read. Bill was able to recognize and pronounce each word correctly as well as read at an appropriate pace for a third grader. When Mr. Taylor administered the Dynamic Indicators of Basic Early Literacy Skills (DIBELS) Oral Reading Fluency (ORF) measure to his class at the beginning of the school year, Bill scored 120. This score indicated that Bill was not at risk for reading fluency problems. Mr. Taylor observed that Bill did not use much expression when he read aloud. Also, Mr. Taylor was concerned about Bill not being able to answer comprehension questions. Bill appeared to be a "word caller," that is, someone who can accurately decode words but cannot give meaning to what he has read.

Mr. Taylor had attended a summer workshop on reading comprehension prior to this school year and learned about the MAZE assessment for reading comprehension (see http://www.aimsweb.com/measures/maze/description.php). After consulting the Florida Center for Reading Research (http://www.fcrr.org/), Mr. Taylor's district endorsed the MAZE assessment, purchased the materials, and encouraged the K–8 teachers to use MAZE when appropriate. During the MAZE assessment, students read silently a 150- to 400-word passage using the cloze procedure. Every seventh word is deleted and replaced with three words enclosed in parentheses. The student is asked to circle the correct word. A score is given for the passage by determining the percentage that the student got correct. Bill's baseline score on the MAZE was 60%. Mr. Taylor continued to assess Bill once a week using the MAZE and found over a four-week period that Bill's reading comprehension scores remained in the 58% to 62% range.

Although Mr. Taylor had five years of teaching experience, he was not sure how to help Bill to progress with reading comprehension. Mr. Taylor asked the student support team for assistance. The student support team suggested that Mr. Taylor try some strategies to help Bill think more about what he was reading. These are strategies that good readers often use, so some also may be beneficial to other students in the class. Although Mr. Taylor frequently asked his students questions about what they read, he had not explicitly taught them that there are strategies that good readers often use before, during, and after reading. The student support team encouraged Mr. Taylor to write questions on the board and call students' attention to them before the story is read. Next, Mr. Taylor should model how good readers begin to answer questions while they read. He also could show a non-example to illustrate that by reading too quickly and just calling the words that he likely will not understand what he has read. Finally, Mr. Taylor could plan some follow-up activities after reading to help students to reinforce and remember what they have read. For example, students like Bill could be taught to use a story map to help answer the important questions. Then the story map could be used as a writing tool to explain the different perspectives of two story characters. Figure 5.1 summarizes the tier one intervention Mr. Taylor used in his classroom.

Mr. Taylor immediately implemented the before, during, and after reading strategies in his classroom and introduced the class to story maps. While other students were silently reading and completing their story maps or answering story questions, Mr. Taylor spent at least 20 minutes daily helping Bill's small reading group with their story maps. Mr. Taylor took a few observation notes to help document the progress of the students like Bill that he worked with in the small group for the after reading strategy. In addition, Mr. Taylor continued to assess Bill and his three peers in the group weekly using the MAZE assessment for reading comprehension. Figure 5.2 illustrates Bill's reading comprehension scores.

After using the before/during/after reading strategy for five consecutive weeks until the end of the grading period, Mr. Taylor observed that Bill still had a great deal of difficulty with reading comprehension. Bill's MAZE scores for reading comprehension during the tier one intervention ranged from 58% to 63%, confirming that Bill had not progressed with his reading comprehension.

At the end of the first grading period, Mr. Taylor attended a staff development workshop on Collaborative Strategic Reading (CSR), which involves four strategies used together. First, students learn to preview, which is a before reading strategy. The click and clunk strategy helps them to learn and use language to indicate when they comprehend what they have read and when they do not. Another during reading strategy is get the gist to help students summarize what they have read. Wrap-up, the after reading strategy, enables students to generate and answer questions about what they have learned. Mr. Taylor began to teach his students the CSR process at the beginning of the second grading

Supplements to General Curriculum	Classroom Time (Facilitated by Teacher)	Student-Teacher Ratio
Before Reading Strategy— Teacher writes questions on board and calls students' attention to them. Also, teacher reminds students the importance of preparing to read.	10 minutes daily	20 to 1
During Reading Strategy— Teacher models how good readers answer questions while they read.	5 minutes daily	20 to 1
After Reading Strategy— Teacher provides follow-up activity such as using a story map to help answer questions. Then the story map could be used to write an essay on the different perspective of two story characters.	20 minutes daily (Teacher meets with small group that includes Bill to provide extra help with story map, answering questions, and essay writing.)	4 to 1

Figure 5.1 Summary of Bill's Tier One Intervention

Week	Intervention	Score
1	Baseline	60%
2	None	58%
3	None	62%
4	None	59%
5	Before/During/After Reading with Story Map	60%
6	Before/During/After Reading with Story Map	62%
7	Before/During/After Reading with Story Map	58%
8	Before/During/After Reading with Story Map	63%
9	Before/During/After Reading with Story Map	61%

Figure 5.2 Bill's Reading Comprehension Scores

period. He especially encouraged students to use the click and clunk language to show when they were and were not comprehending information.

Mr. Taylor was fortunate to have Melinda, a graduate student from the local university, start her field experience in his classroom during the beginning of the second grading period. Melinda had learned about CSR in her university studies and was eager to see it applied in a classroom. At first Mr. Taylor and Melinda co-taught the CSR lessons. The before reading aspect of CSR, preview, was done as a whole class prior to reading the day's selection. As the majority of the students in the class became familiar with the CSR routine, Mr. Taylor and Melinda were able to take turns working individually with Bill's group for 45 minutes daily. First, Mr. Taylor and Melinda expected Bill to use the click and clunk language when they were working one-on-one on Bill's story map. After Bill used this language freely one-on-one with the teacher, Mr. Taylor expected Bill and his peers to use the language during small reading group time. Although Bill improved on the number of comprehension questions he answered correctly, his scores were not considered passing. As Bill and his peers read the day's selection aloud in small group, Mr. Taylor or Melinda presented get the gist, a second during reading aspect of CSR in game-like format. Bill worked with a partner in his group to see if they could beat the other pair in the group by summarizing what they had read in exactly 20 words. The final aspect of CSR was wrap-up, where students generated and answered questions. Once again, Melinda or Mr. Taylor helped Bill and the peers in his small group to learn how to generate questions and to answer them. When Melinda noticed that Bill really seemed to like and respond to the game-like format of get the gist, she suggested to Mr. Taylor that wrap-up be presented to Bill's small group as a game.

Bill came from a single-parent household. His mother worked outside the home, so Bill and his older brother stayed with their grandmother after school. Bill's mother and grandmother did meet with Mr. Taylor about Bill's reading problems and were willing to do what they could to help. Mr. Taylor showed them the get the gist aspect of Collaborative Strategic Reading. Bill and his brother liked video games, so Bill's mother and grand-mother were not surprised when Mr. Taylor indicated that Bill was beginning to respond to strategies such as get the gist and wrap-up when they were presented in game-like format. Bill's grandmother was willing to work with Bill for at least 20 minutes three times a week on get the gist and wrap-up. During the meeting, Bill's mother mentioned that Bill liked acting and wanted to be an actor someday. That gave Mr. Taylor the idea that he could incorporate some improvisational drama activities into reading. Once students like Bill had read and were familiar with a story or passage, then they could act out the meaning for their classmates. Bill and his small group liked the improvisational drama activities and began asking if they could write their own scripts. Mr. Taylor and Melinda were so impressed that they asked Bill and his peers in the small group to do several presentations for the entire class. See Figure 5.3 for a summary of the tier two intervention for Bill.

Bill's reading comprehension scores improved with the tier two intervention. See Figure 5.4 for Bill's reading comprehension scores for tier two. Mr. Taylor found that Bill needed the additional structure that Collaborative Strategic Reading provided. Too much of Mr. Taylor's before, during, and after strategies implemented in tier one were teacher driven. Bill later shared with Mr. Taylor that he became bored when the teacher was always "doing every-thing" and often daydreamed about things that interested him. With CSR, Bill felt like he got to participate in the process in ways that he felt comfortable. In addition, Bill told Mr. Taylor and Melinda that he did not mind performing in

Supplements to General Curriculum	Classroom Time (Facilitated by Co-Teachers)	Student-Teacher Ratio
Before Reading Strategy—CSR (preview)	10 minutes daily	20 to 1
During Reading Strategy—CSR (click and clunk, get the gist) After Reading Strategy—CSR (wrap-up, story map, and improvisational drama)	45 minutes daily (One of the co-teachers meets with small group that includes Bill to provide extra help with CSR strategies, story map, and improvisational drama activities.)	1 to 1 and 4 to 1
Family Assistance		
Bill's grandmother worked with him for at least 20 minutes three times a week on get the gist and wrap-up (answering questions in a game-like format). Sometimes Bill and some of his friends performed at home and at school their own improvisational drama skits that went along with what they had read.		

Figure 5.3   Summary of Bill's Tier Two Intervention

Week	Intervention	Score
10	CSR Introduction	60%
11	CSR—Preview	62%
12	CSR—Clink and Clunk	66%
13	CSR—Get the Gist	69%
14	CSR—Wrap-up	72%
15	CSR—Wrap-up with Story Map	75%
16	CSR with Story Map	78%
17	CSR with Story Map	79%
18	CSR with Story Map and Improvisational Drama	82%

Figure 5.4   Bill's Reading Comprehension Scores With Tier Two Intervention

front of the class when he and his buddies could write the scripts. Mr. Taylor continued to assess Bill during the tier two intervention using the MAZE assessment for reading comprehension and was proud to report that by the end of the second grading period, Bill's reading comprehension was now at 82% or B level. The intensity of the tier two intervention, and additional time spent on it, appeared to be just what Bill needed.

CONCLUSION

Too many students read the words on the printed pages without understanding or remembering what they read. It will be very difficult for them to become lifelong learners if they can't obtain meaning from what they read. The NRP identified seven categories of text comprehension instruction that are supported by research (NICHD, 2000): (a) comprehension monitoring, (b) cooperative learning, (c) use of graphic and semantic organizers, (d) question answering, (e) question generation, (f) story structure, and (g) summarization. The NRP suggested that reading comprehension strategies should be taught in combination as multiple strategies. This chapter has focused on several of the multiple strategies that teachers can select to help improve their students' reading comprehension as well as several strategies that teachers can use together. Through the use of multiple strategies, all students, including those with learning difficulties, can obtain the most benefit for the time invested and have a variety of strategies to use in other classes, later in school, and in the real world for the rest of their lives.

WHAT'S NEXT?

In Chapter 6, you will find strategies for teachers to use in content area instruction in the elementary and middle grades, with a focus on reading and studying school textbook chapters, content area vocabulary development, and comprehension strategies. Some of the comprehension strategies in Chapter 5 also may be helpful in teaching content area literacy.

REFERENCES

Afolayan, J. A. (1992). Documentary perspective of bibliotherapy in education. *Reading Horizons, 33,* 137–148.

Alvermann, D., Dillon, D. R., & O'Brien, D. G. (1987). *Using discussion to promote reading comprehension.* Newark, DE: International Reading Association.

Bauer, M. S., & Balius, F. A., Jr. (1995). Storytelling: Integrating therapy and curriculum for students with serious emotional disturbances. *Teaching Exceptional Children, 27*(2), 24–28.

Baumann, J. F., & Bergeron, B. S. (1993). Story map instruction using children's literature: Effects on first graders' comprehension of central narrative elements. *Journal of Reading Behavior, 25,* 407–437.

Bidwell, S. M. (1990). Using drama to increase motivation, comprehension, and fluency. *Journal of Reading, 34*(1), 38–41.

Block, C. C., & Israel, S. E. (2004). The ABCs of performing highly effective think-alouds. *The Reading Teacher, 58*(2), 154–167.

Borders, S., & Paisley, P. O. (1992). Children's literature as a resource for classroom guidance. *Elementary School Guidance & Counseling, 27,* 131–139.

Boulineau, T., Fore, C., III, Hagan-Burke, S., & Burke, M. D. (2004). Use of story-mapping to increase the story grammar text comprehension of elementary students with learning disabilities. *Journal of Learning Disabilities, 27,* 105–121.

Brown, J. S., Collins, A., & Duguid, P. (1989). Situated cognition and the culture of learning. *Educational Researcher, 18*(1), 32–42.

Casteel, C. P., Isom, B. A., & Jordan, K. F. (2000). Creating confident and competent readers: Transactional strategies instruction. *Intervention in School and Clinic, 36,* 67–74.

Choate, J. S., Enright, B. E., Miller, L. J., Poteet, J. A., & Rakes, T. A. (1995). *Curriculum-based assessment and programming.* Boston: Allyn & Bacon.

Climo, S. (1989). *The Egyptian Cinderella.* New York: HarperCollins.

Cornett, C. E., & Cornett, C. F. (1980). *Bibliotherapy: The right book at the right time.* Bloomington, IN: Phi Delta Kappa Educational Foundation.

Davis, Z. T. (1994). Effects of prereading story mapping on elementary readers' comprehension. *Journal of Educational Research, 87,* 353–360.

Dupont, S. (1992). The effectiveness of creative drama as an instructional strategy to enhance the reading comprehension skills of fifth-grade remedial readers. *Reading Research and Practice, 31*(3), 41–52.

Dymock, S. (2007). Comprehension strategy instruction: Teaching narrative text structure awareness. *Reading Teacher, 61*(2), 161–167.

Emery, D. W. (1996). Helping readers comprehend stories from the characters' perspectives. *The Reading Teacher, 49,* 534–541.

Fink, L. S. (2008). *Book report alternative: Examining story elements using story map comic strips.* Retrieved April 6, 2008, from http://www.readwritethink.org/lessons/lesson_view.asp?id=236.

Foley, M. M. (2000). The (un)making of a reader. *Language Arts, 77*(6), 506–511.

Gambrell, L. B. (1996). What research reveals about discussion. In L. B. Gambrell & J. F. Almasi (Eds.), *Lively discussion! Fostering engaged reading* (pp. 25–38). Newark, DE: International Reading Association.

Gambrell, L. B., & Chasen, S. P. (1991). Explicit story structure instruction and the narrative writing of fourth- and fifth-grade below-average readers. *Reading Research and Instruction, 31*(1), 54–62.

Gardill, M. C., & Jitendra, A. K. (1999). Advanced story map instruction: Effects on the reading comprehension of students with learning disabilities. *Journal of Special Education, 33*(1), 2–17, 28.

Gauthier, L. R. (2001). Coop-Dis-Q: A reading comprehension strategy. *Intervention in School and Clinic, 36,* 217–220.

Gray, C. (2007). *GIST: A summarizing strategy for use in any content area.* Retrieved April 6, 2008, from http://www.readwritethink.org/lessons/lesson_view.asp?id=290.

Hager, D., & Vaughn, S. (1995). Parent, teacher, and self-reports of the social competence of students with learning disabilities. *Journal of Learning Disabilities, 28,* 201–215.

Hagood, B. F. (1997). Reading and writing with help from story grammar. *Teaching Exceptional Children, 29*(4), 10–14.

Henry, L. (2005). *Building reading comprehension through think-alouds.* Retrieved April 6, 2008, from http://www.readwritethink.org/lessons/lesson_view.asp?id=139.

Idol, L. (1987). Group story mapping: A comprehension strategy for both skilled and unskilled readers. *Journal of Learning Disabilities, 20,* 196–205.

Idol, L., & Croll, V. J. (1987). Story-mapping training as a means of improving reading comprehension. *Learning Disability Quarterly, 10,* 214–229.

Johnson, D. W., Johnson, R. T., & Holubec, E. J. (1994). *The new circles of learning: Cooperation in the classroom and school.* Alexandria, VA: Association for Supervision and Curriculum Development.

Kelin, D. A., II. (2007). The perspective from within: Drama and children's literature. *Early Childhood Education Journal, 35*(3), 277–284.

Klingner, J. K., & Vaughn, S. (1998). Using collaborative strategic reading. *Teaching Exceptional Children, 30*(6), 32–37.

Klingner, J. K., Vaughn, S., Arguelles, M. E., Hughes, M. T., & Leftwich, S. A. (2004). Collaborative strategic reading: "Real world" lessons from classroom teachers. *Remedial & Special Education, 25*(5), 291–302.

Liang, L. A., & Dole, J. A. (2006). Help with teaching reading comprehension: Comprehension instructional frameworks. *Reading Teacher, 59*(8), 742–753.

Manning, M. (2002). Self-monitoring reading. *Teaching K–8, 32*(4), 103–104.

Mathes, P. G., & Fuchs, D. (1997). Cooperative story mapping. *Remedial and Special Education, 18*(1), 20–27.

Montague, M., & Graves, A. (1993). Improving students' story writing. *Teaching Exceptional Children, 25*(4), 36–37.

Moss, D. M. (1989). *Shelley: The hyperactive turtle.* Bethesda, MD: Woodbine House.

Myracle, L. (1995). Molding the minds of the young: The history of bibliotherapy as applied to children and adolescents. *The Alan Review, 22*(2), 36–40.

National Institute of Child Health and Development. (2000). *Teaching children to read: An evidence-based assessment of the scientific research literature on reading and its implications for reading instruction* (Report of the National Reading Panel). Retrieved September 20, 2008, from http://www.nichd.nih.gov/publications/nrp/findings.cfm.

O'Neill, C., Lambert, A., Linnell, R., & Warr-Wood, J. (1976). *Drama guidelines.* Portsmouth, NH: Heinemann.

Oster, L. (2001). Using the think-aloud for reading instruction. *Reading Teacher, 55*(1), 64–69.

Ouzts, D. T. (1991). The emergence of bibliotherapy as a discipline. *Reading Horizons, 31,* 199–206.

Palincsar, A. S., & Brown, A. L. (1984). The reciprocal teaching of comprehension-fostering and comprehension-monitoring activities. *Cognition and Instruction, 1,* 117–173.

Pardeck, J. T. (1995). Bibliotherapy: An innovative approach for helping children. *Early Child Development and Care, 110*, 83–88.

Pressley, M., Brown, R., El-Dinary, P. B., & Afflerbach, P. (1995). The comprehension instruction that students need: Instruction fostering constructively responsive reading. *Learning Disabilities Research and Practice, 10*, 215–224.

Raphael, T. (1982). Questioning-answering strategies for children. *The Reading Teacher, 37*, 377–382.

Rawls, W. (1976). *Summer of the monkeys.* Garden City, NJ: Doubleday.

Rogoff, B. (1990). *Apprenticeship in thinking: Cognitive development in social context.* New York: Oxford University Press.

Rosenblatt, L. M. (1982). The literary transaction: Evocation and response. *Theory into Practice, 21*, 268–277.

Rosenshine, B., & Meister, C. (1994). Reciprocal teaching: A review of the research. *Review of Educational Research, 64*, 479–530.

Ruckdeschel, S. (2007). *Scaffolding comprehension strategies using graphic organizers.* Retrieved April 6, 2008, from http://www.readwritethink.org/lessons/lesson_view.asp?id=95.

Schmitt, M. C., & O'Brien, D. G. (1986). Story grammars: Some cautions about the translation of research into practice. *Reading Research and Instruction, 26*, 1–8.

Smolkin, L. B., & Donovan, C. A. (2002). "Oh excellent, excellent question!": Developmental differences and comprehension acquisition. In C. C. Block & M. Pressley (Eds.), *Comprehension instruction: Research-based best practices* (pp. 140–157). New York: Guilford.

Sousa, D. A. (2001). *How the special needs brain learns.* Thousand Oaks, CA: Corwin Press.

Sridhar, D., & Vaughn, S. (2000). Bibliotherapy for all: Enhancing reading comprehension, self-concept, and behavior. *Teaching Exceptional Children, 33*(2), 74–82.

Stanfa, K., & O'Shea, D. (1998). The play's the thing for reading comprehension. *Teaching Exceptional Children, 31*(2), 48–55.

Stein, N., & Levine, L. (1990). Making sense out of emotion: A goal-directed analysis of action. In N. Stein, B. Leventhal, & T. Trabasso (Eds.), *Psychological and biological approaches to emotion* (pp. 45–73). Hillsdale, NJ: Erlbaum.

Strother, D. B. (1989). Developing thinking skills through questioning. *Phi Delta Kappan, 71*, 324–327.

Swanson, P. N., & DeLaPaz, S. (1998). Teaching effective comprehension strategies to students with learning and reading disabilities. *Intervention in School and Clinic, 33*, 209–218.

Vaughn, S., & Klingner, J. K. (1999). Teaching reading comprehension through collaborative strategic reading. *Intervention in School and Clinic, 34*, 284–292.

Vaughn, S., Klingner, J. K., & Bryant, D. P. (2001). Collaborative strategic reading as a means to enhance peer-mediated instruction for reading comprehension and content-area learning. *Remedial and Special Education, 22*, 66–74.

Vygotsky, L. S. (1978). *Mind in society: The development of higher mental psychological processes.* Cambridge, MA: Harvard University Press.

Wagner, B. J. (1988). Does classroom drama affect the arts of language? *Language Arts, 65*, 46–56.

Wilhelm, J. D. (2001). Think-alouds boost reading comprehension. *Instructor, 110*(4), 26–28.

Reading Comprehension in the Content Areas 6

Strategies Presented in This Chapter Include

✓ KWPLS: Know, Want to Know, Predict, Learned, Summarize

✓ Analogies Instruction

✓ The Possible Sentences Strategy

✓ A Vocabulary Self-Collection Strategy

✓ GRITS: A Guided Reading in Textual Settings

✓ ReQuest: Asking Self-Declared Questions

✓ Idea Circles

✓ Intra-Act: Sharing Perspectives

✓ Question-Answer Relationships

✓ RTI Case Study for Reading Comprehension in the Content Areas

CONTENT AREA READING AND THE BRAIN

While most reading instruction in Grades K–3 is done as part of basal reading instruction and emphasizes reading skills specifically, reading in subsequent years involves reading of content area texts as well as continued instruction in basal readers. Because content area reading tends to emphasize the content rather than specific reading skills, the brain regions involved in the reading process may function a bit differently. By the time most students are exposed to content area reading, they have mastered many of the initial reading skills discussed in Chapters 1, 2, 3, and 4 of this book (e.g., phoneme manipulation, phonics, and simple vocabulary). In short, they have reached a high level of automaticity in decoding words, such that actual mental efforts in phoneme recognition are somewhat reduced, whereas more effort is involved in extracting meaning from the text. The research on brain involvement in reading has shown this picture quite clearly in the form of brain scans. For advanced readers—typically the readers involved in content area reading—the areas of the brain that tend to be most active are not Wernicke's area (which, as you recall, deals with auditory discrimination) or the visual cortex (which has primary responsibility for "seeing" the letters on the page), but Broca's area, which is where meaning is attached to words. Consequently, reading in content areas is, to some degree, slightly different from earlier reading in terms of brain function.

The picture described above holds true for the average to good readers who have acquired the phonemic awareness, phonics, vocabulary, and comprehension skills that they need to apply to content area reading. Students with learning difficulties still may be struggling with some or all of these skills, which can make content reading laborious. Thus, if efforts are spent on decoding and pronouncing words as well as determining the meaning of numerous vocabulary words, students with learning difficulties do not comprehend or obtain the necessary meaning from what they read. In addition, students in content classes are expected to learn, remember, and apply a wealth of facts and concepts in each content class. In earlier chapters, we have mentioned how students with learning difficulties have difficulty remembering information because they have not been able to process it in a way that it can be remembered. Because of limited background knowledge, these students may not be able to relate the new information to what they have already learned. In addition, students with learning difficulties may not have good organization and study habits that will enable them to work with content information effectively.

Some of the comprehension strategies and tactics discussed in Chapter 5 can be applied to content area reading. For students with learning difficulties, it is important to give them practice in using newly learned strategies in a variety of classes, so they can see that the strategies are valuable learning tools to be used often. This chapter will present additional strategies for teachers to use in content area instruction in the elementary and middle grades with a focus on reading and studying chapters in school textbooks, content vocabulary development, and comprehension strategies.

Reading expository text in content area classes may pose problems for students with reading difficulties or students who have not learned appropriate strategies to help them read and remember important information. To compound the difficulty of students' comprehending expository text, some content area teachers in Grades 4 through 12 fail to provide instruction in the comprehension process (DiCecco & Gleason, 2002). If students, particularly those with reading problems, are expected to read chapters and answer comprehension questions, then they need to be provided some instruction on how to examine text structure and explain important information (Beck, McKeown, Hamilton, & Kucan, 1998; Durkin, 1978/1979; Gillespie & Rasinski, 1989). For example, the following words can help students identify text structures.

Sequence				Compare and Contrast	
first	second	before	while	yet	but
after	initially	finally	either	like	unlike
next	earlier	later	although	similarly	opposites
when	now	then	less than	more than	most
Cause and Effect			Problem/Solution		
because	since	thus	propose	conclude	a solution
if . . . then	therefore	as a result	the problem	the question	evidence is
consequently	nevertheless	then . . . so	reason for	research shows	
on account of	for this reason	due to			

SOURCE: Adapted from Alvermann and Phelps (1998, p. 210) and Fountas and Pinnell (2001, p. 402).

Even young children can be taught to start looking for some of these cue words when they are reading. For example, words such as first, second, and third indicate that several things are being mentioned in a particular order or sequence. Young students learn that words such as earlier, later, and now give an indication of time. They also can be taught to compare two people, places, things, or ideas. For example, second or third grade students may find the similarities and differences of Alaska and Hawaii during a social studies activity. Young students begin to learn about cause and effect when they find the answers to questions such as the following: Why did that happen? What caused that to happen? What did the people think or what did they do when that happened? Some of the questioning and story map strategies in Chapter 5 can help young students with learning difficulties identify problems and solutions. Perhaps using the story maps or the drama strategies discussed in Chapter 5 will help to make abstract concepts such as sequencing, comparison, cause and effect, and problem solution more concrete for students with learning difficulties.

Graphic organizers (GOs) can help students learn to explore text structures and determine the relationships among concepts to elicit meaning from text information that they read. While the concept of GOs was described initially in Chapter 4 as an effective way to teach vocabulary, we explore the idea here as a mechanism for content area reading instruction. These visual depictions or illustrations label the relationships among key concepts to make them more explicit (see Hudson, Lignugaris-Kraft, Miller, 1993; Moore & Readance, 1984; Novak & Gowin, 1984). Graphic organizers often use spatial arrangements, geometric shapes, lines, and arrows to display text structure and identify relationships (Darch, Carnine, & Kame'enui, 1986). In a study of middle school students with learning disabilities, DiCecco and Gleason (2002) found that GOs aided students with learning disabilities in recalling relational knowledge, particularly when they were asked to write essays to assess their knowledge of the content material.

In a meta-analysis of graphic organizer research, Moore and Readance (1984) found that teachers who used GOs indicated that they felt more competent in teaching the content material to students. More specifically, they perceived being more organized, more in control of learning activities, and more aware of learning task demands. DiCecco and Gleason (2002) cautioned that effectively incorporating graphic organizers into instruction is more than showing students a graphic organizer on an overhead projector. It includes teacher modeling, guided practice, and review. Ellis (2000) suggested a means of scaffolding instruction using graphic organizers (see Teaching Tip 6.1). Larkin (2001) also provided some general scaffolding tips that are applicable to scaffolding graphic organizer instruction as well (see Teaching Tip 6.2).

TEACHING TIP 6.1

Scaffolding Graphic Organizer Instruction

Ellis (2000) noted that the scaffolding or support provided by a teacher or peers can be represented as a four-stage process in which more support is provided at first through the modeling of teacher-constructed GOs. Then teacher mediation is provided when the graphic organizers are co-constructed by the teacher and students, peer mediation is used when students develop or complete graphic organizers in cooperative learning procedures with peers, and finally self-mediation occurs when students independently construct or complete graphic organizers. This continuum of scaffolding or support may be represented as:

I do it	We do it	Students do it	You do it
Teacher develops GO and presents it to students	Teacher and class co-construct GO	Students work in pairs or small groups to construct GO with minimal, if any, teacher assistance	Individual student constructs GO without assistance

SOURCE: Adapted from Ellis (2000, p. 7).

TEACHING TIP 6.2

General Guidelines for Effective Scaffolding

Larkin (2001) provided general guidelines suggested by teachers for effective scaffolding. These guidelines are applicable to graphic organizer instruction.

- *Identify students' background knowledge.* To help students learn new information, incorporate some information that they already know. For example, if students were asked to complete a graphic organizer in which they were to compare and contrast information about United States presidents, asking them to compare attributes of more current presidents (i.e., Bill Clinton and George W. Bush) may help them to learn information about the presidents with whom they are less familiar (e.g., Franklin D. Roosevelt and Herbert Hoover).

... Scaffolding steps

- *Begin with what students can do.* When incorporating graphic organizers into instruction, plan some easier tasks first. Some students may be lost if they were asked to compare and contrast specific U.S. presidents, but if they first completed a fact sheet for each of the presidents (e.g., Bill Clinton, George W. Bush, Franklin D. Roosevelt, and Herbert Hoover), then they could later use that information to complete the compare and contrast graphic organizers.

- *Help students achieve success quickly.* This is tied closely to *begin with what students can do.* By providing lessons and activities where students can do the work, their self-esteem grows because they view themselves as being successful. Quick and continued success may be what some students need to break their cycle of academic failure.

- *Know when it's time to stop.* Students need drill and practice to aid their learning, but the sure way to turn students off to learning is to overdo the drill and practice. Thus, plan meaningful ways in which students can use graphic organizers (e.g., taking notes, preparing study guides, as a test alternative) rather than require the same old work with GOs day in and day out.

- *Help students to be independent when they have command of the activity.* Don't let your students remain teacher dependent when they have mastered using particular graphic organizers. Encourage and help them to use GOs on their own in other classes and in real life situations, since the teacher will not always be there for assistance. The key to effective scaffolding is helping students to move toward independence by providing support when needed and *gradually* lessening it and removing it as it is no longer needed.

Griffin and Tulbert (1995) reviewed literature on graphic organizer research to glean recommendations for classroom practice, which include

- GOs are more effective when used with expository texts as opposed to lecture activities.
- GO instruction is more effective if vocabulary is the criterion measure used (Moore & Readance, 1980, 1984).
- GOs are more effective when constructed using the following steps (Horton & Lovitt, 1989):
    - Divide chapters into approximately 1,500-word passages.
    - Construct an outline of main ideas in the reading passage.
    - Select a GO format to fit the structure of the information.
    - Both teacher and students prepare versions of the GO.

KWPLS (KNOW, WANT TO KNOW, PREDICT, LEARNED, SUMMARIZE)

Originally, KWL was designed to help students think about what they already knew about a topic (i.e., activate background knowledge), determine what they want to know about the topic, and then (after reading the passage) review what they have learned about the topic (Ogle, 1986, 1989). KWL works well for students of many ages to help them make connections among previously learned information and new information to be learned as well as ask questions about their learning. A printable version of a KWL chart suitable for Grades PreK–12 is available at http://www.eduplace.com/graphicorganizer/pdf/kwl.pdf. For example, younger students in science class may be studying plants. Prior to beginning a unit or the lessons on plants, the students and teacher together could fill out a KWL chart on plants.

KWL Chart on Plants

What we know	What we want to find out	What we learned
Plants are living things.	What do plants need to live?	Plants need water, sunlight, and nutrients to live.
Some animals eat plants.	What do you call those who eat plants?	Herbivores eat plants.
Many plants are green.	What causes plants to be green?	Chlorophyll is the substance that makes plants green.
Some plants grow tall.	What are some kinds of plants that grow tall?	Corn and sunflowers are plants that grow tall.

A sample lesson by Finnegan and Manning (2007) uses KWL to help students in Grades 3–5 learn about the perspectives of slaves and slave owners. The lesson is intended for five one-hour sessions. Although the book the students read in the lesson is fiction, students must tap into their background knowledge about slavery and the Underground Railroad. In the lesson, students also refer to their KWL charts to help with some related writing projects.

KWPLS is a variation by Larkin (2001) on the KWL strategy and graphic organizer that not only helps students to accomplish the K step, the W step, and the L step, but also encourages students to make predictions before reading and during reading (i.e., the P step—predict) and to summarize main ideas after reading (i.e., the S step—summarize). Each student is given a copy of the blank KWPLS graphic organizer and will need to be instructed in how to use the KWPLS strategy and GO sheet.

A reproducible blank copy of KWPLS may be found on page 203. See Teaching Tips 6.1 and 6.2 on scaffolding GO instruction and general guidelines for effective scaffolding to help you determine how to introduce a new GO to your students.

KWPLS is designed to help students pay attention to the things that good readers do in the before, during, and after reading sequence. The KWPLS GO is designed to guide students through the before, during, and after sequence, but be sure to caution your students not to fill in the shaded boxes. For example, they cannot fill in the have learned box prior to reading the chapter or passage. They also cannot complete the know box for background knowledge during or after reading to encourage them to examine background knowledge prior to reading. You might explain to your students that they will continue to use background knowledge during reading and after reading, but it will only be necessary to record it on the KWPLS sheet prior to reading. See the blank KWPLS sheet on page 203.

	K *Know*	W *Want to know*	P *Predict*	L *Learned*
	LOOK AT:	*Title →*	*Pictures →*	*Headings*
Before Reading				
During Reading				
After Reading				
Summarize main ideas in one sentence				

	K Know	W Want to know	P Predict	L Learned
	LOOK AT:	Title →	Pictures →	Headings
Before Reading	• The U.S. National Government has three branches. • The President is the head of the Executive Branch. • The President is elected to a four-year term of office.	• What are the three branches of U.S. government? • What are some of the powers of each branch? • How are members of each branch selected?	• The three branches of U.S. government are the House of Representatives, the Senate, and the President. • Only the President can make laws. • The members of each branch are elected directly by the people.	• The three branches are the legislative, executive, and judicial. • The U.S. Congress has the primary responsibility to make laws. • Members of Congress are elected directly by the people.
During Reading		• The Constitution gives the power to declare war to which branch? • How many members are in the U.S. House of Representatives? • How many justices are on the U.S. Supreme Court?	• The Constitution gives power to declare war to the Congress. • There are 100 members in the U.S. House of Representatives. • There are 50 justices on the U.S. Supreme Court.	
After Reading		• How is the Chief Justice of the U.S. selected? • What is the length of term of office for a U.S. Representative? • What is the length of the term of office for a U.S. Senator?	• The Chief Justice of the U.S. is selected by the other justices. • Representatives are elected for four years. • Senators are elected for six years.	• The Constitution gives Congress the power to declare war. • There are 435 representatives. • There are nine justices on the Supreme Court.

Summarize main ideas in one sentence   The powers of the U.S. national government are divided among the legislative, executive, and judicial branches.

On the sample KWPLS sheet on page 204, students are learning about the three branches of U.S. national government. Before reading they are asked to look at the title, pictures, and headings of the passage or chapter that they will be reading and record information that they already know about the U.S. government branches (K) and what they want to know (W). Then they are to predict (P) what information they might learn from reading the selection. During reading, they are asked to continue to formulate questions about what they want to know (W), continue to make predictions (P), and record new information that they learned (L). After reading, students are asked to continue to record information that they want to know (W), make predictions (P), and list additional information that they learned (L). At any point in this process, students may reexamine their predictions and place an X through those predictions that they learned are incorrect. Students may want to wait until after reading and recording all of the KWPL information to reexamine their predictions, or the teacher may have a follow-up activity where students work with a peer buddy to reexamine their predictions. Finally, students are asked to look over their almost completed KWPLS sheet to make one summary (S) statement that captures the essential information learned from the reading. Students with learning difficulties can benefit from using the KWPLS sheet to help them sort out essential information from the trivial and to feel comfortable in making predictions. These students likely will need guidance to follow the steps in using the sheet. Teacher cues and covering (with a blank piece of paper) the row(s) of the sheet not being used at any particular time will aid these students.

ANALOGIES INSTRUCTION

In content area reading, students with learning difficulties often encounter abstract ideas that may be difficult to comprehend because they do not or cannot relate the ideas to their own background knowledge and experiences (McKenna & Robinson, 2002). Glynn (1996) and others have noted that the use of analogies can help to make abstract content interesting and understandable. By connecting new with known information, students can deepen their understanding of content material read (Kuse & Kuse, 1986). Glynn offered the following suggestions for teaching with analogies (TWA):

1. *Introduce the new concept.* Graphic organizers may be used to help identify the characteristics and background information about the new concept.

2. *Review a familiar concept* to be presented through an analogy.

3. *Identify the features* of both new and familiar concepts.

4. *Explain the similarities* of the two concepts.

5. *Explain the differences* where the analogy breaks down or no longer applies.

6. *Draw conclusions.* In other words, what are the big ideas that students need to remember about the new concept?

Suggesting several analogies and asking students to critique them at the end of a unit can modify the TWA activity (McKenna & Robinson, 2002). Students must decide which analogies work and which don't. After students have had experience working with analogies, then they may be ready to suggest their own analogies.

A Venn diagram may assist younger students in making comparisons through analogies (printable version available at http://www.eduplace.com/ graphicorganizer/pdf/venn.pdf). For example, young students in a social studies class may want to compare fighting in a war to being sick. When individuals are fighting in a war or are sick, they may be told what they have to do and may not get to eat the foods that they want to eat. Fighting in a war is different from being sick because children can get sick, but likely will not fight in a war.

Synectics is a form of analogous comparison by comparing something that is new or difficult with something that is familiar in order to stretch one's thinking. Larkin (2001) developed a synectics graphic organizer to help students stretch their thinking while learning about the Choctaw Indians during a social studies lesson (presented on page 207). Students use the GO to compare concepts about the Choctaws (new ideas) with concepts that are familiar.

The partially completed GO gives students practice in completing various parts of the analogy. For statements 1 and 2 in the far left column of the GO, students are asked to supply a familiar concept with which to compare the statements. For statements 3 and 4, students are given a familiar object, but must explain a comparison that can be made with the statements. For statements 5, 6, and 7, students are asked to supply both a concept or object with which the statement can be compared and the comparison to be made. Until students with learning difficulties are familiar with using the synectics sheet, the teacher may want to supply a partially completed sheet in which students only list the concept or object for comparison, because the comparison is already made (e.g., as in statements 1 and 2). Then students may work on sheets in which they only make the comparison, because the familiar object or concept for comparison is given (e.g., as in statements 3 and 4). Finally, students may be ready for a combination of either the familiar concept or object being given or the comparison being given (e.g., as in statements 5, 6, and 7).

Other ideas for helping students to think by analogy can be found in a sample lesson found on the Journey North (2006) Web site at http://www .learner.org/jnorth/tm/hotdog.html. In the lesson, "How Is a Hot Dog Like a Shoe?" students use and explain analogies to show their comprehension of new concepts. Suggestions are given for both younger and older students.

REFLECTIVE EXERCISE 6.1
GUIDING PRINCIPLES FOR TEACHING CONTENT

In the preceding section, we noted that GOs help students to explore text structures and determine the relationships among concepts to elicit meaning from text information. Therefore, helping students to explore text structures and determine relationships among concepts to elicit meaning could be considered a guiding principle for teaching

(Continued on page 208)

Choctaw Loss of Homeland

Directions: Making comparisons between two objects or ideas will help you to express your feelings and ideas. Fill in the blanks to complete the analogies.

1. The Choctaw signing the Treaty of Hopewell with the U.S. government	is like		because	it establishes peace and friendship.
2. In the 1700s the Spanish establishing forts on the borders of Choctaw land	is like		because	they try to protect their interests.
3. The U.S. government and missionaries attempting to "civilize" the Choctaw by teaching them the values of the non-Indian society	is like	a razor	because	
4. The United States trying to acquire additional Choctaw land	is like	a candy bar	because	
5. Promises made to the Choctaw by the U.S. government	are like		because	
6. Shawnee chief Tecumseh's urging the Choctaw council to rise up against white intruders	is like		because	
7. The loss of the Choctaw homeland	is like		because	

207

REFLECTIVE EXERCISE 6.1 (Continued)

content. Think about other principles that might guide you in teaching content lessons to make those lessons more meaningful to students. If you are having difficulty thinking of those on the spot, ponder this topic as you are planning your lessons, driving home from school, or during a few minutes of quiet time. Also, think about guiding principles as you read the remainder of this chapter. You may want to add principles such as helping students to develop, tap into, and use their background knowledge; helping students to make predictions about what they read and check their predictions; and summarizing what they have learned. These reading tactics are supported by the research (National Institute of Child Health and Development [NICHD], 2000) and should be used in every classroom. Keep your list of principles accessible and review it periodically. You might want to discuss some of these principles with your colleagues and share some ideas.

POSSIBLE SENTENCES

The possible sentences activity is a pre- and postreading strategy that will help students with learning difficulties to learn content area vocabulary by (a) drawing upon their background knowledge of a topic, (b) making predictions about possible sentences that might appear in their reading, and (c) using partial knowledge about selected vocabulary words (Buehl, 2001; Stahl & Kapinus, 1991). In this activity, students are instructed to create possible sentences using both known and unknown vocabulary terms from the reading passage and then to examine the truth of those sentences using the reading passage.

The possible sentences activity was used with fifth-grade students in two studies and was found to improve students' vocabulary and factual information recall (Stahl & Kapinus, 1991). In one study, Stahl and Kapinus reported that a structured discussion of predicting how key vocabulary words will be used in a reading passage as opposed to only a general discussion of that passage seemed to improve recall of that passage.

Stahl and Kapinus (1991) noted the following steps in the possible sentences strategy:

1. The teacher selects approximately six to eight words (i.e., usually key concepts) that might pose difficulty for the students (e.g., barometer, humidity, meteorology).

2. Then the teacher chooses four to six additional words that are familiar to the students (e.g., rain, clouds, predict).

3. Next, the teacher puts the ten to twelve words on the board or overhead transparency along with a short definition if necessary.

4. Students are asked to think of possible sentences containing at least two of the words in the forthcoming reading passage or chapter. This forces students to examine the relationships (e.g., synonyms, antonyms, superordinates, subordinates, and examples) among words.

5. The teacher then puts the student contributions on the board or transparency. All predictions are included and the accuracy or inaccuracy of the predictions is not discussed at this time.

6. When students have included all words in at least one sentence, they are instructed to read the passage or chapter.

7. After the reading, the class discusses whether the sentences could or could not be true based on what they have read. True sentences are left as is on the board, while students discuss ways to modify untrue sentences. The discussion aspect may help students with both high and low background knowledge of the topic. Thus, listening to others' contributions can help those students who are less willing to participate. In addition, comparing the sentence contexts created prior to reading to those after reading the passage or chapter requires students to pay attention to words in context. Finally, through generating sentences, reading the passage or chapter, and in the follow-up activities, students receive multiple exposures to their vocabulary words.

Note that this strategy can be used for students with learning difficulties at various grade levels by selecting vocabulary words that students may not know but will encounter in the materials they will be reading. Another option is to use the strategy to help young students improve their listening vocabulary. Thus, in Step 6 the teacher may read the passage to the students or they may listen to the passage via audiotape, videotape, CD, or DVD.

VOCABULARY SELF-COLLECTION STRATEGY (VSS)

The vocabulary self-collection strategy (VSS) helps students acquire and remember content area language for specific subjects (Haggard, 1986; Vacca & Vacca, 2002). Through VSS, students decide the importance of particular concepts and use contextual clues to establish meaning. Students with learning difficulties especially can benefit from practice in using context clues. Once students have read and discussed a reading assignment, they can begin using VSS. The following summarizes the VSS steps:

1. *Teacher models.* The teacher nominates a word and models the VSS procedures (i.e., how to respond to the three questions in Step 4) for students.

2. *Select teams.* Teams may be teacher selected or student selected and should consist of two to five students.

3. *Nominate a word.* Each team chooses a word from the text selection to emphasize. The word should be one that they believe is important enough to share with the class and that they would like to learn more about.

4. *Present the word.* A spokesperson from each team identifies its nominated word and responds to these questions:

    a. *Where is the word located in the text?* The spokesperson may either read the passage containing the word or describe the context of how the word is used.

    b. *What is the meaning of the word?* The team members determine the meaning of the word using context clues from the passage and additional references if needed.

    c. *Why is this word important to learn?* The team must justify why its nominated word is important enough to be emphasized.

The teacher's role is to write the nominated words and their meanings on the board or overhead transparency and facilitate class discussion by encouraging students to ask questions or provide additional clarification.

5. *Record nominated words.* Students record nominated words and their meanings in a learning log or vocabulary notebook. These vocabulary lists may be reviewed and studied on a regular basis. The students may see these words several times again when their teacher includes the words in practice or extension activities.

Like in the possible sentences strategy, VSS may be used to help younger students with learning difficulties to hone their listening skills and increase their content area vocabulary. The teacher may guide students in listening for new words while he or she reads a passage.

The results of VSS research are promising. Ruddell and Shearer (2002) studied three classes of middle school students during an intensive reading intervention for 45 minutes a day. All of the 17 participants read two to four years below grade level. For VSS, each student nominated one word at the beginning of the week for the class list. The class had discussions through the week to determine the final list. At the end of the week, students were tested and expected to spell each word, explain the word definition, and write a good sentence using the word. The researchers found that the students increased the breadth and depth of their vocabulary knowledge and demonstrated abilities for learning new words strategically and independently. The students chose important, challenging, and interesting words. Also, the researchers noted that students would be more invested in learning self-selected words rather than lists from commercially prepared materials.

It was noted on the Southwest Educational Development Laboratory (2008) Web site that with vocabulary strategies such as possible sentences and VSS students could be encouraged to use words from other cultural contexts. Also stated was that VSS has been shown to be effective with second language learners.

 REFLECTIVE EXERCISE 6.2
SELECTING IMPORTANT VOCABULARY

You have just read about two strategies for helping students to learn content area vocabulary. In the VSS strategy, students nominate vocabulary words that they believe are important. Beyond the words that the students nominate, how will you determine the other vocabulary words that they need to learn? Students with learning difficulties can be overwhelmed with too many vocabulary words. This "spray and pray" instructional approach often means that the teacher exposes students to a large number of vocabulary terms and spends little time helping the students fully learn the terms and their meanings. Therefore, the teacher has to pray that the information will be retained.

Sometimes teachers feel pressured to cover content material rapidly to address curriculum standards or policies. Why not consider making a plan that not only helps students to meet curriculum standards, but more important, helps them to remember and use the vocabulary terms that they do learn? Don't forget that students with learning difficulties will need regular review to maintain and generalize the vocabulary words they have learned.

GUIDED READING IN TEXTUAL SETTINGS (GRITS)

McKenna (2002) indicated that students in upper elementary grades require extensive support when reading nonfiction. Some guided reading formats expect students to read large amounts of material without providing the necessary scaffolding for them to do so. Although background building, prereading activities, and postreading discussions provide support before and after silent reading, they do nothing to give students needed guidance during silent reading.

To address this problem (i.e., lack of support for students during silent reading), McKenna (2002) developed guided reading in textual settings (GRITS), which incorporates a number of research-validated strategies. These strategies include (a) charting—arranging information in rows and columns, (b) graphic organizers—arranging information in a flexible format such as a semantic map or Venn diagram to make abstract information more visible, (c) reading guides—providing questions and tasks for students to do while reading to help them stay on track, (d) think-alouds—modeling of one's thinking during reading and discussion, (e) walk-throughs—helping students to preview what they will be reading, and (f) analogies—comparing new and abstract ideas to those ideas that are familiar and concrete. Thus, GRITS employs many of the strategies and ideas that have already been discussed in this and other chapters.

McKenna (2002) found that GRITS provided the scaffolding that third grade students needed to comprehend science-related nonfiction. Prior to GRITS instruction, 24 of the students scored below instructional-level criteria as compared to 18 students who would not receive the four GRITS lessons. When the students were assessed at the end of the academic year, 22 of the 24 GRITS students met the criteria as opposed to 11 of the 18 non-GRITS students. McKenna concluded that students who participate in GRITS lessons tend to improve their grade-appropriate nonfiction reading skills, even in the absence of teacher support. When teachers teach students to use GRITS, they can assume that (a) students have little prior knowledge of the topic they will be reading, (b) students are not skilled at strategically reading nonfiction, (c) students are not accustomed to monitoring their comprehension while reading, and (d) students can be easily distracted, frustrated, or bored while reading (McKenna). Use the following steps to implement GRITS in your classroom.

Advance Preparation. Read the nonfiction passage ahead of time to look for terms, ideas, and so on that could pose difficulty for students. Think of questions and comments that may aid students when they come to difficult points. Decide how much information should be read and discussed at one time. For new and difficult information, one paragraph may be sufficient. For other information, students may be able to read and comprehend two or three paragraphs at one time. Prepare a reading guide for each part (i.e., one paragraph alone or two to three paragraphs together) of the selection. Use charts and graphic organizers if appropriate (McKenna, 2002). If students have not yet been introduced to reading guides, you may want to include some lessons first to help students become familiar with reading guides. Essentially, reading guides help students to look for particular information as they read. A reading guide may be in the form of a blank or partially completed graphic organizer that students finish as they read and locate the necessary information. Be sure to help students with learning difficulties become familiar with the information that is contained on the reading guide prior to reading the text selection.

Before Reading. Help students perform a walk-through of the selection prior to reading (McKenna, 2002). This includes focusing first on pictures and graphics and then asking students to make predictions about the pictures prior to reading the captions. Finally, have students examine the subheadings and help them to recognize how the selection is organized using the subheadings. Another prereading task is to build background knowledge. This is accomplished by discussing any introductory material contained in the selection (e.g., terms, guiding questions). Next, read the first paragraph aloud to help the class further build background by discussing terms, asking questions, and making predictions.

During Reading. Once the background is built, ask students to silently read the next paragraph (McKenna, 2002). If students have difficulty, provide assistance as needed. Then ask a student to read aloud the same paragraph. Ask students questions to help them connect the new information just read with background knowledge. Teacher think-alouds can help students learn how to process the new information. Suggesting analogies also can aid students in relating the new information to what they already know and understand.

After Reading. Ask students to complete the part of the reading guide that pertains to the paragraph just read and discussed (McKenna, 2002). Monitor and provide assistance as needed while students are completing the reading guide. Repeat the during reading and after reading steps (i.e., silent reading, oral rereading, discussion, and guide) throughout the entire selection, working on a paragraph or a small section (e.g., two to three paragraphs) at a time.

Follow-Up Activities. The final step in GRITS is to facilitate a postreading discussion of the entire selection using the completed reading guide (McKenna, 2002). Discussion topics should not be limited only to the reading guide.

REQUEST: ASKING SELF-DECLARED QUESTIONS

Although ReQuest originally was used for one-on-one instruction, this strategy easily can be adapted to help students in a content area classroom think while they read (Vacca & Vacca, 2002). Thus, the students ask self-declared questions in an active search for meaning. As noted in earlier chapters, students with learning difficulties need practice in formulating good questions that will guide their reading. Vacca and Vacca (pp. 207–208) outlined the following rules and adaptations for using ReQuest in the content area classroom:

1. Teacher and students silently read the same text segment. The teacher should consider using short passages (i.e., even those of one or two sentences) for students who have difficulty with comprehension.

2. After the teacher closes the book, students question their teacher. The teacher can show students that it is human to err while he or she is in the "hot seat" being questioned. Encourage students to ask the types of questions that a teacher might ask. The teacher may ask the students for clarification if he or she does not understand a question being asked. Variations: Have students alternate the role of questioner for each question in order for more students to participate in the activity. Have students work in ReQuest teams of three or four students that participate against each other with the teacher being the facilitator.

3. The teacher and students exchange roles. That is, the teacher asks the students about the text segment read. Students should be cautioned that "I don't know" is not an acceptable answer. If they do not know an answer, then they must explain why they do not know the information being queried. Students may justify their answers by making reference to the text. The teacher should model asking good questions and asking a variety of kinds of questions to help students improve their questioning techniques.

4. Steps 1, 2, and 3 are repeated for each section of text read.

5. Students make predictions about the remainder of the reading material assigned. When students have processed sufficient information to make predictions about the remainder of the reading assigned, the teacher will ask students to make their predictions and justify why they chose these predictions. The teacher should encourage students to speculate or take a risk with their predictions.

6. Students silently read the remainder of the reading material assigned.

7. The teacher facilitates a class discussion of the material just read.

IDEA CIRCLES

Teachers may be familiar with literature circles (also known as literature study groups and book clubs) in which a small group of students read the same story, poem, article, or book and individuals within the group perform a specific task to help facilitate a discussion (Daniels, 1994). The group meets regularly and rotates the following possible discussion roles at each session (adapted from Vacca et al., 2003):

- *Discussion director.* Generates discussion questions, convenes the meeting, and solicits contributions from the other group members.
- *Literary luminary/passage master.* Reads aloud important, memorable sections of the text.
- *Connector.* Helps group members connect real world ideas with text readings.
- *Illustrator.* Provides a graphic response to the text.
- *Summarizer.* In one or two minutes, highlights the key points and gist of the day's reading at the end of the meeting.
- *Vocabulary enricher/word wizard.* Records interesting or unfamiliar words encountered during reading and uses a dictionary or glossary to provide definitions during the literature circle.
- *Investigator/researcher.* Provides related background information (e.g., information about author, historical events, geography).

When the intended reading and discussion is finished, the information is shared with the larger community (e.g., class, school; Daniels, 1994). See Teaching Tip 6.3 to help students know how and what to share.

Idea circles, similar to literature circles, are peer-led small group discussions (i.e., three to six students) of concepts with the information obtained from multiple text sources (Guthrie & McCann, 1996; Vacca et al., 2003). The interaction rules (described in Teaching Tip 6.3) must be discussed explicitly, particularly for students with learning difficulties. If students read different informational books, then they can bring unique information to the idea circle discussions. You may want to have all students read a common passage from a text and then ask each of them to choose different related readings from books or reputable Internet sites. For students who struggle with decoding or even for younger students, listening to a teacher read books or listening to books on audiotape may be an option.

Make sure that all students know the goal of the idea circle. In the beginning, tell students what they must accomplish and the amount of time they have to work on the task. Setting a timer may be helpful for students with learning difficulties to assist them with monitoring their time. Students may have to collaboratively or individually complete a sheet to guide discussion within 15 minutes. A variation is to have students individually prepare guided discussion sheets prior to the idea circle meeting and then they collectively prepare one sheet summarizing the information brought to and

TEACHING TIP 6.3

Helping Students Share Information in Circle Activities

Some teachers may be afraid to turn their students loose with cooperative activities such as circle discussions. One key to making these successful learning activities for students is to make sure that students know and practice the rules.

How to Share

- Keep conversation going and avoid long pauses
- Respond to questions asked by other group members
- Give elaborative responses—tell why you responded as you did
- Challenge other group members' interpretations of the reading
- Clarify questions, responses, and ideas
- Remain on task
- Include all group members when discussing
- Give all group members a turn

What to Share

- Written responses supporting the discussion
- Questions to clarify and spark interest
- Personal reflections and background knowledge
- Activities that help construct meaning and support ideas
- Interpretations that involve higher-order thinking (i.e., go beyond literal interpretation)
- Feelings about the text read
- Real world connections (e.g., books, movies, television shows)
- Evaluation of the text read

SOURCE: Adapted from Goatley (1997).

contained in the discussion. A blank reproducible guided discussion sheet and a sample discussion sheet appear on pages 216–217. Final products resulting from the idea circle may be either individual or group efforts. Vacca et al. (2003) suggested that students might pool their efforts and prepare a graphics presentation for the class on their topic.

A sample lesson using idea circles and differentiated instruction can be found at http://www.bridgew.edu/Library/CAGS_Projects/LDUBIN/idea%20circles.htm. The content areas are science and language arts for third grade. In this lesson, the concept of idea circles is employed when students explore one concept using multiple texts. The differentiation of the lesson occurs because different levels of texts are used for student's different understandings of the concept and their differing ability levels. Also, the different texts may take into account the varied interests and learning styles of the students (Bridgewater State College, 2003).

Idea Circles Discussion Guide

Subject: _____ Topic: _____ Grade: _____

Information needed	Source
Important facts	
Opinions and perspectives	
Misconceptions	
Positive features	
Negative features or problems	

Idea Circles Discussion Guide	
Subject: _____ Science _____ Topic: _____ Birds _____ Grade: _____ 3 _____	
Information needed	*Source*
Important facts about birds • Kinds • Where they live • How they fly • How they reproduce	• Video watched in class • Classroom poster • Textbook • Encyclopedia
Opinions and perspectives • Protecting birds • Killing birds	• Interview friends and family • Organization web sites
Misconceptions • All birds fly	• Web sites
Positive features of birds • Beauty and music • Eat insects and worms	• Video • Web sites
Negative features or problems • Carry diseases • Make messes	• Textbook • Magazines

INTRA-ACT: SHARING PERSPECTIVES

When students with learning difficulties read content area materials, they need to not only comprehend what they have read, but also be able to participate in perspective sharing. In other words, they need to assess their own reactions to the material and be willing to hear the reactions of others. Intra-Act provides the groundwork for such reflective discussions (Vacca & Vacca, 2002). Students should work in small groups (i.e., four to six students, one of whom is the team leader) through the following four phases of Intra-Act (adapted from Vacca & Vacca, pp. 236–238.):

1. *Comprehension.* The teacher facilitates student comprehension by introducing the text selection and helping students to use effective prereading strategies such as
   • Activating and building background knowledge
   • Making predictions about the content to be learned

   The student team leader initiates and sustains a seven- to ten-minute (less for younger students) discussion of the text material read. Group members may add information or ask clarification questions.

2. *Relating.* The team leader shifts the discussion (seven to ten minutes, or less for younger students) from important ideas in the reading to individual reactions to what students have read.

3. *Valuation.* The team leader distributes a game sheet to each group member. A reproducible blank game sheet is included below. The game sheet contains four declarative statements based on the reading for which students may have differing opinions. Each student establishes personal meaning by agreeing (circling A) or disagreeing (circling D) with each statement. Next, each student must predict how each of his or her team members will respond by circling A or D for each statement under the column for each respective group member's name.

Intra-Act Game Sheet

Group Member Names →					
Statements ↓					
1.	A D	A D	A D	A D	A D
	____	____	____	____	____
2.	A D	A D	A D	A D	A D
	____	____	____	____	____
3.	A D	A D	A D	A D	A D
	____	____	____	____	____
4.	A D	A D	A D	A D	A D
	____	____	____	____	____

4. *Reflection.* Each member scoring his or her game sheet begins the reflection phase of Intra-Act. As each group member indicates his or her response for each of the four statements, the remaining group members note whether their predictions are the same as the actual member's response. A plus sign (+) is placed on the blank line for each prediction that is the same as the respective member's response. A dash (–) is placed on the blank line for each prediction that is not the same as the respective member's response. The teacher facilitates the reflection phase to help students reflect on what they have learned. Students should be given adequate time to discuss and challenge each other's perspectives. The teacher may need to provide extra assistance to younger students with learning difficulties in recording their game sheets. Another option would be for the teacher to guide the students through verbalizing their perspectives and then record the information on the board or an overhead transparency.

Students with learning difficulties will need repeated participation in Intra-Act activities to help them learn their discussion roles. The teacher may want to have a class debriefing each time Intra-Act is used to help students determine what they learned from the process and how they can improve the process in the future.

QUESTION-ANSWER RELATIONSHIPS (QAR)

After students have read content area selections, teachers often ask them to answer questions either orally or in writing to demonstrate their comprehension of the material. With the size of current content texts and the length of chapters, students with learning difficulties may be overwhelmed by the amount of information they must search to locate answers to end of the chapter questions or other questions asked by the teacher. Students need to learn how to recognize the resources they will need for answering particular questions. For example, Bos and Vaughn (2002, p. 186) noted three arbitrary categories in which students must be able to distinguish between literal and inferential questions:

1. *Textually explicit.* Information can be obtained directly from the text material read, with only minimal use of the reader's background knowledge.

2. *Textually implicit.* Information can be obtained from the text material read, but the reader is required to activate background knowledge to use along with text information.

3. *Scriptually implicit.* Information cannot be located in the text, but must be obtained solely from the reader's background knowledge.

Swanson and DeLaPaz (1998) suggested that teachers show students how to identify question-answer relationships and then give them opportunities to label different kinds of questions according to the relationships. Teachers will need to make sure that students examine both the question and the answer to label the appropriate relationship. Rather than using the terms *explicit* and *implicit*, students with learning difficulties will find it easier to differentiate between "in the book" and "in my head" kinds of questions. Teachers should give students practice in answering both kinds of questions and ask them to reflect on how they knew the answers. For example, young students learning about the state in which they live (e.g., Georgia) might have to determine whether the following are "in the book" questions or "in my head" questions.

- What is the name of the state where I live? (in my head)
- What is the capital of the state where I live? (in my head)
- How many counties are in the state where I live? (in the book)
- What are the names of two towns or cities in the state where I live? (in my head)
- What is the name of the governor in the state where I live? (in the book)
- What are the main crops that are grown in the state where I live? (in the book)

Raphael and Au (2005) noted that reading independently is not a prerequisite for receiving QAR instruction. A first grade teacher could introduce her students to QAR language through listening comprehension when the teacher reads aloud to the students. The teacher encourages her students to ask questions about the story, which she writes on sticky notes. Then she models for the students whether their questions can be answered by information *In the Book* or information *In My Head*. A sixth-grade teacher also could introduce his students to *In the Book* and *In My Head* language of QAR by having the class read a passage followed by the two types of questions.

After students are comfortable with *In the Book* and *In My Head*, then they can learn the subcategories of each (Raphael & Au, 2005). The subcategories of *In the Book* are *Right There* and *Think and Search*. The subcategories of *In My Head* are *Author & Me* and *On My Own*. *Right There* answers are found in one place in the text. Answers for *Think and Search* questions mean that the answer is in the text, but the reader needs to combine different parts of the text to locate the answer. *On My Own* answers mean that the reader needs to tap into his or her own ideas and background experiences. For answers to *Author & Me* questions the reader will not find the answer in the text, but must think about how the text information and information that he or she knows fit together.

A sample lesson by Dennis-Shaw (2007) that helps students in Grades 3–5 to use question-answer relationships to aid reading comprehension can be found at http://www.readwritethink.org/lessons/lesson_view.asp?id=227. It is recommended that the lesson be conducted in three 60-minute sessions on consecutive days. In the lesson, students learn about the different types of question-answer relationships, answer literal and inferential questions as well as determine how and where to locate the answers, work in pairs and small groups to apply a self-questioning strategy to identify different types of questions and their answers in a text, and create questions to show their understanding of different types of QAR.

RTI CASE STUDY FOR READING IN THE COMPREHENSION AREAS

Chantelle is a fourth grade student in Mrs. Sandler's class. When Mrs. Sandler reviewed Chantelle's academic reports for Grades K–3, she noticed that Chantelle seemed to make average grades in all subjects. For the first three weeks of fourth grade, Chantelle continued to make average grades in all subjects. Then Mrs. Sandler observed that Chantelle was struggling with her reading comprehension, particularly in social studies and science. During language arts class, Chantelle did well with her reading decoding. She could pronounce almost every word and read fluently. Mrs. Sandler soon realized that Chantelle had developed coping strategies to help her with reading comprehension. Chantelle listened carefully as other students and the teacher read aloud. She often would question her friends as to what they thought the passage that she had just read was about. Chantelle also would pay careful attention to pictures and could remember class discussions about stories read from previous days and weeks.

One day, Mrs. Sandler had an individual conference with Chantelle. She asked her to read an unfamiliar grade level social studies passage. As anticipated, Chantelle read every word fluently. When Mrs. Sandler asked Chantelle questions about the passage she had just read, Chantelle was embarrassed that she could not answer the questions. Reluctantly, Chantelle read an unfamiliar passage from the science text for her teacher. Mrs. Sandler noticed that Chantelle read most of the words fluently, but struggled with some of the unfamiliar science vocabulary. Once again, Chantelle could not answer the questions that her teacher asked about the science text passage. Mrs. Sandler assured her now tearful student that she would help her learn to answer questions about what she had read.

Mrs. Sandler found that some of her other fourth graders were struggling with science and social studies vocabulary, so for a tier one intervention she decided to pre-teach vocabulary for these content areas. Each week, Mrs. Sandler prepared a list of science vocabulary words and a list of social studies vocabulary words complete with definitions for the students to put in their notebooks. Mrs. Sandler went over the vocabulary words at the beginning of each class on Monday prior to the students reading a new chapter. In addition, Mrs. Sandler introduced her students in science and social studies to a KWL chart. She modeled for her students how they could fill in what they already knew about a given topic, what they wanted to know, and then later after reading a chapter what they have learned. As most of the students began to understand how the KWL chart worked, Mrs. Sandler gradually removed some of the teacher and whole class support so that students were expected to complete the weekly KWL charts for science and social studies in pairs or individually. Mrs. Sandler noticed that Chantelle needed help from her peer buddy and sometimes the teacher to complete her KWL charts. Weekly social studies tests were given on Thursdays and weekly science tests were given on Fridays in Mrs. Sandler's room. The pre-taught vocabulary and the KWL charts were enough to boost the science and social studies grades of the lower-functioning students in Mrs. Sandler's class to passing. Chantelle improved with this tier one intervention, but she could not consistently make passing grades. She still struggled with answering the reading comprehension questions that accompanied each science and social studies chapter and she struggled with similar questions on the weekly tests. Figure 6.1 summarizes the tier one intervention Mrs. Sandler used in her classroom. Figure 6.2 illustrates Chantelle's reading comprehension scores for her weekly science and social studies tests.

Supplements to General Curriculum	Classroom Time (Facilitated by Teacher)	Student-Teacher Ratio
Before Reading—Teacher pre-teaches science and social studies vocabulary and students put vocabulary words with definitions in their notebooks.	Mondays Science—20 minutes Soc. Studies—20 minutes	25 to 1
Before Reading—Teacher models how to complete the K (Know) and W (Want to know) sections of the KWL chart.	Daily 4 days Science—10 minutes Soc. Studies—10 minutes	25 to 1
During Reading—Teacher models how to begin completing the L (Learned) section of the KWL chart	Daily 4 days Science—5 minutes Soc. Studies—5 minutes	25 to 1
After Reading—Teacher models how to finish completing the L (Learned) section of the KWL chart.	Daily 4 days Science—5 minutes Soc. Studies—5 minutes	25 to 1

Figure 6.1   Summary of Chantelle's Tier One Intervention

Week	Intervention	Science Score	Soc. Studies Score
1	Baseline	75%	77%
2	None	74%	75%
3	None	70%	72%
4	None	44%	52%
5	Pre-teach Vocabulary and KWL Chart	50%	55%
6	Pre-teach Vocabulary and KWL Chart	58%	60%
7	Pre-teach Vocabulary and KWL Chart	60%	64%
8	Pre-teach Vocabulary and KWL Chart	70%	72%
9	Pre-teach Vocabulary and KWL Chart	64%	68%
10	Pre-teach Vocabulary and KWL Chart	66%	69%

Figure 6.2   Chantelle's Reading Comprehension Scores for Science and Social Studies

At the end of the nine-week grading period, a tearful Chantelle stayed after school one day to tell Mrs. Sandler, "You promised me you would help me learn to answer questions about what I read and I still got D's in science and social studies. I tried really hard and it didn't work. My mom is not going to be happy with me or you." Mrs. Sandler assured Chantelle that she would try something else until they found a solution to this problem. She was disturbed by Chantelle's emotional outburst and even more disturbed that Chantelle's efforts were not helping her to be successful in science and social studies.

Mrs. Sandler talked to other fourth and fifth grade teachers in her school to come up with ideas that she could try that would provide more intensive instruction or tier two intervention for Chantelle and a few of her struggling peers in science and social studies. One idea was to make use of cooperative groups. Most of the students in Mrs. Sandler's class were successful with the science and social studies routine of pre-taught vocabulary and KWL charts. Mrs. Sandler thought that the KWPLS strategy might be more challenging for them and they could work in small groups using it. These students could hone their prediction and summarization skills. That would give Mrs. Sandler time to work with Chantelle and a small group (i.e., five) of her peers more intensely for about 30 minutes in science and 30 minutes in social studies each day for four days a week. For two weeks, Mrs. Sandler worked with Chantelle's group on analogies instruction. The students learned to use their background knowledge to make comparisons between known information and new information they were learning. The next three weeks, Mrs. Sandler worked with the small group on the possible sentences strategy. Of course she reminded Chantelle's group to continue using the analogies they learned earlier. For the next four weeks, Mrs. Sandler worked with this group on question-answer relationships. Once again, some review time was spent on the previously learned strategies, analogies, and possible sentences.

In order to not call unwanted attention to Chantelle's group for fear that they might be teased by peers, Mrs. Sandler often rotated the group membership as students learned the strategies and could perform them on their own. No one seemed to notice that Chantelle was usually in the group. Also, Mrs. Sandler had group members to help her "teach" the strategies to other classmates. Chantelle delighted in being able to "teach her classmates." Learning new strategies seemed to be exciting for students in Mrs. Sandler's class, so almost all of the students wanted to find out about strategies that they did not already know. See Figure 6.3 for a summary of the tier two intervention for Chantelle.

The tier two intervention was successful for Chantelle. See Figure 6.4 for Chantelle's reading comprehension scores for science and social studies during tier two. Mrs. Sandler continued to reinforce and offered many opportunities for her students to practice the analogies, possible sentences, and question-answer relationship strategies. In fact, Mrs. Sandler and her students were asked to teach some of the strategies to another fourth grade class.

CONCLUSION

This chapter presented strategies for teachers to use in content area instruction for students with learning difficulties in the elementary and middle grades,

Supplements to General Curriculum	Classroom Time (Facilitated by Teacher)	Student-Teacher Ratio
Before Reading—Teacher pre-teaches science and social studies vocabulary and students put vocabulary words with definitions in their notebooks. (ongoing)	Mondays Science—20 minutes Soc. Studies—20 minutes	25 to 1
Small Group— Analogies Instruction (2 weeks) Possible Sentences (3 weeks) Question-Answer Relationships (4 weeks)	Daily 4 days Science—30 minutes Soc. Studies—30 minutes	5 to 1
Small Group— Review and further application of Analogies Instruction Possible Sentences Question-Answer Relationships (11 weeks)	Daily 4 days Science—20 minutes Soc. Studies—20 minutes	5 to 1

Figure 6.3   Summary of Chantelle's Tier Two Intervention

Week	Intervention	Science Score	Soc. Studies Score
11	Pre-teach Vocabulary Analogies Instruction	70%	72%
12	Pre-teach Vocabulary Analogies Instruction	73%	76%
13	Pre-teach Vocabulary Possible Sentences	71%	73%
14	Pre-teach Vocabulary Possible Sentences	75%	78%
15	Pre-teach Vocabulary Possible Sentences	76%	78%
16	Pre-teach Vocabulary QAR	70%	71%
17	Pre-teach Vocabulary QAR	72%	75%
18	Pre-teach Vocabulary QAR	72%	76%
19	Pre-teach Vocabulary QAR	76%	80%
20–30	Pre-teach Vocabulary Review Analogies, Possible Sentences, and QAR	76–80%	80–85%

Figure 6.4   Chantelle's Reading Comprehension Scores With Tier Two Intervention

with a focus on reading and studying chapters in school textbooks, content vocabulary development, and comprehension strategies. During the first reflection exercise in this chapter, you were asked to generate a list of guiding principles for teaching content area literacy and to add to the list and talk with colleagues about their ideas as you read through this chapter. You now may wish to consult Teaching Tip 6.4, Instructional Practices to Promote Content Area Literacy, to see if there are additional teaching principles you would like to add to your list or learn more about. You also may wish to consult Chapter 5, Gaining Meaning From Reading. Some of the comprehension strategies in that chapter also may be helpful in teaching content area literacy.

 TEACHING TIP 6.4

Instructional Practices to Promote Content Area Literacy

Teachers can do so many things to help students with content area literacy. You will note that the strategies presented in this chapter incorporate a number of the following best practices. Keep this list handy to review periodically which of the best practices you currently are incorporating into your instruction and those that you would like to incorporate.

Before Reading

1. _____ Assess students' background knowledge.
2. _____ Help students access and add to their background knowledge.
3. _____ Introduce new vocabulary terms and stress relationships among them.
4. _____ Ensure that students know the specific purpose for reading a particular selection.
5. _____ Help students preview the selection to be read.
6. _____ Encourage students to make predictions about what they will read.

During Reading

7. _____ Encourage students to self-question the selection.
8. _____ Ask students to note unknown words and concepts and to use references if needed.
9. _____ Remind students to take notes or record key ideas on graphic organizers.

After Reading

10. _____ Relate discussions to the specific purpose determined prior to reading a particular selection.
11. _____ Encourage all students to participate in class discussions.
12. _____ Encourage students to question and challenge each other's contributions to class discussions.
13. _____ Promote written interaction of teacher with students as well as students with peers.
14. _____ Provide opportunities for students to extend vocabulary knowledge.
15. _____ Relate new material to previously learned material.
16. _____ Make explicit real-world connections to the material read.
17. _____ Assist students in summarizing and synthesizing information that they have read.

(Continued)

☞ **TEACHING TIP 6.4** (Continued)

Other

18. _____ Help students develop good study habits.
19. _____ Discuss test preparation and test-taking strategies with students.
20. _____ Modify reading assignments and instructional practices to meet individual student and class needs.
21. _____ Incorporate alternative means of assessment (e.g., projects, reports, graphic organizers, drama presentations, PowerPoint presentations).
22. _____ Incorporate technology when appropriate.
23. _____ Provide opportunities for student choices.
24. _____ Provide access to a variety of print materials related to specific content areas.
25. _____ Use teacher read-alouds and picture books in instruction.

SOURCE: Adapted from McKenna and Robinson (2002, pp. 49–50).

REFERENCES

Alvermann, D. E., & Phelps, S. F. (1998). *Content reading and literacy: Succeeding in today's diverse classrooms* (2nd ed.). Boston: Allyn & Bacon.

Beck, I. L., McKeown, M. G., Hamilton, R. L., & Kucan, L. (1998). Getting at the meaning: How to help students unpack difficult text. *American Educator, 22*(1,2), 66–71, 85.

Bos, C. S., & Vaughn, S. (2002). *Strategies for teaching students with learning and behavior problems* (5th ed.). Boston: Allyn & Bacon.

Bridgewater State College. (2003). *A sample lesson combining idea circles and differentiated instruction.* Retrieved May 4, 2008, from http://www.bridgew.edu/Library/CAGS_Projects/LDUBIN/idea%20circles.htm.

Buehl, D. (2001). *Classroom strategies for interactive learning* (2nd ed.). Newark, DE: International Reading Association.

Daniels, H. (1994). *Literature circles: Voice and choice in one student-centered classroom.* York, ME: Stenhouse.

Darch, C., Carnine, D., & Kame'enui, E. J. (1986). The role of graphic organizers and social structure in content area instruction. *Journal of Reading Behavior, 28,* 275–294.

Dennis-Shaw, S. (2007). *Guided comprehension: Self-questioning using question-answer relationships.* Retrieved May 4, 2008, from http://www.readwritethink.org/lessons/lesson_view.asp?id=227.

DiCecco, V. M., & Gleason, M. M. (2002). Using graphic organizers to attain relational knowledge from expository text. *Journal of Learning Disabilities, 35,* 306–320.

Durkin, D. (1978/1979). What classroom observations reveal about reading instruction. *Reading Research Quarterly, 14,* 481–533.

Ellis, E. S. (2000). *Strategic graphic organizer instruction.* Tuscaloosa, AL: Masterminds.

Finnegan, K., & Manning, E. (2007). *Critical perspectives: Reading and writing about slavery.* Retrieved May 4, 2008, from http://www.readwritethink.org/lessons/lesson_view.asp?id=1060.

Fountas, I. C., & Pinnell, G. S. (2001). *Guiding readers and writers grades 3–6: Teaching comprehension, genre, and content literacy.* Portsmouth, NH: Heinemann.

Gillespie, C., & Rasinski, T. (1989). Content area teachers' attitudes and practices toward reading in the content areas: A review. *Reading Research and Instruction, 28,* 45–67.

Glynn, S. (1996). Teaching with analogies: Building on the science textbook. *The Reading Teacher, 49,* 490–492.

Goatley, V. (1997). Talk about text among special education students. In S. I. McMahon & E. Raphael (Eds.), *The book club connection.* New York: Teachers College Press.

Griffin, C. C., & Tulbert, B. L. (1995). The effect of graphic organizers on students' comprehension and recall of expository text: A review of the research and implications for practice. *Reading & Writing Quarterly, 11*(1), 73–89.

Guthrie, T. J., & McCann, A. D. (1996). Idea circles: Peer collaboration for conceptual learning. In L. B. Gambrell & J. F. Almasi (Eds.), *Lively discussion! Fostering engaged reading* (pp. 87–105). Newark, DE: International Reading Association.

Haggard, M. R. (1986). The vocabulary self-collection strategy: Using student interest and world knowledge to enhance vocabulary growth. *Journal of Reading, 29,* 634–642.

Horton, S. V., & Lovitt, T. C. (1989). Construction and implementation of graphic organizers for academically handicapped and regular secondary students. *Academic Therapy, 24,* 625–640.

Hudson, P., Lignugaris-Kraft, B., & Miller, T. (1993). Using content enhancements to improve the performance of adolescents with learning disabilities in content classes. *Learning Disabilities Research & Practice, 8,* 106–126.

Journey North. (2006). *How is a hot dog like a shoe?* Retrieved May 4, 2008, from http://www.learner.org/jnorth/tm/hotdog.html.

Kuse, L. S., & Kuse, H. R. (1986). Using analogies to study social studies texts. *Social Education, 50,* 24–25.

Larkin, M. J. (2001). Providing support for student independence through scaffolded instruction. *Teaching Exceptional Children, 34*(1), 30–34.

McKenna, M. C. (2002). *Help for struggling readers: Strategies for grades 3–8.* New York: Guilford.

McKenna, M. C., & Robinson, R. D. (2002). *Teaching through text: Reading and writing in the content areas* (3rd ed.). Boston: Allyn & Bacon.

Moore, D. W., & Readance, J. E. (1980). A meta-analysis of the effect of graphic organizers on learning from text. In M. L. Kamil & A. J. Moe (Eds.), *Perspectives in reading research and instruction: Twenty-ninth yearbook of the National Reading Conference* (pp. 213–217). Washington, DC: National Reading Conference.

Moore, D. W., & Readance, J. E. (1984). A quantitative and qualitative review of graphic organizer research. *Journal of Educational Research, 78*(1), 11–17.

National Institute of Child Health and Development. (2000). *Teaching children to read: An evidence-based assessment of the scientific research literature on reading and its implications for reading instruction* (Report of the National Reading Panel). Retrieved September 20, 2008, from http://www.nichd.nih.gov/publications/nrp/findings.cfm.

Novak, J. D., & Gowin, D. B. (1984). *Learning how to learn.* New York: Cambridge University Press.

Ogle, D. M. (1986). K-W-L: A teaching model that develops active reading of expository text. *The Reading Teacher, 39,* 564–570.

Ogle, D. M. (1989). K-W-L: The know, want to know, learn strategy. In K. D. Muth (Ed.), *Children's comprehension of text: Research into practice.* Newark, DE: International Reading Association. (ERIC Document Reproduction Service No. ED304672)

Raphael, T. E., & Au, K. H. (2005). QAR: Enhancing comprehension and test taking across grades and content areas. *Reading Teacher, 59*(3), 206–221.

Ruddell, M. R., & Shearer, B. A. (2002). 'Extraordinary,' 'tremendous,' 'exhilarating,' 'magnificent': Middle school at-risk students become avid word learners with the vocabulary self-collection strategy (VAA). *Journal of Adolescent & Adult Literacy, 45*(5), 352–363.

Southwest Educational Development Laboratory. (2008). *Building reading proficiency at the secondary level: A guide to resources.* Retrieved May 4, 2008, from http://www.sedl.org/cgibin/mysql/buildingreading.cgi?showrecord=23&1 =description.

Stahl, S. A., & Kapinus, B. A. (1991). Possible sentences: Predicting word meanings to teach content area vocabulary. *The Reading Teacher, 45,* 36–43.

Swanson, P. N., & DeLaPaz, S. (1998). Teaching effective comprehension strategies to students with learning and reading disabilities. *Intervention in School and Clinic, 33,* 209–218.

Vacca, J. L., Vacca, R. T., Gove, M. K., Burkey, L., Lenhart, L. A., & McKeon, C. (2003). *Reading and learning to read* (5th ed.). Boston: Allyn & Bacon.

Vacca, R. T., & Vacca, J. L. (2002). *Content area reading: Literacy and learning across the curriculum* (7th ed.). Boston: Allyn & Bacon.

Resources

Commercially Available Reading Programs

Reading and Literacy Programs Reviewed Include

✓ SRA Reading Programs

✓ Orton-Gillingham Failure Free Reading Program

✓ The Herman Method for Reversing Reading Failure

✓ Earobics Literacy Language Program

In addition to the programs reviewed in Chapters 1–6, a number of other reading programs are used widely in the field for students with learning disabilities and other reading disorders. When considering which programs to use for any RTI intervention at any tier, teachers have the responsibility of making certain that any commercial program they select is supported by scientific research. The quickest and easiest way to do that is to check Web sites that present reviews of research support for the various commercially available supplementary reading programs. Two such Web sites are

Florida Center for Reading Research (http://www.fcrr.org)

University of Oregon (http://reading.uoregon.edu/curricula/)

In addition, several of the most commonly used reading programs that have not been discussed at length in the text are presented below. These include the SRA (Scientific Research Association) direct instruction programs, the Orton-Gillingham reading method, the Herman Method for Reversing Reading Failure, and Earobics. All of these commonly used programs have scientific support, and these are described here to assist you in your selection of appropriate supplemental reading materials.

THE SRA READING PROGRAMS

Description of the Program

In response to the need for research-based reading interventions, SRA/McGraw-Hill offers Open Court Reading (SRA/McGraw-Hill, 2002), a systematic method balancing literature and phonics instruction designed to improve both reading fluency and comprehension. Open Court Reading is designed such that no assumptions are made about students' prior knowledge. Each skill is systematically and explicitly taught in a logical progression, to enable understanding and mastery (SRA/McGraw-Hill, 2002). Phoneme-based instruction emphasizing letter sounds is the hallmark of this program as recommended by the National Reading Panel (NRP; National Institute of Child Health and Development [NICHD], 2000). The Open Court Reading program includes educational materials and strategies for kindergarten through sixth grade. A scaffolded approach is used to build skills, and the reading materials are based on the real world for meaningfulness and application of ideas. Reading material is selected to reflect the world in which students live and add to their general knowledge foundation.

Reading instruction uses a broad-based approach. Students receive planned instruction in the areas of decoding of letter sounds, comprehension, inquiry and investigation (learning how to apply what you have read), and writing. There are also applications for teaching spelling, vocabulary, grammar, usage and mechanics, penmanship, and listening, speaking, and viewing (SRA/McGraw-Hill, 2002), making this a comprehensive literacy program.

Open Court promises fluent, confident readers by the end of first grade. This program as outlined by the SRA Web site (see www. sra4kids.com) is intended to

- Develop children's print awareness through reading aloud
- Encourage phonemic awareness through games, puppets, and language activities
- Teach the alphabet and how it works with Pre-Decodable and Decodable Books, Alphabet Cards, Chart materials and carefully structured activities for kindergarten classrooms
- Teach sound/spelling associations systematically using Sound/ Spelling Cards
- Teach blending as a strategy for accessing unfamiliar words with Sound/Spelling Cards and encourage children to build fluency and read context independently using Decodable Books in Levels 1–3
- Develop spelling strategies through Dictation and WordBuilding Activities
- Each three-part lesson includes:

  Part One—*Preparing to Read:* Sounds and letters; phonemic awareness; phonics and fluency; and word knowledge

  Part Two—*Reading and Responding:* Comprehension skills and strategies; and inquiry

  Part Three—*Language Arts:* Spelling; vocabulary; writing process strategies; writer's craft; English-language conventions; grammar, usage, and mechanics; listening, speaking, and viewing; penmanship; and basic computer skills

In addition, SRA offers the Corrective Reading program designed for students with reading problems or who are at risk for reading failure. This program has been extensively tested in public school classrooms, and this research base documents the efficacy of this program. Corrective Reading includes a scripted presentation approach (i.e., recommended teacher instructional dialogue is explicitly stated in the instructional manual), and complete learning materials needed for each lesson. Like the Open Court Reading program, Corrective Reading allows students to work in a decoding program, a comprehension program, or both.

This program includes a point system based on realistic goals to motivate students who often expect to fail. It is designed to accelerate student learning for those children who are behind their peers in reading skills. Each skill is broken down into subskills, which are taught through direct instruction and practiced until mastery level of each skill is achieved. The high level of proficiency allows students to generalize learned skills to other settings. This program is broader in scope and sequence than the Open Court program.

The SRA Corrective Reading program includes the following features:

- Field-tested in reading, spelling, language arts, and math problems
- Tightly scripted lesson plans leave no guesswork for teachers
- Interactive lessons require frequent verbal responses from students
- Teachers monitor and correct errors immediately
- Lessons are presented to small groups of students
- Students are grouped by performance level
- Frequent assessment of student progress means no child fails
- Presentation books provide maximum effectiveness and efficiency during instruction
- Totally integrated skillbooks, textbooks, and authentic literature support the skills and strategies

Whereas the SRA programs are similar in many ways and emphasize the instructional mandates of the NRP (NICHD, 2000) report, there are notable differences between these programs. Table 1 presents a summary comparison of these programs.

Table 1   Characteristics of SRA programs

Program	Features	Supplementary Materials	Support
Open Court (K–6)	Pretests Phonemic awareness Blending Oral practice Comprehension strategies	Activity books Collections for young scholars Web site activities	Professional development Web site resources Online support
Corrective Reading (PreK–12)	Phonics High-frequency practice Extensive review Scripted presentation	All materials included	Professional development Web site resources Online support

Research Support

These curricula are supported by many studies, including these two recent examples. A study completed in Lee County, Alabama, evaluated the effectiveness of the Corrective Reading program with fourth grade and seventh to tenth grade students who were at risk for reading failure. At-risk students were defined as students who scored below the 23rd percentile on the *Stanford Achievement Test*. Selected students were pulled out of the general education classroom to receive approximately 60 hours of instruction in Corrective Reading. Target students in the fourth grade improved an average 10.5 percentile points on the *Standard Achievement Test* compared to the district average loss of 3.5 percentile points. Sixty-six (80%) of the at-risk students made significant gains and 44 moved out of the at-risk category (SRA/McGraw-Hill, 2002).

A study conducted in California compared schools using the Open Court program with schools using traditional basal series. Participating students included those with limited proficiency in English and from low socioeconomic backgrounds. Schools from 41 school districts enrolled approximately 137,000 students. Scores for these students were compared to students' scores from 274 randomly selected schools with similar demographic make-ups. These schools used traditional language programs. Students in the Open Court schools achieved gain scores on the *Stanford Achievement Test, 9th Edition*, in total reading of 19.2% for second-grade and 12.7% for third-grade students compared to 12.3% for second-grade and 7.2% for third-grade students in schools not using the program.

THE ORTON-GILLINGHAM FAILURE FREE READING PROGRAM

Description of the Program

The Orton-Gillingham–based reading programs, produced by the Institute for Multi-Sensory Education (ISME; 2002), are based on the Orton-Gillingham method of reading instruction developed by Dr. Samuel T. Orton and educator Anna Gillingham (see www.ortongillingham.com). Originally intended for use with children with learning disabilities, these programs currently are used with all struggling readers at the elementary level. The methodology uses phonetics and emphasizes visual, auditory, and kinesthetic learning styles. Perhaps the best known of these programs is the Failure Free Reading Program.

In this program, interactive group instruction begins by focusing on the structure of language and gradually moves toward reading. The programs are both language based and success oriented. They provide students with immediate feedback and a predictable sequence that integrates reading, writing, and spelling. In addition, the phonetic strand is placed into existing curricula, allowing flexibility in topics for the classroom teacher. The organized process is intended to offer phonetic, sequential, and success-oriented programs for teachers and parents to use to enhance children's skills in reading, spelling, and writing.

Using the ISME Orton-Gillingham programs, students are taught explicitly reading, handwriting, and written expression skills as one logical body of knowledge—thus this represents the more comprehensive literacy approach (see discussion in Chapter 1). Learners move step by step from simple to more complex material in a sequential, logical manner that enables students to master important literacy skills.

The comprehension component of the program was designed to improve students' ability to read for comprehension and retention by allowing students to participate in reciprocal teaching activities (see Bender, 2008, for a description of reciprocal teaching). Students learn and remember material more effectively as they assist their peers in learning the presented curriculum.

Important concepts of the Orton-Gillingham method, as outlined by the Institute for Multi-Sensory Education Web site (www.orton-gillingham.com), include an emphasis on

- Phonemic awareness
- Syllabication patterns for decoding and encoding
- Multisensory techniques for sight words
- Reciprocal teaching methods for the reading classroom
- Advanced spelling techniques
- Informal assessment
- Guidelines for weekly lesson plans
- Multisensory strategies for reading, writing, and spelling

Teacher training and support are important components of this program. Several training program formats are available from ISME including an initial Overview for Staff Development, a 16-hour core training program, and a 30-hour comprehensive training program. College credit from the University of Michigan at Dearborn is available for teachers in these programs. In addition to these more comprehensive group-training programs, there also are training resources that include classroom consultation, refresher workshops, lessons in Greek and Latin roots, and training for individual teachers.

Research Support

In a study conducted by Barney Rankhorn and Grace England (1998), the authors investigated the use of the Failure Free Reading Program with special education students with severe reading disabilities. The program was used to supplement instruction for approximately seven months. Thirty-nine students from a suburban school district in a southwestern state participated in this study. Students with learning disabilities represented 52% of the special education population (Rankhorn & England, 1998). The scores for each student's most recent performance and individually administered IQ assessments were secured from school records. All students with learning disabilities demonstrated a minimum discrepancy of 20 points between measured IQ and achievement.

First, teachers were trained in the Failure Free Reading Program. Each student was pretested and posttested using tests of letter-word identification, word attack, reading comprehension, and dictation. Next, students participated in a daily instructional period of 30 minutes maximum using the printed materials for the Failure Free Reading Program. Comparisons of reading achievement as measured by the posttests and expected ability and achievement were completed to evaluate the effects of the pilot program. Reductions in discrepancies between reading achievement and expected ability were significant in all areas evaluated. Average posttest discrepancies were reduced to one standard deviation of 15 points or less between expected and achieved performance. In addition, decreases in discrepancies between pretest and posttest scores for comprehension were substantial (63% to 85%). At the conclusion of the study, 31% of the students exhibited severe discrepancies in reading achievement (i.e., letter and word identification); this represented more than a 50% drop for this group from the beginning of the school year in the number of students exhibiting a significant level of discrepancy (Rankhorn & England, 1998).

THE HERMAN METHOD FOR REVERSING READING FAILURE

Description of the Program

The Herman Method for Reversing Reading Failure is a multisensory, bi-hemispheric brain-based approach to help students compensate for their visual and auditory processing problems (Herman Method Reading Institute, 2002). This program is based on the Orton-Gillingham philosophy and is a remedial program for struggling readers at all grade levels.

This program is separated into 20 sequential levels of instruction for reading with each level containing a spelling and handwriting component to reinforce reading skills. Daily lesson plans with specific goals and objectives for teaching each skill are included in two teacher guides. Each level also includes a review of previous skills so students are able to maintain skill levels that they have achieved. While this program was designed for students with learning disabilities, it also offers effective teaching strategies for nondisabled students experiencing difficulties in acquiring reading skills.

Several aspects of the Herman Method make it an effective strategy for teaching reading. First, the Herman Method coordinates visual, auditory, kinesthetic, and tactile information for teaching each reading and spelling skill. This multisensory approach is intended to assist students in compensating for problems with retention, visual and auditory processing, spatial orientation, and sequencing by accessing both hemispheres of the brain. Second, the method uses a comprehensive approach to teaching a variety of literacy and language skills. Decoding, encoding, structural analysis, sight words, contextual clues, and dictionary skills are included. Further, there is a consistent emphasis on comprehension skills. Finally, the program is success oriented. Skill levels range from simple decoding to independent reading with multiple opportunities for review and reinforcement of skills to ensure that mastery is obtained. Program activities include phrase list reading, sentence cards, software programs, workbook activities, computer instruction, practice readers, and reading games

(Herman Method Reading Institute, 2002). Teachers can find additional information on this program at the company Web site (www .hermanmethod.com).

Research Support

The effects of commercially produced software on phonemic awareness of students using the Herman Method for teaching reading was evaluated in a study by Lynne Bowman (1999). Participants in this study were 13 middle school students (ages 11 to 15) in a self-contained special education classroom. All students were identified as learning disabled or functionally delayed according to the state of Tennessee guidelines for eligibility. These students were similar in reading ability. Students were separated randomly into two groups. The experimental group of seven students used the Herman Method and program software. The control group of six students did not use the software program, but received instruction using the Herman Method for the direct instruction portion of the class. Each student received 25 minutes of reading instruction and 25 minutes of handwriting instruction daily. All students in the study also used the computer for 25 minutes each day. Three days each week the treatment group's computer time was spent using the Herman Method's "Curious George Learns Phonics" interactive software. A repeated measures design was used to analyze the pretest and posttest data. The pretest was given before any reading instruction began. The test given to both groups consisted of an assessment of word analysis and decoding skill.

These data were analyzed using an independent *t*-test. All students using the Herman Method improved significantly on each of the posttreatment assessments. In addition, those using the software also improved in their ability to work with rhyming words, while the control group did not (Bowman, 1999). This research provides evidence to validate the Herman program.

EAROBICS LITERACY LAUNCH

Description of the Program

Cognitive Concepts' Earobics Literacy Launch is a research-based supplemental reading program designed to provide elementary reading students in prekindergarten through third grade with the fundamental skills required for reading success. The goal of this program is to facilitate the transition from spoken language to print. Similar to the Fast ForWord Program described in Chapter 2, this reading instructional program draws heavily from the recent brain compatible instructional research as a base for many of the activities in the curriculum. A combination of technology, multimedia tools, and print materials are used to accomplish the goal of developing students' skills in fundamental language areas.

Earobics Literacy Launch also integrates technology into classroom activities. The technology component adjusts to the needs of each student by providing systematic, individualized instruction. Student achievement is easily documented and can be evaluated with built-in data reporting. Important components of the program as outlined by the Cognitive Concepts literature (2002) and Web site (www.earobics.com) include

- Scientifically based
- Research proven
- Improvement in student performance for phonological awareness, vocabulary, fluency, phonics, reading comprehension
- Ensures success of existing literacy curriculum
- Integrates technology into the classroom
- Supports English Language Learners

The Earobics program maintains a high interest level by providing students with a wide variety of activities. Phonemic awareness is developed using interactive Earobics software. The software games are not only engaging for students, but also adapt to each student's skill level. Students work through lessons at their own pace. Classroom activities, songs, and chants strengthen language enrichment skills. They are designed to encourage the acquisition of vocabulary, language concepts, and the production of sounds, words, and sentences. Hands-on activities, letter and word cards, and alphabet manipulatives are used to teach knowledge of letters and sounds. This knowledge of letters and sounds is expanded into word analysis. Abilities such as decoding, spelling, and recognizing sight words are developed through manipulating letters on alphabet mats and practicing the identification of words both in isolation and in context.

As students master skills, they experience sounds and stories while reading with teachers or independently. Materials used in the program include big books, little books, take-home books, talking CD-ROM books, and books on audiocassettes and videotapes. Composition skills are incorporated as well, through shared writing activities with Earobics Literacy Launch literature and materials.

Research Support

Cognitive Concepts (2002) offers empirical evidence for the efficacy of the Earobics Literacy Launch program. A pilot study was completed in January 2001 in the Newport Public School System to examine the effectiveness of the Earobics Literacy Launch program. Kindergarten students from eight schools participated in the 12-week study. Students were divided into a control group of 293 students and an experimental group of 292 students. All students were administered the Phonemic Awareness Test (Parts A and B) as a pretest. A posttest version of the Phonemic Awareness Test (Parts A and B) was administered after the study was completed. Part A of this test assesses students' abilities to identify initial and final sounds of words and to identify rhyming words. Part B assesses students' skills in blending phonemes into words and segmenting words into syllables and phonemes. Teachers of the students in the Earobics group received teacher resource materials consisting of lesson plans, group activities, and information on classroom management. These teachers also were given training in the program, which consisted of an overview of the literacy research, practice with the Earobics materials and software, and sessions on relevant topics. Students in the experimental group used the Earobics software for a minimum of three 20-minute sessions per week. They also received instruction with correlated activities, literature, and multimedia materials. Students in the control group received phonemic instruction, but did not use the Earobics software or materials.

An analysis of pretest and posttest scores revealed that students using the Earobics program increased the percentage of correct answers on the Phonemic Awareness Test: Part A by an average of 34 percentage points, while students in the control group increased by only 29 percentage points. The increase achieved by the students using the Earobics program was statistically higher than that obtained by the control group students. In addition, students in the group using the Earobics program improved by an average of 39 percentage points on the Phonemic Awareness Test: Part B. Students in the control group increased by an average of 25 percentage points on the same test. The scores for the Earobics group were again statistically higher than for the control group.

REFERENCES

Bender, W. N. (2007). *Differentiating instruction for students with learning disabilities: Best teaching practices for general and special educators* (2nd ed.). Thousand Oaks, CA: Corwin Press.

Bowman, L. M. (1999). *Curious George meets Herman: The effects of commercially produced phonics software on phonemics.* Johnson Bible College, TN: NIA Educational Technology and Bible Research Project.

Cognitive Concepts. (2002). *Solutions for literacy and learning: Earobics.* Retrieved August 18, 2002, from http://www.earobics.com.

Herman Method Reading Institute. (2002). The Herman Method for Reversing Reading Failure. Retrieved July 26, 2002, from www.hermanmethod.com.

Institute for Multi-Sensory Education. (2002). Retrieved July 26, 2002, from www.ortongillingham.com.

National Institute of Child Health and Development. (2000). *Teaching children to read: An evidence-based assessment of the scientific research literature on reading and its implications for reading instruction* (Report of the National Reading Panel). Retrieved May 23, 2002, from http://www.nichd.nih.gov/publications/nrp/findings.cfm.

Rankhorn, B., & England, G. (1998). Effects of the Failure Free Reading Program on students with severe reading disabilities. *Journal of Learning Disabilities, 31*(3), 307–312.

SRA/McGraw-Hill. (2008). A site for preK–8 teachers. Retrieved July 24, 2002, from http://www.sraonline.com.

Glossary

Advance organizer: A preview or outline of learning tasks presented in oral or written form prior to beginning the body of the lesson to help students (a) focus on the lesson, (b) understand the teacher's expectations for the task, and (c) connect new and previously learned information.

Affix: Usually a prefix or suffix that is attached to a base or root word.

Alphabetic code: The relationships between letters and the sounds they represent.

Alphabetic principle: Characters that represent sounds.

Analogy phonics: Students learn new words by using analogies to familiar words. Also known as word families. For example, cat, hat, and sat are in the at word family. Students may learn the new word mat by being familiar with other words that are in the at family.

Analytic phonics: Students analyze letter–sound relations from familiar words.

Anchored instruction: Use of video examples to provide a situational context, or anchor for learning a new vocabulary term or new concept. By providing video examples of a shark attack, students with learning difficulties can master vocabulary terms such as *feeding frenzy* more easily.

Angular gyrus: A region of the brain responsible primarily for processing of written language and other language functions.

Automaticity: Instant decoding of letters or other stimuli, such that the brain processing involved in decoding these letter sounds is automatic.

Background knowledge: Knowledge that students have based on experiences or previously learned information.

Base word: A word to which prefixes or suffixes may be added.

Broca's area: A region of the brain responsible for language, also active in the reading process.

Cloze procedure: A structured fill-in-the-blank activity in which a student uses the content and context of the reading passage to select the vocabulary terms that correctly fill in the blanks in the reading passage.

Collaborative strategic reading (CSR): A strategy to improve reading comprehension using heterogeneous groups in multilevel classes.

Comprehension: To understand and attribute meaning to what is read or heard.

Concept circles: Using sections within a circle to teach various aspects of a particular concept. A divided circle (divided into quarters, or fifths—whatever is appropriate) is drawn with the related subcomponents written into each portion of the divided circle. Students work to describe the relationships between the vocabulary terms in the circle.

Configuration clues: A sight-word instructional technique that involves drawing boxes around letters in words to concentrate on the shape of the word in order to learn the word.

Consonant blend: Two or three letter combinations of consonants that are blended together. Each letter sound is pronounced quickly to form the blend (e.g., bl, cl, scr, squ).

Consonant digraph: Two consonant letters that form one sound (e.g., sh, th).

Content area reading: Reading in subjects where students learn content (e.g., facts, concepts) as opposed to learning skills (i.e., how to do something).

Context clues: A sight-word instructional technique that involves using other text or pictures presented in the text to determine the meaning of new words.

Coop-Dis-Q: A strategy that combines teaching tactics from cooperative instruction, group discussion, and questioning tactics.

Decoding: To determine what sounds particular letters make to decipher words.

Developmental instruction: Instruction that is based on students' needs and current levels of performance.

DIBELS: An informal assessment of early literacy, from the Dynamic Indicators of Basic Early Literacy Skills, Sixth Edition.

Distributed practice: Instruction that involves consistent, active engagement with the new material distributed over a period of time in order to ensure mastery and long-term retention. Research has shown that practice distributed over a period of days is much more effective for learning than the same amount of practice provided all in one day.

Drop Everything and Read (DEAR): A widely used reading practice in which students are assigned to do silent reading for a specified number of minutes each day. According to the National Reading Panel, research has not documented the effectiveness of silent reading programs.

Embedded phonics: An implicit approach in which students learn phonics when it is embedded in text reading.

Expository text: Information that is explained or related to explanation.

Fluency: Also referred to as reading fluency, it involves display of effective reading skills, with decoding words at a high level of automaticity. This is demonstrated by a student reading entire words and even phrases together, with appropriate voice intonation and pauses for punctuation.

fMRI: Functional magnetic resonance imaging, a recently developed nonradiological technique that measures the brain's use of oxygen and glucose during the thinking process, and from that information, physicians can determine which brain areas are most active during various types of educational tasks.

Graphemes: The squiggly lines on a page that represent printed letters.

Graphic organizers: A visual representation of relationships between vocabulary terms or concepts in a reading text.

Guided reading in textual settings (GRITS): A reading comprehension strategy used for teaching students in the elementary and middle grades in content areas.

Homograph: Words that are spelled alike but pronounced differently and have different meanings (e.g., tear—make an opening, tear—moisture when one cries).

Hypertext function: A set of software design principles that allow for the presentation of reading texts that have various instructional options built into the program. When using hypertext software programs, a student reading a text may click on a vocabulary term in the text and the software will present either a definition of the term, an illustration, a picture, a video, or a pronunciation of the term.

Inference: Meaning is not readily evident.

Irregular words: Words that do not follow the general rules for spelling or word formation; in the English language, these words account for approximately 15% of all words.

IT-FITS: A learning strategy acronym used to help a child learn new vocabulary terms by creating a keyword for the term.

Learning strategy: A cognitively based series of steps or tasks, which can assist a child in completing an assignment or school task such as learning a new vocabulary term.

Literal: A term used to represent the lowest level of reading comprehension, or understanding the text exactly as stated.

Modeling: Performing part or all of a task to demonstrate to others how it is done.

Multi-tiered intervention: A series of increasingly intensive interventions aimed at a particular educational deficit or behavioral problem.

National Reading Panel (NRP): A panel of reading experts who published a report on reading instruction in 2000.

No Child Left Behind: Federal legislation, passed in 2001, which emphasizes reading instruction.

Onset: The initial sound—usually a consonant sound—in a word.

Paired associate learning: The pairing of two stimuli together—a word and a picture. When this pair is shown to a child with a reading difficulty very frequently, each stimulus takes on the meaning of the other.

Performance monitoring: Refers to repeated assessments of the academic performance of a student during an RTI intervention.

Phoneme: The smallest sound that can change the meaning of a word.

Phonemic awareness: The first term used to describe phonemic instruction, which represents a child's ability to detect different phonemes.

Phonemic manipulation: A more recent term than phonemic awareness that represents a child's ability to manipulate phoneme sounds in various ways, including detecting phonemes, segmenting words into phonemes, and other skills beyond mere awareness of phonemes.

Phonics: The mapping of sounds to letters or letter combinations, as well as the ability to decode unknown words based on those letter–sound relationships.

Phonological instruction: A term used to represent phonemic instruction in addition to instruction in interpretation of all speech sounds, including syllables and whole words.

Pyramid of intervention: A series of educational interventions, commonly including three intervention levels, in which the first level on the bottom of the pyramid is aimed at all students in general education, the second level or tier is aimed at small groups needing more intensive assistance, and the third tier, usually depicted at the top of the pyramid, is directed at individuals needing extensive remedial assistance.

Response to Intervention: a process by which a student's performance during a particular educational intervention or a series of interventions, is monitored in order to indicate how the student benefited from the interventions. This is now allowed as one way to document the possibility of a learning disability.

Rime: The latter part of a word that includes the vowel and all that follows.

Root word: A synonym for base word, but typically refers to a base word of Greek origin.

RTI: See Response to Intervention.

Scaffolded instruction: A form of instruction in which students are provided with supports when needed and then the supports are removed gradually as students demonstrate that they are no longer needed.

Semantic feature analysis: Involves a pictorial representation of the relationships between vocabulary terms, in the context of likenesses and differences.

Semantic web: Sometimes referred to as a semantic map, this is a form of graphic organizer that presents the web or map of relationships between vocabulary terms or concepts in a reading text.

Sight-word instruction: Includes instructional techniques that do not depend exclusively upon a student's ability to associate sounds with specific letters; examples would include rote memory of whole words, use of context clues to decode new words, and any attempts to master instant word lists.

Silent sustained reading (SSR): A widely used reading practice in which students are assigned to do silent reading for a specified number of minutes each day. According to the National Reading Panel, research has not documented the effectiveness of silent reading programs.

Synectics: A form of analogous comparison that involves comparing something new or different with something familiar.

Synthetic phonics: Students are taught explicitly to convert letters into sounds or phonemes and blend them to form words. Students learn sounds first and use them to create words.

Tier one: The first level of a series of educational or behavioral interventions aimed at the same educational problem.

Tier two: The second intervention in a series of educational or behavioral interventions aimed at the same educational problem.

Tier three: The third intervention in a series of educational or behavioral interventions aimed at the same educational problem.

Venn diagram: A type of graphic organizer in which two circles intersect to illustrate similarities and differences.

Visual cortex: An area of the brain which is located at the lower rear, responsible for visual discrimination of letters and other visual stimuli.

Wait time: The period of time between when a teacher finishes asking a question and when an answer is called for. On average, teachers will wait only 2 or 3 seconds, while 8 to 10 seconds is recommended to allow students with slower processing to consider their answers and raise their hands.

Wernicke's area: A region of the brain responsible for various types of language functions, including auditory processing and comprehension.

Word family: See analogy phonics.

Index

CORWIN
A SAGE Company

The Corwin logo—a raven striding across an open book—represents the union of courage and learning. Corwin is committed to improving education for all learners by publishing books and other professional development resources for those serving the field of PreK–12 education. By providing practical, hands-on materials, Corwin continues to carry out the promise of its motto: **"Helping Educators Do Their Work Better."**